EUTHANASIA

EUTHANASIA

G. C. Oosthuizen
H. A. Shapiro
S. A. Strauss
(Editors)

Human Sciences Research Council
Publication No. 65

1978
OXFORD UNIVERSITY PRESS
Cape Town

Oxford University Press

OXFORD LONDON GLASGOW

NEW YORK TORONTO MELBOURNE WELLINGTON

IBADAN NAIROBI DAR ES SALAAM CAPE TOWN

KUALA LUMPUR SINGAPORE JAKARTA HONG KONG TOKYO

DELHI BOMBAY CALCUTTA MADRAS KARACHI

Copyright © 1978 Oxford University Press

ISBN 0 19 570143 7

The authors gratefully acknowledge the financial assistance of the Human Sciences Research Council, the Natal Council of Churches and the University of Durban-Westville in connection with the publication of this work. Opinions expressed in the work or conclusions reached are those of the author concerned and must in no instance be regarded as a reflection of the sponsors.

Set in 10pt on 12pt Times Roman
Printed and bound by Pioneer Press, 17 Shelley Road, Salt River, Cape
Published by Oxford University Press, Harrington House, Barrack Street, Cape Town 8001, South Africa

CONTENTS

PSYCHIATRIC, PSYCHOLOGICAL AND NURSING ASPECTS OF EUTHANASIA

FOREWORD

This book completes a very successful symposium on euthanasia. So much was said and such deep insights shared that it would have been a pity if nothing had been recorded for posterity. The Symposium offered unique contributions to the problems of saving life without excessive suffering and of remaining humane despite modern technology.

The Symposium was organized by the Natal Council of Churches and the University of Durban-Westville; this happy blending of religious and secular values ensured a balanced attempt at defining the concept euthanasia.

Durban, with its various population groups, represents the meeting-place of East and West, of Europe and Africa. Selecting Durban as a venue ensured a universal approach to a problem that touches man's very essence. The international flavour was guaranteed by the presence of Prof. U. P. Hämmerli of the University of Zürich, of 'Council of Europe'-fame, and also by our own Prof. Chris Barnard. The East was represented by the valuable contributions on Buddhism, Hinduism, Islam and Judaism. The South African and African points of view were also represented.

This foreword would not be complete without a tribute to the Principal and staff of the University of Durban-Westville, who so generously provided their time and facilities for the Symposium. My thanks also to the workers of the Natal Council of Churches.

The Symposium became possible by means of a very substantial donation from the Ethical Drug Foundation, for which generous contribution we are most grateful.

Finally, I should like to acknowledge the work of the Editors, Prof. G. C. Oosthuizen (Theological), Prof. H. A. Shapiro (Medical) and Prof. S. A. Strauss (Legal). To Prof. Oosthuizen I offer a special word of thanks for seeing his 'brainchild', the Symposium, through all its various successful stages.

GEORGE PURVES
Chairman
Natal Council of Churches

ACKNOWLEDGEMENTS

The symposium on euthanasia has drawn attention from far and wide. The bringing together of people from various professions for the purpose of discussing matters that affect their specific disciplines is something that rarely occurs. This is the third symposium of this type organized thus far in South Africa. The first centred on the ethics of tissue transplantation, and the second on termination of pregnancy.

The success of such a symposium inevitably depends on the quality of the contributions; quality has been a notable aspect of this symposium. A special word of thanks goes to those who prepared and delivered the papers at the University of Durban-Westville under the auspices of its Department of Science of Religion and the Natal Council of Churches.

The symposium was a great success according to those who attended it. Because the papers were in general of such good quality the Human Sciences Research Council agreed to give a substantial amount towards the publication of this material. The University of Durban-Westville and the Natal Council of Churches contributed smaller amounts for this purpose. To all these institutions we express our appreciation.

We hope this book will be of help to those who wish to be enlightened on some of the many questions pertaining to euthanasia, a subect that has become most pertinent in our complex techno-scientific age.

G. C. OOSTHUIZEN
Director of Symposium

LIST OF CONTRIBUTORS

W. G. M. ABBOTT, B.A., B.D. (Durban)
Secretary, Natal Council of Churches

B. A. BALKISSON, B.Sc. Hons. (S.A.), M.Sc. (U.D.W.)
Registered Clinical Psychologist

C. F. BARNARD, M.Med., M.D., D.Sc. (Cape Town), M.S. Ph.D.
(Minn.), F.A.C.S., F.A.C.C.
Professor and Head of the Teaching Department of Cardiac
Surgery in the University of Cape Town

M. G .T. CLOETE, M.A., D.Phil. (Pretoria)
Professor of Criminology in the University of Durban-Westville

ROGER H. ELLIS, B.A. Hons. (Natal), M.A. (Cantab.), B.Litt.
(Oxon.)
Senior Lecturer in Divinity in the University of Natal

G. C. K. FÖLSCHER, M.Comm (Pretoria)
Senior Lecturer in Economics in the University of Durban-
Westville

V. Z. GITYWA, M.A. (Fort Hare), D.Phil.
Professor of Anthropology in the University of Fort Hare

G. C. GOOSEN, Th.D. (Rome)

H. GRANT-WHYTE, B.A., M.B., Ch.B. (Cape Town),
F.F.A.R.C.S (England and Ireland), F.A.C.A. (U.S.A.)
Emeritus Professor of Anaesthetics in the University of Natal

U. P. HÄMMERLI, M.D. (Zürich)
Professor of Medicine in the University of Zürich

T. JENKINS, M.B., B.Sc.
Professor and Head of the Department of Human Genetics,
School of Pathology, S.A. Institute for Medical Research at the
University of the Witwatersrand

N. K. LAMOND, B.Soc.Sc. Hons. (Natal), M. Litt. (Aberdeen)
Professor of Nursing in the University of Natal

M. G. H. MAYAT, M.B., Ch.B. (Wits), Dip. Og. (Cape Town),
M.R.O.G. (London), F. Co. and G.

T. P. MISHRA, M.A. (Agra), Ph.D.
Senior Lecturer in Sanscrit in the University of Durban-Westville

S. SALMAN NAVDI, M.A. (Karachi), Ph.D. (Chicago)
Professor of Islamic Studies in the University of Durban-Westville

G. C. OOSTHUIZEN, M.A., M.Th., S.T.M. (W.T.S.N.Y.), D.Phil. (S.A.), Th.D. (V.U. Amsterdam)
Professor of Science of Religion in the University of Durban-Westville

A. V. OPPERMAN, B.A. Hons., M.B., Ch.B. (Pretoria), M.D. (Rand)

M. S. PATERSON, M.B., B.Ch. (Rand), O.P.M. (London)

B. G. RANCHOD, B.A. LL.B. (Cape Town), LL.D. (Leiden)
Professor of Law in the University of Durban-Westville

B. ROBINSON
Senior Journalist

H. SCHLEMMER
Clinical Psychologist, King George V Hospital, Durban

L. SCHLEMMER
Director, Centre for Applied Social Science at the University of Natal

H. A. SHAPIRO, Ph.D., M.B., Ch.B., F.R.S.S.Af.

F C. SHAW, B.A.(S.S.)(Natal), M.S.M. (McGill)
Professor of Social Work in the University of Natal

P. C. SMIT, B.A. LL.B. (Stell.), LL.D. (O.F.S.)
Associate Professor of Law in the University of the Orange Free State

H. W. SNYMAN, M.B., Ch.B., M.D. (Groningen)
President of the South African Medical and Dental Council

M. STEIN, M.B., B.Ch. (Wits), F.R.C.S. (Edin.), D.A. (R.C.P.S.I.), D.G.O. (Trinity)

S. A. STRAUSS, B.A. (Stell.), LL.B. (O.F.S.), LL.D. (S.A.)
Professor of Law in the University of South Africa

J.D. VAN DER VYVER, B.Comm., B.A. Hons., LL.B. (P.U. for C.H.E.), LL.D. (Pretoria)
Professor of Law in the Potchefstroom University for Christian Higher Education

L. H. VAN LOON, B.Sc. (Eng.), P.R. Eng.
Part-time Lecturer in Science of Religion in the University of Durban-Westville

ABNER WEISS, M.A., Ph.D.
Rabbi Professor in the University of Natal

AN INTRODUCTION TO THE EUTHANASIA DEBATE

S. A. Strauss

Life is perhaps the most self-evident quality of man. Yet man has never ceased to marvel at the wonder of life. Often he has become cynical of life and has exclaimed: 'There's naught in this life sweet!' (Fletcher). Often he has been brought to desperation by the visitations which are part of life, and has bewailed life as 'an ill whose only cure is death' (Prior), as 'nothing but a journey to death' (Seneca). But he has always grieved over the briefness of life: 'A life is but a span', Shakespeare wrote, probably referring to the distance from the tip of his thumb to the tip of his little finger.

In the end man clings to life and rejoices in it.

How rich and strange the human lot,

How warm the tints of life . . . ? (Watson)

In a graveyard in Surrey, England, there is a century-old stone on which these words are inscribed:

If life were merchandise that men could buy

The rich would live and none but poor would die.

Even primitive Neanderthal man forty thousand years ago buried lumps of bloodstone (haematite) with his dead, probably associating the red substance with the essence of life and hoping — if not believing — that it may restore life to the deceased. Boshier and Beaumont (1972)[1] have described the use of red ochre in funerary practice through the ages as 'pandemic'.

Men who had come to grips with violent death have often related that they had felt no fear and that in a split second many happy memories of their lives had flashed through their minds. Psychologists explain this as a reminder to the man in mortal danger that life has been a worthwhile experience and that it is worth clinging to with all the power at his disposal. Even serious injuries inflicted with violence have brought no pain where the victim was face to face with death. David Livingstone, the great missionary-explorer of Africa, told of an attack on him by a lion who sprang on him and caught his shoulder, crushing it. 'The shock,' he wrote, 'produced a stupor similar to that which seems to be felt by a mouse after the first shake of the cat. It caused a sort of dreaminess in

1

which there was no sense of pain nor feeling of terror, though quite conscious of all that was happening.'

No wonder then that the hallmark of Western civilization — if not always upheld in practice — is the respect for life. It is reflected in the constitutions and legal codes of our culture, in the programmes for social betterment and in the spectacular advances of medicine in our century. The spirit of the Hippocratic oath persists in the 1948 Declaration of Geneva whereby the doctor pledges himself in the following terms, *inter alia*: 'The health and life of my patient will be my first consideration.'

Perhaps the juridical, social and scientific preoccupation with the sanctity of life in our civilization has in recent times largely shifted from preservation of life to *the quality of life*. Naturally, life and the quality of life are concepts that can never be divorced, but increasing emphasis is put on the quality of life as a dominant consideration. In any debate on contraception, abortion and euthanasia, the concept 'quality of life' immediately comes to the fore because it postulates the prevention or termination of life in order to prevent life of 'lesser quality' and to enhance the quality of life for those who remain behind. This, of course, is a debatable point, for who am I to judge the quality of life of another? So we shall have to look to our theologians and philosophers for guidance. 'Quality of life' is a concept on which we should ponder deeply at a symposium such as this.

If life is the most self-evident quality of man, the termination of life would invariably have been given a high priority in his reasoning. Religious thought revolves largely round the mystery of death. Mankind grapples unceasingly with the riddle of existence and has sought reassurance from religion that existence is not without purpose and that there is life — and even happiness — beyond the grave. But the discussion is primarily concerned with the unknown *Jenseits,* the other side. Strangely, but only naturally, there is an avoidance of reflection on death and the process of dying. Even in its 'clinical' modern form, death is still feared by many. Some dread the pain or agony or utter loneliness which they believe will accompany death. Some are fearful of the possibility of eternal retribution which may await them *Jenseits.* Others who claim to reject any suggestion of life beyond the grave, fear 'the call into oblivion'.[2]

Freud was right when he said that basically no one believes in his own death: 'Subconsciously each of us believes in his own immortality.' Whilst his thoughts may turn and return to the perplexing question of what lies beyond the Styx, man is inclined to push to the back of his mind contemplation of *himself as dying*. In modern society death ideally takes place in a clinical situation. What happens when a person dies, what the dying person's psychological processes are or may conceivably be, are not ordinarily topics for discussion in the *salon*. Yet the death of a beloved one is one of the deepest emotional experiences that a human being may experience.

It is, therefore, almost impossible to discuss euthanasia in cold, unemotional terms. We find ourselves in an area where the cold rhetoric of law and the dispassionate vocabulary of medicine are of little avail. Almost any stand on euthanasia will be affected by one's own impressions of the death of a beloved, by some uneasiness, perhaps subconsciously, of one's own dying 'one day', by an abhorrence of human suffering in general, by one's deepest religious beliefs in the eternal destiny of man, and by one's sense of propriety.

Van den Berg's (1969)[3] eloquent plea for legalized euthanasia is essentially a treatise on a series of tragic cases of vegetating human beings who are the products of what he terms 'medische macht', the power of modern medicine. To him, the exercise of this power results in cruelty. He expresses himself in emotional terms:

. . . . Ongepast is het volstrekt onbekwamen, lang verslagenen, stervenden en reeds gestorvenen voort te doen vegeteren . . . . Dat is in ieder geval wreed.

He concludes with an appeal to his colleagues, the doctors, to put an end to this cruelty.[4]

Even more emotional are the terms used by Ficarra,[5] the American doctor and lawyer, who argues from the premise of natural and Divine law. He describes the custom of some primitive peoples to kill or abandon parents worn out with age or disease.

As civilization progresses mercy killing tends to disappear. Instead of killing their aged parents, men began to pride themselves in caring for the helpless old folks.[6]

'[When] we adopt euthanasia in any form,' he says, 'we are on the path back to the jungle.'[7] 'When one considers mercy killing, the proponents of this evil are flirting with moral insanity. It is of such depravity that one shudders at its evil consequences and resurrects within the mind the cavilistic sentiments of a triskaidekaphobe.'[8] To Ficarra the euthanasia issue is part of the conflict between two systems of thought; between that system which recognizes its obligation to God and His Law and the other system which claims

3

that men need have no higher motive than the gratification of their own desires. Moreover, mercy killing is a false mercy.

For the physical evils which we suffer here have a value in perfecting the higher nature of man. They bring out in the sufferer and those around him qualities of the soul — patience, consideration of others, and gentleness — which might otherwise never come in existence.[9]

I have quoted only a single view at either extreme of the spectrum of current thought on euthanasia. They may be multiplied almost *ad infinitum*. To me they manifest the truth that the justifiability or otherwise of euthanasia is in the final analysis, like abortion, a matter of individual conscience, irrespective of what the law says. Let us bear in mind in our discussions that even though it may be possible to legislate for or against abortion and euthanasia, it will be impossible to pour individual conscience into a legislative mould.

We cannot disregard the extra dimension given to the euthanasia debate by modern 'medical power'. To a certain extent life and death have become controllable phases in individual existence. Medicated survival, as it has been termed, has afforded dramatic proof of the skill of the modern doctor and medical scientist. But it has raised serious questions concerning the quality of life. Is there any sense, from the humanitarian point of view, in continuation of the medicated survival of a Karen Quinlan? Can we still reason in the absolute terms of life as a divine gift which no man may take? Do we in fact have *life* here? We shall expect our theoleogians and doctors to give us guidance on these questions.

Perhaps a solution may be sought in the distinction between active and passive euthanasia. Active euthanasia, it may be said, is the inducement of death through a positive act; passive euthanasia, on the other hand, is the discontinuation of medical treatment in a terminal case so as to let the patient die. Active euthanasia, it may be reasoned, ought to be criminal; passive euthanasia lawful. We shall have to turn to the lawyer to tell us whether this distinction is justifiable on the basis of traditional legal thought. Is there a juridical distinction between the administration of a drug to a suffering patient, causing his death, on the one hand, and pulling the switch of a resuscitating machine, thereby hastening the death of the patient, on the other? Are not both these actions positive acts in terms of the law which would satisfy the *Makali* test?[10]

The true enquiry is whether the deceased would have died when he did but for the [accused's] unlawful act. If this enquiry gives an affirmative answer, [the accused] is responsible for the death because he caused it to take place when he did, that is to say because he hastened it.[11]

And yet we sense that there is a difference. In the former situation the doctor has not attempted with all the means at his disposal, to prolong the life of the patient. In the latter, the doctor has used every technique at his disposal in order to save and prolong the life of the patient, and has only pulled the switch when it has become absolutely clear that the patient cannot perform the basic function of respiration on his own, and that medically and morally there is no sense in keeping him alive artificially. Will a traditionally narrow juridical test of causation be of any avail in solving this problem? Must the jurist not seek the solution along the lines of expansion of the grounds of justification for the taking of life? But then, surely, it is also conceivable that the *boni mores,* 'die regsgevoel' or juristic notions of society, may declare the classic type of euthanasia, the *Hartmann* (1975)[12] situation, as justifiable in law? And what about the two anaesthesia situations described by Glanville Williams:[13] In the first, a patient is suffering from an incurable disease accompanied by excruciating pain. The doctor administers the minimum dosage of drugs necessary to make the pain endurable, knowing that such dosage will probably also cause death. In the second, a patient is suffering from a painful and incurable disease and a drug is administered. Steadily increasing doses have to be administered because of the resistance which is a consequence of the habitual administering of the drug. This means that unless the patient dies beforehand due to another cause, a point must be reached when the dosage becomes fatal. Williams is of the opinion that in neither of these cases the doctor's conduct would be unlawful, and his argument is very convincing. In the British case of *Adams* — quoted by Williams[14] — the judge instructed the jury in the following terms: 'If the first purpose of medicine, the restoration of health, can no longer be achieved there is still much for a doctor to do, and he is entitled to do all that is proper to relieve pain and suffering, even if the measure he takes may incidentally shorten life.' Will our doctors support this view? Will our courts be prepared to follow this bold precedent?

As a result of the first heart transplants, the euthanasia debate assumed yet another dimension. The necessity of controlled euthanasia with a view to make human organs available for transplantation purposes has been proposed. Dempster[15] is in agreement with this view. He argues that euthanasia should be legalized so as to enable surgeons to obtain on a planned basis the best organs for transplantation purposes. In particular he has in mind the type of case where the prospective donor is a terminal patient whose circulation is artificially maintained by a respirator. The law should be adjusted, he argues, so as to enable doctors to switch off the respirator when they are of the opinion that the patient will never recover. Planned euthanasia, by switching off the respirator either before or after the organ has been removed, does in fact exist by private arrangement, Dempster says, but no doctor is at ease about performing it. The community should decide if legalized euthanasia is desirable. 'It is very probable that the public wants good organ transplantation and will quickly adjust its ethics accordingly,' he concludes.

To what extent has the medical profession already accepted these views? To what extent has society shown itself prepared to approve of such practices? Furthermore, will the courts — usually on the conservative side — be prepared to sanction them?

Are we entitled at all, in the euthanasia debate, to introduce utilitarian arguments — or, by so doing, are we whittling away the very foundations of our civilization, setting out on the 'path back to the jungle', in the words of Ficarra? The law has generally assumed a utilitarian approach to the affairs of man, instead of a Utopian or an absolute, fundamentalist one. I am not suggesting that the law has lost sight of religious and moral principles, but in many areas of human conflict, and in particular conflict of human ideals, the law has been compelled to seek a compromise between absolute principle and expediency. An example is the legal regulation of abortion. The process of abandonment or 'adaptation' of principle and acceptancy of expediency has generally been a slow and painful one. Italy is perhaps the best current example. But it has become a truism that if the ways and desires of man prove conclusively that the legal and social machinery can never hope to eradicate an evil, a legally regulated evil is still better than an unregulated one.

The words of St Thomas of Aquinas are very apposite in this context:

Human law aims to lead men to virtue, not all at once, but gradually. Therefore it does not require of the average imperfect man the standard of perfection attained by the virtuous, i.e. it does not prohibit everything that is sinful. If it did, the average imperfect man, unable to observe the law's requirements, might fall into complete lawlessness . . . . The laws would come to be despised and, through contempt of law, men might become more depraved than ever.[16]

In a different context Chief Justice Rumpff in the case of *S. v. Goliath*[17] gave expression to the same fundamental notion by intimating that the law does not necessarily enforce the highest ethical standards:

> In the application of our criminal law, in cases when the actions of an accused are judged according to objective standards, the principle is applied that no more is expected from the accused than is reasonable, reasonable here meaning that which can be expected of the average person in the particular circumstances.[18]

I have specifically mentioned abortion because there seems to be a certain parallel between euthanasia and abortion. In both instances there is the need — I do not wish to call it the *desire* — to terminate life for the sake of other interests: in the case of abortion essentially the interests of the pregnant woman, and in some cases that of the unborn child as a 'potential' human being; in the case of euthanasia the interests (or presumed interests) of the patient and (perhaps primarily?) of his next of kin. But how far can this parallel be drawn? This is an aspect which is bound to come up in any debate on euthanasia. It has been suggested that because the law allows abortion — albeit only conditionally — *ergo* the law should allow euthanasia.

This argument undoubtedly has a certain ring of validity. But the supposed parallel must be scrutinized very closely. Euthanasia involves the termination of a life which has virtually come to its end and which is already ebbing.

Abortion, on the other hand, involves the taking of a life which is at its very inception and which is full of potential promise. There are circumstances in which the law allows abortion — e.g. where the foetus was conceived in rape — where by no stretch of imagination would the law allow the deliberate termination of that life once the child has been born and is perfectly normal and healthy. Any comparison sought between abortion and euthanasia has very definite limitations.

Perhaps the lawyer will argue that the law as it stands today in South Africa — and in other countries as well — is ideal. Brand the mercy-killer as a murderer, but do not punish him at all; postpone sentence idefinitely (*De Bellocq's* case);[19] or, if the law says that murderers *shall* be punished, impose a sentence which is only nominal, for example, imprisonment until the rising of the court (*Hartmann's* case). Thereby the law registers society's disapproval in the strongest terms, and yet it is a 'registration' only, because the law then extends the utmost leniency to the accused. But is this a solution? Is it still criminal law which is applied when, although we say that murder is our most serious crime and that capital punishment, *sub condicione,* is in fact the prescribed punishment, yet we recognize a class of murderer that we do not want to punish at all? Have we not thereby transformed criminal law into criminal non-law? In a discussion such as this, we should realize that the criminal law as a social instrument has its limitations. But the matter does not end there. Where a medical practitioner is involved in euthanasia, it does not concern only the criminal law. Professional ethics also become involved. Would the Medical Council have struck Dr Hartmann off the roll if the court's verdict was that the accused was not guilty of murder because his act of killing was an act of mercy?

Assuming the present legal position to be untenable, how does society set about to correct it? Does it leave it to the courts to slowly evolve a set of rules — a process which may take decades or perhaps even longer? Or does it declare euthanasia as lawful by means of legislative action? Buchenwald and Belsen still cast a gloomy shadow on any suggestion of positive legalization of euthanasia, and post World War II euthanasia movements have been notably unsuccessful. It has often been said that legalized euthanasia is open to abuse. This is too true. But it is also true of all man's rules and institutions. Man is a corruptible being. But must this deter legal regulation of euthanasia? Surely it is not beyond the imagination of men to devise a scheme in a democratic society which will ensure the maximum safeguard against abuse? The memories of Buchenwald and Belsen will hopefully remain alive in the minds of civilized men forever. But in our thought on the vexed and perhaps insoluble problem of euthanasia we must not be shackled forever by these memories.

In ending this brief introduction to our discussion I must raise the question with which I should really have started: What is euthanasia? How do we define this concept? The word is Greek in its origin and in its classical sense probably referred to a certain attitude towards death: a happy and, if possible, also honourable death — *felici vel honesta morte mori.* It is only during the 19th century that the word came to be used in the sense of aid to the dying and the destruction of 'useless' lives.[20] Today it is widely used as a synonym for mercy-killing. Whatever may be the correct meaning of the word, in talking about euthanasia we should try and define the ambit of our discussion. Do we include the withholding of medical treatment on the doctor's sole initiative? Do we include the refusal of medical treatment on the part of the patient? Do we include involuntary mercy-killing? And, incidentally, in the case of voluntary mercy-killing, are we convinced that in the case of the terminal patient there is invariably a real consent on his part?

I have started by referring to man's overwhelming desire to live, his instinct of survival. Perhaps it is only fitting to end in saying that pain and suffering may torment man until his only desire is to live no more. That desire we should also respect.

1. Boshier, A., & Beaumont, P., 'Mining in Southern Africa and the Emergence of Modern Man', *Optima*, March 1972.
2. Biörck, G., *Second Thoughts on Life and Death,* paper read before the First World Meeting on Medical Law, at Ghent, Belgium, in 1967.
3. Van den Berg, J. H., *Medische Macht en Medische Etiek,* 1969.
4. Ibid., 48.
5. Ficarra, B. J., *Surgical and Allied Malpractice,* 1968.
6. Ibid., 814.
7. Ibid.
8. Ibid., 808.
9. Ibid.
10. *S v. Makali* 1950 (1) SA 340 (N).
11. Ibid., 343 - 4.
12. *S v. Hartmann* 1975 (3) SA 532 (C).
13. *The Sanctity of Life and the Criminal Law,* 1957.
14. Ibid., 288 - 9.
15. Dempster, W. J., 'Legalize Euthanasia for Transplants', *Codicillus,* October 1958, Vol. 9, No. 2, 13.
16. The words are quoted by C. Daly in *Morals, Law and Life,* 1966, 21.
17. 1972 (3) SA 1 (A).
18. Ibid., 25. (Translated from Afrikaans.)
19. First reported in 32 (1969) THRHR 392; see now 1975 (3) SA 538 (T).
20. Ehrhardt, H., *Euthanasie und Vernichtung 'Lebensunwerten' Lebens,* 1965, 7.

Religious and Ethical Aspects of Euthanasia

AN ANGLICAN VIEWPOINT

Roger H. Ellis

In August 1975 the Church of England Information Office published
*On Dying Well: An Anglican Contribution to the Debate on
Euthanasia*[1] being a report from the Board for Social Responsibility.
In March 1976 the General Synod of the Church of England
received and welcomed the report. Thus in a real sense my task of
representing the Anglican view on euthanasia is made the more
simple as an informed and responsible report of the Anglican
position can easily be summarized and a report acknowledged by
the General Synod of the Church of England comes as close to
expressing an Anglican viewpoint as one could wish.[2] Thus the
main lines of this paper will be a highlighting of the more important
conclusions reached in *On Dying Well* with some personal reflec-
tions when necessary.

Terminology is invariably a problem when discussing concepts
such as this and certainly becomes one when dealing with euthanasia. The report rejects the phrase 'right to die' as suffering from
'a dangerous ambiguity' and this especially as 'it serves to mask
three quite distinct demands'.[3] As terminology will be central to our
Symposium I quote in full, with the 'three demands' being as
follows:

   (i) that the individual should in principle be free to determine
      whether he shall live or die and that, in the event of his
      choosing to die he should be entitled to be assisted in so
      doing by the medical profession, except in so far as his
      rights are limited by the general interest;

  (ii) that a doctor should with the patient's consent be free,
      under certain safeguards, to end the patient's life in cases
      (if there are such) where it is medically impossible to control
      the pain;

 (iii) that

      (a) a patient *in extremis* should not be subjected to
         troublesome treatments which cannot restore him to
         health, and

      (b) doctors may use drugs to control pain even at the risk
         of shortening life.[3]

The Report goes on to argue — and I believe rightly — that (iii) does not involve euthanasia at all for it does not involve deliberately killing the patient though under (iii) (b) notice must be taken of Joseph Fletcher, an Episcopalian renowned for his Situation Ethics, who has given currency to the term 'indirect euthanasia' or 'anti-dysthanasia', i.e. refusal to prolong an ugly or painful state.[4] Thus while forms (i) and (ii), which involve direct intervention to cause death, are not recognized by the Report as being ethical, two of the final set of conclusions allow for (iii) in the following terms:[5]

(1) In its narrow current sense, euthanasia implies killing and it is misleading to extend it to cover decisions not to preserve life by artificial means when it would be better for a patient to be allowed to die. Such decisions, coupled with a determination to give the patient as good a death as possible, may be quite legitimate.[6]

(2) Nor should it be used to cover the giving of drugs for the relief of pain and other distress in cases where there is a risk that they may marginally shorten the patient's life. This too we think legitimate.[7]

Thus the clear position is adopted that a patient *in extremis* should not be subjected to troublesome treatment which cannot restore him to health nor should drugs to control pain be withheld even if it hastens death. This, the report affirms, is not voluntary euthanasia. More so it suggests in strong terms that 'much, though not all, of the case for voluntary euthanasia would be met by wider recognition of the limits to be set upon attempts to prolong life when further treatment offers no reasonable hope of recovery or significant alleviation.'[7] To the present writer this is a point to be made most central as it is the primary contribution that the theologian can make in this medico-ethical debate. As Joseph Fletcher so rightly reminds us 'the problem of anti-dysthanasia is . . . . a problem of medical success, not of medical failure',[8] and so within this context the theologian can offer a positive understanding of death which asserts that death has both a Godward as well as a manward direction. Thus death is not intrinsically negative, prolonging of life can be in reality a prolonging of death and allowing death can be the right and loving thing to do. To this we must return later, but the point remains that the medical world needs an assurance that a good death [a literal *eu* (= good) *thanatos* (= death)] is not a failure, not a negativity to be avoided regardless, but under God can be a positive to be embraced.

But, as its main contribution to the debate the Report offers the insights expressed in its Conclusions 4 and 5:[9]

(4) If all the care of the dying were up to the standards of the best, there would be few cases in which there was even a *prima facie* argument for euthanasia; better alternative means of alleviating distress would almost always be available if modern techniques and human understanding and care of the patient were universally practised.

(5) It should be the aim to improve the care of the dying in hospitals and hospices and in their homes to as near this standard as the money and the staff available will allow. We think that, at present, ignorance and mistaken ideas are a greater obstacle than shortage of money or staff.

These conclusions can well be summarized as an opposition to euthanasia by affirmation of a gospel for the dying, through society's development of better medical care and of a more compassionate approach to terminally ill patients. It is along these lines that the main burden of the Report runs; alongside it is the firm contention that to legalize deliberate killing of the dying, i.e. any form, even of voluntary euthanasia, would cause greater evils than it would remove.[11] The grounds for this assertion are well spelt out in their seventh and final conclusion which deals explicitly with the problems that would be brought about by a change in legislation. It reads as follows:[12]

(7) However, to justify a change in the law in this country to permit euthanasia, it would be necessary to show that such a change would remove greater evils than it would cause. We do not believe that such a justification can be given; for

(a) such cases are very few, and would be fewer still if medical, and in particular hospital, practices were sounder;

(b) a change in the law would reduce the incentive to improve these practices;

(c) the legalization of euthanasia would place some terminal, and even some non-terminal, patients under pressure to allow themselves to be put away — a pressure which they should be spared;

(d) it would also, in practice, be likely to result in recourse to euthanasia in many cases in which it was far from morally justified, and performed for unsound reasons;

(e) in the rare cases (if such there are) in which it can be justified morally, it is better for medical men to do all

15

that is necessary to ensure peaceful dying, and to rely on the flexibilities in the administration of the law which even now exist, than to legalize euthanasia (which would have to be subject to rigid formalities and safeguards) for general use;

(f) although there may be some patients whose relationship with their doctor would not suffer, we believe that for the great majority of patients their confidence in doctors would be gravely weakened.

And for myself this final point embraces a precious possession, one never to be forgotten by the medical world and one which the laity must strive to have maintained. To it we must return later.

With the main conclusions now stated our attention must turn to the theological arguments supporting them, for the Christian should never forget that moral debate takes place within a context of religious belief and hope. Further, I doubt if we realize with sufficient clarity that our underlying concepts of God largely determines the shape of our theological and ethical thinking. In my experience of debate on euthanasia it has usually been necessary to clear the theological ground first.[13] Indeed the Report rightly focuses the theological consideration upon the doctrine of God as Creator. Herein comes the delicate balance between saying that the whole created order is a gift from God and ultimately depends on him while also asserting that men are called to exercise that freedom under God and to be his fellow workers. Regarding the former position, the conclusion reached can be that euthanasia should not be carried out, since respect for God's creation and the consequent value of human life prohibit it. On the latter argument that man must share as co-worker with God, the conclusion can emerge, (also based on the value of human life), that the act of physical destruction could be a morally creative act for a greater value could be achieved in a person's life, *taken as a whole,* if he knew that at a certain stage of his dying he would be painlessly put to death rather than be allowed to linger on, feeling himself a burden to others as well as to himself.[14] In this sense his death could be seen as a good.

The Report is desperately honest in weighing up the strengths and weaknesses of both positions though it finally argues against the latter on two grounds:

(i) Firstly, on an understanding of death which sees death as the destruction of man himself thus forcing man to a faith which throws itself fully on the love of God — a faith in what God can and will achieve. Interestingly Hugh Trowell, a chaplain/doctor, in his work on euthanasia allows himself a personal opinion only on his final page, and here he asserts:

> Dying and death can only be transformed, and its dolours mitigated by those who have thought out their position with regard to death. It is the unthinking man who cannot face the dark night. . . . This situation needs to be transformed; it has to be redeemed. . . . He gave life to us, when there was not life; to him we yield our lives in death to be held safe and secure.[15]

(ii) Secondly, the report raises the stark issue as to whether voluntary euthanasia, in the sense of direct killing, even with the patient's consent and even if appearing in that existential situation to be morally justifiable, might still not be questionable in the light that 'agape is better expressed and more freely nourished by the careful accompanying of a person in his dying'.[16]

The final point of the theological section is treated with equal honesty in recognizing differing positions and here turns its attention to exceptional cases. The concern as expressed is whether we are restricted to a choice between an absolute prohibition of euthanasia and an absolute permission of it. They admit that this cannot be, for there might well be, indeed from time to time there are, highly unusual cases in which the general principle that euthanasia should not be, has to be overthrown. This is brave and honest and agapaic ethics and is expressed in their sixth conclusion. It reads:[17]

(6) In situations in which, for any reason, the techniques referred to in (Conclusion) 4 . . . . are not available (as might happen, for example, in the jungle, in emergencies and accidents, or in war, where medical aid is lacking or insufficient) exceptional cases could conceivably arise in which deliberate killing would be morally justified as being in the best interest of the person concerned.

So it is interesting to note that in the section relating to the Law, the plea is again made to let the law stay as it is for no law, no professional ethic, can be built upon exceptional cases and yet there will always be exceptional cases. It would hardly be possible in legislation to specify these cases precisely enough in advance to prevent the categories of exceptional cases being continuously expanded, under both good and bad pressures, which will always exist.[18] Indeed, the whole euthanasia debate has been bedevilled by the differing interpretation of 'when' euthanasia can be administered; this uncertainty must play no insignificant role in our weighing up of the ethical concerns in the debate.

As the present writer reads the Report and as he understands the Anglican position, four points can be considered central. They are as follows:

(i) the underlying ethical position can be firmly stated viz., the value of the human being and the sanctity of life. This is both theological and instinctive and the Report rightly warns us that 'in matters so fundamental to our well being as those of life and death, we interfere at our peril with deeply felt attitudes and convictions.[19] This is a basic proposition in any medico-ethical discussion[20] but although the main lines laid down are clear the principle allows for interpretation, hence the next point.

(ii) that troublesome treatment for a person *in extremis* or the administration of drugs to control pain even if life is thereby shortened, is not euthanasia at all but an extension of Christian *agape*. For myself I would have liked this to have been made even more central, for it is here that the 'voluntary euthanasia' does rightly question the medical profession's tendency to 'keep alive' and the questions and concerns that that Society raise with feeling and concern must not be lightly dismissed. Joseph Fletcher, from a different perspective, has also highlighted what can be described as a 'nervousness of one's life being unnecessarily prolonged' by pointing to the undoubted success of medical progress: the prolongation of life — even via a machine — is now within the power of the medical man.[21] Rather, it can be urged, the role mentioned earlier of man through his freedom being a co-worker with God gives to a man a responsibility under God. Thus the moment of death is not in the hands of God — surely freedom denies this?[22] — but the result of our freedom, and one can go on and assert that the responsibility of the creation of life (as in the Abortion debate), and the permitting of death (our present debate), lies deeply within man's power through his freedom, and this becomes his 'terrible responsibility'.[23] Thus with medical advances and successes the control of death has passed forcibly within man's responsibility and, without care, the simple *prolonging* of life can become a prolonging of *death,* if not a denying of death. This is not to speak for

18

direct euthanasia — though Joseph Fletcher would say it did.[24] I wish to underline instead the new set of responsibilities which medical advances have brought about, and to offer the suggestion that the responsibility of freedom under God, (the responsibility of being in the image of God), now includes the action of suspended treatment or the acceleration of pain-killing drugs that will shorten life within the simple prayer of 'Father, we send your child back to you'. Thus the allowing of death can be positively and agapeically viewed, with no sense of direct euthanasia, and now as an expression of our responsibility under God.

(iii) that in all this there be a return to the literal understanding of our basic term 'euthanatos' — 'dying well', and that society as a whole learn what care of the dying entails. By 'the whole of society' I include both minister and doctor — the former too untrained and the latter either doing too much, or, through helplessness, too little. The Report certainly underlines the point that doctors are themselves often inadequate in their care of the dying[25] and the Church with concern for youth, education, evangelism and in-group debate has long neglected this area of real concern. How right the Report is in claiming that the number of cases calling for euthanasia would be reduced if proper and informed care were exercised by all, following the example of Dr Ciceley Saunders, a founder in the Anglican Church of hospices for the dying, and whose writings remain inspirational.[26] Again, in this debate, the Church remains guilty of fine words and indifferent action, and hopefully this symposium will inspire her anew!

(iv) that we leave the Law alone rather than encourage Parliament to widen it to embrace the requests of the 'voluntary euthanasia' societies. The fear here is that what can be humanly practised at present in South Africa could become regimented in difficult legislation. More so the 'voluntary euthanasia' declaration places an unethical burden — if not blackmail — on the doctor, and, finally, that vital trust in the medical world would be undermined. This might appear simplistic but must be viewed alongside the previous points. I believe that the doctors do not need as much protection from law on this matter as they need a positive appraisal of death, which this paper — and the underlying English report — has attempted to give.

19

Two difficult points remain. The first relates to the third conclusion, not yet mentioned here which reads: [27]

(3) We have not examined and therefore have not advanced any conclusion about cases where children are born with severely crippling and incurable defects, or where an attempted cure might, if unsuccessful, leave the patient with such a defect. Our concern has been with *voluntary* euthanasia.'

Thus there is no Anglican position here,[28] but the Report's insistence on the value and the worth of the human person and its acknowledgement of the 'exceptional cases' points in the direction of treating as ethically valid a decision not to allow life to an infant whose quality of life would be such as to render it sub-human, i.e. where to all intents and purposes humanness is not present. Indeed, yet again criteria cannot be laid down here — at least not by the medical layman, and the absence of a paediatrician on the panel of speakers could be a glaring omission — but support has to be given to the practitioner who, in his or her loneliness, is faced with the responsibility as a co-worker under God to make an agapaeic decision based firmly on the value and dignity and sanctity of the human life in which some particular infant will never be able to share. The individual doctor's decision will remain final but the theologian can at least stand by him and support his decision that here the quality of life has fallen below that of a relationship level, which surely is the hallmark of God-intended life. Again, the freedom within man and nature (which can produce such deformity) demands in turn a repeat of that simple prayer: 'Father, we send your child back to you'. A positive appraisal of euthanasia is surely demanded here, the Church cannot expect the doctor to make the lonely decision without the support of a positive ethic of life and death.

The other concern left by the Report relates directly to our life in South Africa. The Report as I have summarized it, along with my own comments, reflects that of a White middle class position in touch with medical attention of a sophisticated kind. The Report admits this in its final paragraph: 'There are still parts of the world where medical facilities are not readily available and where physical suffering can be both acute and prolonged. Such parts of the world pose their own problems, both legal and ethical.[29] Undoubtedly such parts of the world include at least our rural Blacks and many in the townships as well. Has the Anglican anything different to say here? No doubt the Black Anglican has and the White Anglican can only listen in humility, sharing insights with him while remaining aware of the vast difference in situation. If in many of these situations 'dying well' surely cannot be, we must explore again the category of 'exceptional circumstances'. It would be presumptuous of me to say more, other than to acknowledge that I am aware of a wider range of problems than exist in England and with its Health Service and for myself with the comfort of a Medical Aid Society behind me, and that I eagerly anticipate a later contribution which all of us take with utter seriousness.

The ultimate strength of the Anglican Report, and which is its central position, remains its contention that before all else we must be committed to a 'Gospel for the dying' and only in an honest appraisal of what that really involves must we go on to test the ethical validity of euthanasia, provided that, in the end, *agape* — love — is served as Christ willed.

1. Published for the General Synod Board for Social Responsibility by the Church Information Office, London, 1975. Hereafter cited as *The Report*. It should be noted that wherever possible only the views of Anglicans are cited in this contribution.
2. I have found no record of any discussion on euthanasia in the records of the Provincial Synod of the Church of the Province of South Africa (Anglican).
3. *The Report*, 8. The same concern is often expressed. From the Anglican side it comes through forcibly in *Teaching Christian Ethics* a manual for use in Anglican Theological Colleges, S.C.M. Press, London, 1974, 108 ff. See too the entry 'Euthanasia' by Thomas Wood in *A Dictionary of Christian Ethics*, London, S.C.M., 1967, ed. John MacQuarrie, 119 ff.
4. Joseph Fletcher, *Moral Responsibility*, London, S.C.M., 1967, 141 ff. and the chapter 'Euthanasia and Anti-Dysthanasia'. Here Fletcher, working on the principles of his Situation Ethics, goes further than the Report by admitting (150) that he is in favour of the 'direct' method. Thus as an Episcopalian he represents the extreme view within Anglicanism.
5. *The Report*, 61.
6. The same conclusion was reached in an earlier Church Information Office publication "Decisions about Life and Death' London, 1965. cf. Herbert Waddam's *A New Introduction to Moral Theology*, London, 3rd revised edn., 1974, 200 - 1, who takes a similar line but his treatment of the subject is too vague to be helpful.
7. *The Report*, 10.
8. Ibid., 160.
9. Ibid., 61.

10. *The Report* is at pains to demonstrate this and ch. 4 deals with seven case studies (25 ff.) and ch. 5 with 'Further Medical Considerations'.
11. *The Report* deals with this in many places — ch. 2 on 'Moral Considerations' and ch. 6 on 'Legal Considerations'. The latter concludes (60), 'Even if it be conceded that in ethics there are occasions untouched by the present law when it may be justifiable to kill, the rarity of such occasions is such that in England any attempt to legislate for them is almost sure to fail, while the evils to which such an attempt could give rise are so great that the attempt should not be made.'
12. Ibid., 62.
13. *The Report* recognizes this though perhaps less stridently, e.g. 15: 'To the Christian . . . moral reflection and decision are embedded in his total relationship to God, and moral language is delicately interwoven with religious language. Freedom is set within a context of obedience, responsibility within a context of divine invitation and grace'.
14. Ibid., 18. The italics are in the original.
15. *The Unfinished Debate on Euthanasia,* London, S.C.M., 1973, 150. He touches on the same point on p. 133 where he refers to 'the amazing deepening of the dying person'. See *The Report,* 19.
16. *The Report,* 22.
17. Ibid., 61.
18. Chapter 6 of the *Report* deals with the legal considerations which are summed up in Conclusion 7.
19. Ibid., 14.
20. I have developed this point at length in my contribution in *The Ethics of Human Tissue Transplantation,* Cape Town, Timmins, 1972, 87 ff.
21. See *Moral Responsibility,* ch. 9 'Euthanasia and Anti-Dysthanasia', 144 ff, in particular. Care must be taken not to overstate the case here. Trowell, op. cit., 148 and the Report's discussion of Case Histories, 25 ff and Appendix I — 'The Relief of Pain in Terminal Illness' must be borne in mind.
22. This is a basic insight of Process Theology. See as an introduction Norman Pittenger in *A Dictionary of Christian Theology,* ed. Alan Richardson, S.C.M., London, 1967.
23. See the ethical works of J. A. T. Robinson for a development of this and in particular *Christian Freedom in a Permissive Society,* S.C.M., London, 1970, 58 & 63 ff.
24. See under footnote (4) above.
25. *The Report,* ch. 5, 'Further Medical Considerations' and in particular p. 46. It is interesting to note that in the Debate of the General Synod one clerical speaker asserted that the 'gospel of dying' was still far from being accepted by the medical profession 'who had not yet been able to come to terms with the problem of terminal sickness' and a medical member in agreeing asserted that the gospel of dying needed to be understood by the medical profession. See 'Church Times' report of 5 March 1976, 4.
26. See for example the Chapter 'Terminal Care' in *Medical Oncology,*

ed. L. D. Bagshawe, Oxford, Blackwell, 1975, and 'Dimensions of Death' in *Religion and Medicine,* ed. M. A. H. Melinsky, S.C.M., London, 1970.
27. *The Report,* 61. The italics are in the original.
28. An example of the problem with an agapaeic solution is found in H. Trowell, *The Unfinished Debate on Euthanasia,* 137 f.
29. *The Report,* 60.

A ROMAN CATHOLIC VIEWPOINT

G. C. Goosen

Euthanasia, like many other contemporary problems, is extremely complex. It is not a problem that can be answered in a single sentence or paragraph without running the risk of oversimplifying or being patently naive. Any discussion on euthanasia thus requires a certain clarification of one's basic evaluation of matters such as life and death before one can proceed to make oneself, or one's decisions understood. This is particularly important in ethics, which is our concern here. In the past, in Christian ethics or moral theology, there was a tendency to suggest that answers were straightforward and fairly simple if you followed the rules, but little attempt was made to fill in the thinking behind those rules. The result of this approach was that ethics or morals became a sort of question-and-answer game where one put forward a hypothetical moral question, pressed a button (the teacher or textbook) and out popped the answer. This mechanical, facile approach is hopefully a thing of the past.

Changes in moral theology

One of the changes in moral theology today is precisely an attempt to wean people away from the ready-answer approach. *Gaudium et Spes* (No. 34) warns against individuals expecting their pastors to give them detailed answers for every practical ethical problem. Instead the individual should be prepared to act according to his own well-informed Christian conscience, while giving due attention to the teaching of the Church. In moral matters, people must learn to listen to the voice of God in the many ways it can come to them, and then make their own decisions in a given set of circumstances which can never be anticipated one hundred percent in any textbook.

Other changes in moral theology which can only be briefly mentioned here are the attempts to break away from the legalism of the past which bound persons to the letter of the law and crushed the spirit; all decisions seemed ready-made and the individual's duty was merely to follow the rules in a way which kept him an adolescent in moral decision-making. Legalism meant the rigid adherence to the 'natural law' which was seen as a detailed code, nicely drawn up with the help of deductive logic, absolutely normative in all circumstances, ready for automatic application.[1] Together with this went a marked biologism in morality, i.e., a tendency to see some problems, such as contraception, abortion, marital intercourse, euthanasia, etc., only, or mainly, from a biological viewpoint. This biased approach inevitably led to solutions which we must either wholly or partially reject today. Inherent in this latter approach is the neglect of any dialogue with other disciplines such as medicine, psychology, sociology, anthropology, which could help the individual come to a more mature decision. Today we have hopefully dropped a one-sided, casuistic approach in favour of a study of ethical problems in dialogue with other disciplines and on a more pastoral level than formerly. A deepening of our understanding of the problem and a ready appreciation of what other relevant disciplines think on the subject should place us in a position where we can gain deeper insight into the human side of the problem and thus, in the light of the scriptures and the teaching of the Church, come to a more mature solution.

Our attitude to life and death

As euthanasia is an area of moral theology which is concerned with the termination of life, it follows that one's attitude to life and death is going to be reflected in one's attitude towards euthanasia. Or, to express it in another way: the answers one gives to the ethical issues related to euthanasia will depend on the meaning one gives to life and death. If one is penetrated with a thoroughly Christian concept of what life and death are all about, one need not feel over anxious about making this or that particular decision on euthanasia in a given case, however difficult. I think this is true in the same way that a person who is in love with God and his neighbour does not need to fear that he will not know how to act when he comes across a neighbour in distress. In both cases one's ingrained convictions readily translate into actions.

However, to say that our approach to euthanasia depends on our Christian understanding of life and death is a very general statement. Our attitude to many other ethical problems, such as abortion, contraception, sterilization, etc., also depends on this. Although we are mainly concerned here with euthanasia, our

Christian concern for life must obviously extend over the whole span of man's life, and not focus only on isolated moments of life, however important they may be. One of the recurrent pleas from euthanasia societies[2] is the right to die with human dignity, with which I agree, but would insist on adding the right to be born and live with human dignity as well. Our concern for life must be all-inclusive — from the womb to the tomb; if not, we lay ourselves open to charges of selective morality and hypocrisy. Thus, for the Christian, his respect for life in the womb, his concern for the poor and the sick in life, and his attitude towards death, all form part of one general approach to life. Conversely, the abortionist who also advocates active euthanasia is being consistent in his lack of respect for human life.

The value of life

Traditionally, philosophers and theologians have agreed on the *inherent value* of human existence. This appreciation of human life has been especially highlighted by contemporary existential and personalist philosophers. Man is seen as a single unit, as a consciousness present in this world in a material form, as existing in time and space, or in Heidegger's phrase, as 'being-in-the-world'. Man is not so much a being comprising both material and non-material elements, but rather a unity whose characteristic way of being is the body. Furthermore, he is not only being-in-the-world, but being-with-others, i.e. he relates to others, he has an inherent social dimension. In short, man is unique among the living creatures and therefore possesses a special, unique value. Hence, to a certain degree, man's life is inviolable, i.e. he cannot be arbitrarily destroyed like animal life.

Life can also be seen as a process of self-realization, as an opportunity to realize oneself to one's fullest potential. In this sense, self-destruction would be a throwing away of the chances of realizing those qualities and opportunities, and thus anti-life and irrational. From another angle, Heidegger stresses that man's being in this world is a *Sein-zum-Tode,* a being-for-death, and hence self-destruction would be a denial of one's very nature in the world. Man's nature therefore demands that man should accept death, for his entire existence in life is 'towards death'. He should accept death and not inflict it on himself.

The inviolability of human life clearly does not flow from any external quality or characteristic which it may or may not possess,

26

but from an *intrinsic worth* which all accept, although individuals may articulate this in different ways.

Christianity affirms what mankind has said about the inherent value and dignity of human life. It affirms man's basic unity and his living-in-this-world for God and for others, although he has a destiny beyond this world. More than simply living in this world, Christianity affirms life as a participation in the life of God in such a way that earthly life makes possible and prepares for participation in eternal life. Man's life is affirmed and appreciated then for what he *is, not* for what he *has,* or what *use* he might be to society. Man's striving to realize himself is a striving to a fullness of life which has been accomplished in the Incarnation, and it was precisely for this reason that Christ came — so that we might have life to the full.

Facing up to death

Life is one thing, but death quite another and a less attractive reality to face. There are many ways in which man seeks to come to terms with death, some positive, many negative, but wherever he turns, one thing is certain, and that is that man cannot really ignore it for long because sooner or later it will impinge on his life.

One attempt to come to terms with death seems to be that time-honoured way of avoidance, which is never, however, completely successful, since death has the habit of asserting itself in a relentless way. When we are forced to speak of death, we revert to euphemisms. We thus tend to deny death or banish it from the realm of reality. People are said to 'pass away', 'go to their rest', or 'move on'. Death and what reminds us of it, is removed from us not only mentally, but physically as well. Thus the ageing are geographically separated from the rest and banished to 'leisure worlds', 'sunset villages', 'valleys of happiness' or other such bucolic-sounding places. To indulge in this world of make-believe is not really a solution to the problem of death at all, since the stark reality soon enough penetrates this artificial language smokescreen.

Another approach to death is one which is often presented by Albert Camus in his novels. In *The Plague,*[3] for example, death is symbolized by the disease which threatens each and everyone in the city of Oran. No-one escapes death. The wall of death encompasses all. So overwhelming is the presence of this evil that virtues such as love and devotion pale into an abstraction before it. In fact, faced with death and unable to find a rational explanation for it, Tarrow claims, 'Death means nothing to men like me.' For the unbeliever death presents a cul-de-sac that appears absurd and ridiculous. In *The Outsider*[4] we note a certain fatalism in the face of certain death. Meursault does not mind dying as it is the inevitable fate of all men. 'This business of dying,' he muses, 'has to be got through sooner or later.' And thus it is true for all men, of whom Meursault is symbolic, that they are trapped in life as Meursault was in prison, and must await the inevitable sentence of death.

Bacon is reported to have said that 'no man is capable of fully enjoying life if he has not cultivated the habit of thinking serenely on death'.[5] This, I believe, is what the Christian's task is, as regards death. One can only live well and die well if one has come to terms in a meaningful way, with one's personal death. And the Christian way of ensuring a happy death is not Camus' way of money, time and peace of heart, as he suggests in *A Happy Death*.[6]

The Christian should neither seek to avoid death, nor accept it in a fatalistic way. For the Christian death is the end of the natural process of life on earth which comes to an end only to give way to eternal life with God. Man's destiny is, for the believer, so magnificent that he can become so enthusiastic about it to the point of longing, like Paul, 'to be with Christ'. In this sense death can come, in Hamlet's words, 'a consummation devoutly to be wished'! Death is the gateway to eternal happiness and union with Jesus Christ. For the unbeliever, death is merely the dissolution into nothingness of a life that has been so absurd in many ways.

The different kinds of euthanasia

At this point it will perhaps be useful to mention the different connotations given to the word 'euthanasia', as much of the misunderstanding in discussions on euthanasia stems from a lack of defining exactly what one means by the word. In general, the following distinctions are made:

    a. as regards the means use:

        (i) *Passive* or *negative* euthanasia — by this is meant the intended omission of treatment that would probably prolong life; in a more restricted sense it could refer to the omission of treatment in the case of a patient beyond all hope of recovery and for whom it is only a case of prolonging or shortening the death process;

(ii) *Active* or *positive* euthanasia — this refers to the planned use of therapies calculated to induce death sooner than it would normally occur. This kind of euthanasia is sometimes called 'mercy killing'. The direct intention is always to put an end to the life of a patient, although the main motive is often one of compassion;

b. as regards the consent of the patient:

(i) *Voluntary euthanasia* refers to cases where the patient clearly indicates his or her desire that the doctor should accelerate the process of death;

(ii) *Compulsory euthanasia* occurs when people are 'killed' by the State or some other body because they are unfit to live, useless to society, economically unproductive, racially or genetically undesirable, or some other kindred reason.

The Roman Catholic position

Let us now be more specific. Roman Catholics, in the light of all that has been said above, are, and always have been, in favour of euthanasia in the *original meaning* of the word as a *good, easy,* and *tranquil death.* As life is from God it must be respected and people must be allowed to die with dignity. On this point we can fully agree with euthanasia societies. We believe that there is a time for living and a time for dying, and thus Catholic teaching affirms quite clearly that it is wrong to seek to prolong life when all the medical evidence points to the fact that the process of death is well established. Dying persons should be allowed to die if they are beyond recovery. In the past, moralists have been influenced by a certain biologism, and doctors by an exaggerated somatic approach, which saw physical death as the greatest possible evil that could befall man, and thus they strove to preserve life at all costs. Some doctors even saw the death of their patient as a direct insult to their profession! Death is part and parcel of the natural process of entering and leaving this world. To try and reverse this process is futile folly. A sound, commonsense attitude is required here, as the proverb reminds us, 'Thou shalt not kill, yet should not strive officiously to keep alive'.

These are, however, the general guidelines. Once we try to apply these directives in practice we come across many difficulties. (For this reason it is wrong to create the impression, as Catholic morality has often done in the past, that solutions can be arrived at as surely and mechanically as if one were using a computer.) How does one know for certain that the process of death has irreversibly set in? What, for example, does the care of terminal cancer patients entail? Is intravenous feeding in these cases obligatory? Where is the dividing line between neglect of one's duty and 'allowing the patient to die'? How long does one have to be in a comatose condition before the case can be declared beyond hope?

Ordinary and extraordinary means

Again, as a guide to these and other difficult situations, Catholic morality has come forward with a distinction which, even if somewhat vague and hypothetical, does retain much validity today and can be a great help to all concerned. In the case of preserving life, it is said that one is *obliged* to use *ordinary* means, but one is *not always obliged* to use *extraordinary* means.[7]

By the term *ordinary* means is meant 'all medicines, treatments, and operations, which offer a reasonable hope of benefit for the patient and which can be obtained and used without excessive expense, pain or other inconvenience'.[8] By contrast, *extraordinary* means indicate 'all medicines, treatments, and operations, which cannot be obtained or used without excessive expense, pain, or other inconvenience, or which, if used, would not offer a reasonable hope of benefit'.[9]

These two concepts derive from the general distinction between avoiding evil and doing good. One is always obliged to avoid evil, such as taking another's life; but there are reasonable limits to one's duty of doing good. Thus, the duty to preserve life is a duty to do good which has reasonable limits, whereas 'mercy killing' is evil and hence must be avoided.

On the question of where the reasonable limits lie, the individual caring for the patient has to ask himself what God expects of him as regards his duty of preserving life in this particular situation. (And the physician's duty is *primarily* to preserve life, not alleviate pain.) In seeking an answer, he must consider such practical problems as expense, pain, and other inconveniences. It might well be morally wrong, for example, for a terminal patient to spend his life savings on a costly operation. Such a decision might impose undue financial hardship on his family. But let us stress that each case must be judged as it arises and the decision as to ordinary and extraordinary means must be left to the reasonable judgment

30

of prudent and conscientious men.

What complicates the distinction between ordinary and extraordinary means still further is that both terms depend on circumstances of time, place and person. A respirator, for example, might be considered an ordinary means in some urban hospitals, but may be virtually unobtainable in rural areas; an operation costing R2 000 might be no financial burden for a rich family, but could be out of the question for another; for a doctor, 'ordinary' might simply mean what is customary as opposed to unusual treatment, whereas, as pointed out, the ethicist uses non-medical criteria for determining what ordinary and extraordinary means are.[10] In spite of the relativity of these terms, they still maintain a validity insofar as they serve as guidelines and suggest what questions should be asked in the process of decision-making.

From what has been said so far, it can be seen that the Catholic position is a firm NO to active or positive euthanasia, as being in Barth's words, 'an arrogant usurping of the role of God'; but passive or negative euthanasia could be acceptable in certain limited cases, e.g. a therapy which was only prolonging death in a hopeless case could be withdrawn, allowing the patient to die. Along these lines one could speculate whether intravenous feeding is obligatory for a terminal patient whose heart is strong,[11] or whether 'pulling the plug' on a comatose patient is permissible, etc., but these are situations which should be left to the people concerned to decide as they arise. As we said above, the actual decision, the application of the theory, is often agonizingly difficult, but what is more important in a way is the dynamic of the moral decision-making. A thorough Christian understanding of life and death will help the individual to come to his own decision, whereas a completely *utilitarian* or *materialistic* ethic (and this outlook is more common than we think) will logically advocate active euthanasia.

The problem of evil and suffering

If one reads the literature published by the euthanasia societies, one is struck, among other things, by the utter sincerity and deep human compassion of these writers.[12] They are genuinely moved by the pitiable victims of excruciating and humiliating illnesses and suffering. They are moved by suffering which is so inhuman and cruel, that it automatically raises the questions: Why? What is the reason behind it? Why do the good suffer and the bad seemingly get away with their evil deeds? Why do some people suffer so much

31

and others not at all? Why do innocent children have to suffer (this was the stumbling block for Doctor Rieux in *The Plague* '. . . . until my dying day I shall refuse to love a scheme of things in which children are put to torture."). Why should some be born no better than vegetables (a point Joseph Fletcher has used to develop his theory of qualified 'personhood');[13] and finally, *what is suffering*? If no satisfactory answers can be found to these questions, then perhaps it is logical to do what the ancient Indians did and take the incurables to the bank of the Ganges, fill their noses and mouths with sacred mud and throw them into the river; or, as they did on the Isle of Cos — invite the old to a last banquet and during the course of the meal give them a poisoned drink.[14]

One solution to the mystery of suffering is thus active euthanasia. Another way of looking at the problem is to see life as having a positive and negative side. Life as growth, as self-realization, is the positive side, whereas evil and suffering represent the obverse side of the coin, life's negativity. Evil is the antithesis of good as it were, and without good evil is inconceivable. To contemplate and experience evil can thus be a way of knowing good, a means of arriving at an appreciation of what 'good' means. In other words, we can derive something positive from considering its very negativity.

In the sense of what we have just said, Ricoeur refers to suffering as non-being sensed before it is thought.[15] Suffering for him is the most vivid form of self-consciousness, i.e. in suffering consciousness becomes separated, focused and sees itself negated. In this way it heightens one's presence in the world. Descartes and Spinoza likewise saw evil and suffering as a diminution or lessening of being. If one thinks for a moment, not only of suffering, but of ageing, extreme fatigue (which empties and 'nihilates' me), loss of consciousness, sleep and fainting (a certain loss of waking consciousness, or 'absence'), one can see in all these a certain vague experience of 'having to die', a warning or indication of what is ahead. This is valid to a point, but in fact, death remains unique since it can never be partially experienced, it is 'The undiscovered country from whose bourn no traveller returns', and as such, must remain, in Ricoeur's words, 'a stranger to life'.

Pain, suffering, and evil in general, thus all reveal a certain lack of being, a certain negativity which threatens man's being-in-the-world. It forces man to consider himself, to reflect on his mode of being in this world and to contemplate 'the sorrow of his contingency'.

The Christian can readily identify himself with this approach, as indeed Evely has done: 'Suffering and death are the only unavoidable obstacles which compel the most mediocre man to call himself into question, to detach himself from his existence, and to ask himself what would permit him to transcend it.'[16] And I believe that it is precisely in questioning himself and his existence that he can come to a humble acceptance of man's inherent limitations and weaknesses and see them as an expression of his negativity and finitude.

A model of suffering

In the discussion on euthanasia, the emphasis is unfortunately on what is ethically allowed and what is not, with the consequent tendency to neglect the positive side, namely the necessity of dying well. What is urgently needed is not so much an ethic of euthanasia, but of 'benemortasia', as Arthur Dyck has pointed out.[17] And here as Christians, in accepting our suffering as an experience of our finitude, we can turn to Christ to learn the truly 'Christian' response. He experienced suffering and sought consolation. In the garden of Gethsemane, in a moment of death-anxiety, he found no consolation in his best friends, but only in dialogue with the Father, who was constantly at his side and to whom Christ so frequently turned in prayer. Christ knew what mental and physical suffering were all about; he knew what abandonment and loneliness really feel like, especially when he was ridiculed during his trial and betrayed by his especially selected and trained group of followers. Had Christ thought only of himself and his comfort, one could understand, but he spent himself on preserving life, on curing the sick, giving sight to the blind, restoring strength to the paralysed, visiting outcasts, even raising the dead. Can we not see that Christ had to suffer and so enter into his glory, and that we too can turn our suffering into glory? Just as Christ's cry to his Father on the cross ends with joy and consolation (Ps 22), so too we should learn to turn to our Father in suffering and find our consolation in Him.

Suffering, and evil in general, is a constant reminder of our human condition in need of salvation, of the disharmony of the world with itself and with God, which can only be overcome in the death and resurrection of Christ. But in accepting it, suffering can have the effect of making one reflect on one's contingency in this world, of purifying one by helping one to realize that one's true destiny is not here, but in life with God. The greater one's love for this world, the harder this lesson is to learn. Few look forward to suffering, or to the cessation of being-in-the-world which we call death; but with the self-questioning and purification process that suffering can trigger off, comes the clearer Christian vision that the threat of non-being can be turned into a promise of a fuller life, that the darkness of night leads on to the dawn of a new day, and that the Old Jerusalem will be superseded by the New.

I see the problem of suffering as very much at the centre of the euthanasia debate. While certainly doing everything in our power to alleviate suffering, Christians see it as part of our human condition and as a means of spiritual growth, of suffering with Christ. I am well aware that this is far easier to preach than to put into practice, and I certainly do not want to minimize the terrifying dimensions that human suffering can assume. It is clear, however, that here, as in the whole question of euthanasia, one's religious convictions are the decisive factor.

1. F. M. Podimatham, *Relativity of Natural Law in the Renewal of Moral Theology*, Bombay, 1976, 56.
2. E.g. the Voluntary Euthanasia Legislation Society (TES) founded in London by the late Dr Killick Millard in 1935, and the Euthanasia Society of America (ESA) founded in New York in 1938.
3. Penguin Books, 1948.
4. Penguin Books, 1946.
5. L. Derobert, Euthanasia, in *New Problems in Medical Ethics*, ed. D. P. Flood, Cork, Mercier Press, 1956, 278.
6. Penguin Books, 1971.
7. McFadden cites two exceptions to this rule where extraordinary means might be necessary: (i) if the patient is not spiritually prepared for death; and (ii) a patient whose continued existence is vital to the common good. C. J. McFadden, *Medical Ethics*, Philadelphia, Davis Co., 1967, 242.
8. G. Kelly, *Medico-Moral Problems, Part V*, St. Louis, The Catholic Association of the US and Canada, 1957, 6.
9. Ibid.
10. C. E. Curran, *Politics, Medicine and Christian Ethics*, Philadelphia, Fortress Press, 1973, 153f.
11. Intravenous feeding could in some cases be an *ordinary* means of safeguarding life, and as a temporary measure. But in the case cited of a cancer patient who is dying but who has a strong heart, intravenous feeding could either be seen as an *extraordinary* means or as merely a *useless ordinary* means and hence non-obligatory; cf. McFadden, op. cit., 243.
12. The Rev. Charles Potter, founder of the ESA in 1938 stated that mercy was to be their prime objective: 'Perhaps the time has come to forget Moses' "Thou shalt not kill", and listen to the words of

Jesus, "Blessed are the merciful" '. R. F. Drinan, 'Euthanasia: An Emergent Danger', *Hom. Past. Rev.* 50 (1949 - 50), 221, cited by S. Cahill, *Euthanasia: Problematic of Morality and Law,* Rome, 1970, 9.

13. R. A. McCormick, 'Notes on Moral Theology', *Theological Studies* 34, No. 1, 1973, 76.
14. Dérobert, op. cit., 280.
15. P. Ricoeur, *Freedom and Nature: The Voluntary and the Involuntary,* Northwestern University Press, 1966, 450.
16. L. Evely, *Suffering,* London, Burns and Oates, 1967, 95.
17. McCormick, op. cit., 69.

A JEWISH VIEWPOINT

Abner Weiss

The problem of euthanasia is not new. Arguments, for and against, are reported in ancient and in modern times, and the legal situation is well known.[1] However, a number of recent dramatic cases, both at home and abroad, have again focused attention upon the problem, and have served to re-open the discussion.

Any meaningful discussion of the problem of euthanasia demands careful analysis of three fundamental questions: The rights of the patient; the obligations of the physician towards his patient; and the wider social and legal concomitants of 'death control'.[2]

Proponents of euthanasia, in its various forms, argue that the patient enjoys absolute title to life, that he may choose to die with dignity and that his decision to commit suicide is a legitimate option, determined by free choice. Opponents, on the other hand, argue that man does not possess absolute title to his life or to his body, that he is merely a steward of his life, which is a gift he has been privileged to receive and which he is charged with preserving. On this view, suicide is not a legitimate option. Indeed, it is argued, a patient racked with pain may well make an impulsive, ill-considered, request which might be regretted when it is too late.[3]

The physician derives his ethical warrant from the Hippocratic oath, which, on the one hand, requires that he desist from supplying deadly medicine to his patients for the purpose of hastening their demise, or even from offering advice which may lead to suicide, and, on the other, that he relieve suffering. He is guided in his practice by Osler's dictum that the function of the physician is to 'cure sometimes, relieve often and comfort always'.[4] These principles are never more severely tested than when he is involved in the treatment of the terminally ill, when he must comfort and relieve suffering even if he cannot effect a cure. He may undertake symptomatic treatment, relieving the manifestations of the disease without altering its course. He may decide upon palliative therapy, temporarily changing the course of the illness, but not influencing its course in the long run. He may prescribe analgesics or narcotics, tranquillisers and other psychotropic medications to relieve the suffering. By so doing he satisfies the higher principles of medical intent. However, when all these means fail, and unbearable suffering persists, and when the patient begs to be relieved of his agony, his ingrained compassion raises the possibility of his administering some measure primarily intended to shorten the life of his patient. This may involve the active prescription of a drug or regimen whose direct effect will be fatal — for instance, the removal of life-supporting apparatus, or the refusal to embark upon treatment of a new complication in the patient's course, such as pneumonia in a patient suffering from irreversible brain injury. In either case, the adoption of active means of hastening the end, or euthanasia by omission or neglect, the physician is faced with a legal and moral dilemma. Killing is universally sanctioned only in self-defence or by judicial decree. Laws obtaining almost universally are based upon *deontological* considerations, which require an act or deed to be *intrinsically* ethically acceptable — regardless of the *intent* of the deed. The means themselves are judged, and, in these terms, euthanasia is regarded as murder. The physician who opts for euthanasia — active or passive — tacitly rejects deontological standards, invoking *teleological* considerations. These are more forgiving, inasmuch as they seek a higher end (*telos*), or higher principle, by which an action may be judged — the 'end justifies the means' criterion of ideal utilitarianism. In the situation of the terminally ill, the termination of unbearable suffering — a fundamental imperative of the medical ethic — constitutes that higher principle which justifies the means. Accordingly, the moral and legal conflict in which the physician finds himself derives from his being stretched on a teleological frame in one direction and a deontological one in another.[5] Furthermore, not even the teleological considerations are clear-cut. The higher principle is not necessarily satisfied by euthanasia. His judgement is not infallible. There *have* been cases, however rare, of mistaken diagnosis and of remission of 'incurable' illness.[6] The decision not to prolong life withholds from the patient the benefits of a possible — if presently unlikely — medical break-through which may ameliorate his condition. Nor is the dilemma essentially eased by making a distinction between active and passive euthanasia. While the latter may avoid legal conflict, it does not really solve the moral question. Indeed, on teleological grounds, it may be argued that active euthanasia is *more* merciful to the patient, certainly abbreviating his agony — and that of his family — by hastening his demise.[7] Accordingly, without clearly defined guidelines, the physician must despair of doing right, for whatever he does can be judged to be wrong — either deontologically of teleologically.

The problem of euthanasia, moreover, is not exhausted by considering the position of the doctor and his patient. There are wider social and moral issues inherent in 'death control'. Euthanasia may be a first step on a slippery slope. If euthanasia is permitted to the incurably ill, why, logically, should such legislation not be extended to the grossly deformed, the psychotic, the senile?[8] Why should there not be 'the utilitarian incorporation of social advantage through the elimination of vegetable non-contributing members of society'?[9] Why should parents not be spared the suffering and expense of caring for a deformed child? Once the value of the individual human life is made subservient to other principles, therapeutic euthanasia may be extended to encompass eugenic or political euthanasia. 'Self interest may be cloaked in altruism'.[10] The self-serving motives of compassionate relatives and physicians, impecunious families, impatient heirs, and political leaders may be permitted to be expressed as idealism.

Happily, the Jewish tradition is rich in precedent and detailed analysis of the problem, offering guidance to the patient, the physician and the legislator. The object of this paper is to analyse the three aspects of the problem of euthanasia in terms of the legal and ethical norms of the *halakhah* — the Jewish legal tradition.

I

Judaism is, in its essence, a life-affirming faith. 'And thou shalt *live* by them [G-d's commandments]',[11] is the central imperative of Torah. 'I shall not die, but *live*',[12] declares the prophet. Man is charged with preserving, dignifying and hallowing his life. But he is not given absolute title over his life and body — only its stewardship, for life is a gift from G-d, to whom the individual is responsible for its preservation.

> My G-d, the soul with which Thou hast endowed me is pure. Thou hast created it. Thou hast formed it. Thou hast breathed it into me. Thou dost preserve it within me, and Thou wilt hereafter reclaim it and restore it to me in time to come. So long as there is soul within me, I give thanks before Thee, Lord my G-d . . .[13]

Man is never called upon to determine whether life is worth living. G-d is the sole arbiter.[14] From our point of view, life is a gift of infinite value. Since infinity is, by definition, indivisible, it clearly makes no moral difference whether one shortens life by many years or by a few minutes, or whether the person whose life has been shortened by man was young and robust, or whether he was old and physically or mentally debilitated.[15] In these terms, suicide is no less culpable than murder.[16] Judaism does not acknowledge the 'right to die'. Life and death are in the hand of G-d. 'I kill and I make alive'.[17] 'Behold all souls are Mine'.[18] This notion is eloquently and movingly articulated in the *Confession of the Dying*:

I acknowledge before Thee, my G-d and G-d of my fathers . . . that my cure is in Thy hand and my death is in Thy hand . . . And if my appointed time to die has arrived, Thou art righteous [in decreeing] all that befalls me.[19]

This is not to say that Judaism is insensitive to suffering. The term *mita yafah* (a nice death) is used several times in the Talmud,[20] in connection with capital cases, where it was recommended that the anguish of the condemned person should be alleviated with strong drink. The Talmud and later halakhic authorities sanction prayers for death, both by the patient and by those who cannot bear his suffering[21] — but the decision is left to G-d, for even suffering is acknowledged to be part of the Divine plan for man, as in the case of Job, and is rendered meaningful by the faith that conscious life exists beyond the grave.[22]

Accordingly, life in misery is preferred to death with glory or dignity — a sentiment affirmed by the Psalmist: 'The Lord hath chastened me sore; but He hath not given me over to death'.[23] The talmudic account of the martyrdom of Rabbi Hanina ben Tradyon illustrates this position. The Sage was being burned alive at the stake, enwrapped by the parchment scrolls of the Torah. Apparently death was slow in coming, for his watching disciples urged him to open his mouth, ingest the flames, and speed his demise. He refused to do so, declaring that 'it is better that my soul shall be taken by Him who gave it than that I should do any harm to it on my own'.[24]

Clearly, then, the *halakhah* does not grant the right of euthanasia to the patient and considers any request he may make of others to dispatch him quickly to stem from judgment impaired by pain and suffering.[25]

II

The physician, however, *can* be objective in his judgements. What is his professional and ethical mandate? What are the limits of his responsibility? The fact that life and death are ultimately in the hand of G-d does not preclude human participation in the healing process. On the contrary, in reply to a suggestion that one should pray: 'And mayest Thou heal me, for Thou art a faithful healing G-d, and Thy healing is sure, since men have no power to heal and [vainly] occupy themselves [with medicine]', Abaye declared, 'A man should not speak thus, since it was taught "He shall cause him to be thoroughly healed". From this we learn that permission has been given to the physician to heal.'[26] Indeed, *piku'ah nefesh*, the command to save, and preserve human life, takes precedence over all other commandments, and one who fails in this imperative is regarded as having shed blood. Although all men are bound to preserve life, *piku'ah nefesh* particularly defines the calling and the practice of the physician. Jewish law allows him wide discretion in treating his patient, but because of this wide discretion, his legal responsibility is greater than that of any other agents who perform divine commandments. Provided that he adheres to principles of therapy which have already proved successful in preserving human life, or that innovative techniques are responsibly undertaken after consultation with his peers, he is not culpable in cases of failure. Neither the fear of failure nor ungrounded theological reservations should restrain his fulfilment of the command to preserve human life.[27]

> The physician should not refrain from offering his medical services because he fears that he will kill the patient, since he is competent and well-trained. Nor should be abstain on the grounds that G-d alone is the healer of all life.[28]

This interpretation of the obligation to preserve life in no way modifies the conception that life and death are the ultimate prerogatives of G-d. It simply affirms that the physician is entrusted with the responsibility of serving as G-d's agent in the preservation of human life. Just as he is forbidden to shirk his responsibilities, so he is forbidden to exceed his mandate and to arrogate to himself the Divine prerogative of determining who shall live and who shall die.

Obviously, the obligation of the physician to preserve the life of his patient ends with his demise. He is not required to 'revive the dead'.[29] Accordingly, only a precise definition of death and provide a clear indication of the limits of medical responsibility for *piku'ah nefesh*. The *halakhic* criteria are particularly important, since a definition of death cannot be exclusively derived from medical facts or scientific investigations. The physician can do no more than describe the physiological state which he observes. Whether the patient meeting that description is to be treated as a living person or as a corpse is an ethical and legal question.[30] 'Determination of the moment of death, insofar as it is more than a mere exercise in semantics, is essentially a moral and theological problem, not a medical and scientific one.'[31] It is not surprising, therefore, that there is no universally recognized medical definition of death.[32] For the Jew, the *halakhic* criteria of death satisfy the religio-legal requirements of such a definition. Indeed, they are of crucial importance to the believing Jewish physician, because only the presence of these criteria relieves him of the obligation to use all available means in order to prolong the life of his patient.[33] Acceptance of the *halakhic* definition of death allows him to escape the painful dilemma of determining whether continued therapy is actually prolonging the life of his patient or only extending the agony of his death — a dilemma inherent in the absence of a precise definition of the moment of death.[34]

III

The *locus classicus* for the *halakhic* determination of the moment of death is the talmudic discussion of one's obligation with regard to an individual who has been buried alive under a collapsed structure on the Sabbath.[35] The imperative of *piku'ah nefesh* suspends the observance of the Sabbath as long as the patient is alive. One authority demands that, in this case, one should clear the debris from the nostril area of the person buried by the structure, in order to determine whether he is still breathing. Another authority requires that the chest area be exposed in order to test for the presence of cardiac activity. Later halakhic sources accept the first opinion as binding.[36] Rashi, ad loc., explains: 'For at all times life is not evident at the heart but is evident at the nose'. This explanation is based upon the Scriptural text cited by the first authority in the Talmud: 'All in whose nostrils is the breath of the spirit of life'.[37] In deference to the first opinion cited in the Talmud, however, and in view of the intrinsic relationship between cardiac activity and respiration, more recent halakhic authorities have included the presence of pulse with respiration as the two primary signs of life.[38]

In practice, the possibility of coma requires a modification of the definition of death as the absence of the two halakhic life signs, since in deep coma these might not be readily observable.[39] The case of the death of a pregnant woman, close to term, is reported in the Talmud.[40] Since the death occurred on the Sabbath, the question is asked whether a caesarian section may be performed to save the foetus. The Talmud rules that the imperative of *piku'ah nefesh* applies to the foetus, that Sabbath prohibitions should, therefore, be suspended, and that the operation should be undertaken. This ruling is accepted by the author of the *Shulhan Arukh*.[41] In an authoritative gloss, however, Rabbi Moses Isserles suggests that, in practice, the mother may merely have lapsed into coma and that the surgical procedure may be fatal. Since 'we are incompetent to determine the exact moment of death', we should wait awhile. But this waiting period will certainly cause the death of the foetus. It is therefore irrelevant whether the mother has passed out on the Sabbath or on any other day. The operation should not be attempted.[42]

Until recent times, the possibility of coma in the apparent absence of cardiac activity and respiration was of importance only in determining when the patient might be buried: Isserles make no attempt to define the time-lapse, but other authorities rule that a waiting period of twenty[43] or thirty minutes[44] is sufficient after the two life signs have been absent. Ruling that longer periods of coma reported in the Talmud[45] are exceptional, Rabbi Moses Sofer writes that burial should not be unduly delayed: 'Once he lies like an inanimate stone, there being no pulse whatsoever, and if, subsequently, breathing ceases, we have only the word or our Holy Torah that he is dead'.[46] Rabbi Chaim Yosef David Azzulai confirms this ruling. The patient should be buried: 'If once in tens of thousands of cases it happens that he is alive, there does not [devolve] upon us the slightest transgression, for so it has been decreed [by the Torah that he is dead] . . . If we err in these signs [of death], such was His decree, may He be blessed.'[47]

Clearly, therefore, absence of pulse and respiration are merely *signs* of death. Recent medical advances, particularly resuscitatory techniques, have made it quite clear that life can be maintained artificially even in the apparent absence of these life signs. Accordingly, the contemporary halakhic question is whether, when and for how long resuscitation should be attempted.

Since, for most halakhic authorities, respiration and cardiac activity are merely signs of life, and the absence of these signs is merely symptomatic of death — the state of death itself being beyond analytic definition in empirical terms[48] — in the presence of *other* signs of life, death need not be presumed to have taken place.[49] Other signs of life, in fact, *are* recognised by the *halakhah*. Maimonides' comment on the *Mishnah* is noteworthy:

A man does not defile [i.e. is not dead] until his soul departs —
even if he is bleeding to death from a severed artery, and even
if he is moribund . . . Animals, too, do not defile before their
souls depart. Were they decapitated, however, they *would* defile,
in spite of the presence of convulsive movements.[50]

These will occur in some species says [Maimonides] when the
faculty of movement throughout the organism does not originate
from one central source.[51]

Thus the presence of central control is confirmatory evidence of
vitality. If this is indicated by tests showing response to external
stimuli or internal need, and illicitable reflexes, etc. (an EEG, it
should be noted, is of great confirmatory value but is not necessary
per se, since even an isoelectric EEG is not absolutely determinative
of the absence or presence of central control), artificial maintenance
of respiration and circulation is mandatory.[52] Interestingly, the
possibility of artificial maintenance of vital functions is prefigured
in a pre-modern halakhic authority. Rabbi Jonathan Eybeschutz
declared that a fowl without a heart was not necessary dead, since
another organ, theoretically, might have assumed its functions.[53]

IV

The *practical* questions relating to the initiation and discontinuation
of artificial life-supporting therapy, and other problems directly
relating to euthanasia are determined by the halakhic status of the
moribund patient.

The *halakhah* distinguishes between various states of moribundity.
An organism which is regarded as having no chance of survival
beyond twelve months, in spite of the application of all known
therapeutic techniques, is called a *treifah*.[54] It is, nevertheless,
regarded as a living being, and its ephemeral life (*hayyei sha'ah*)
has full halakhic value. Accordingly, one who kills a *treifah* is
guilty of murder.[55] However, if death is imminent (*mitah kerovah
lavo*), in consequence of the organisms having been cut in half, or
of its having been otherwise grossly disfigured by massive injury
(*gistera*), or of massive arterial bleeding (*meguyad*), or of the loss
of a vital organ,[56] it is termed a *neveila me-hayyim*. In the case of
an animal thus afflicted, its ephemeral life is regarded as incon-
sequential, and it is considered to be already dead (*hashuv ke-met*),
although it is physiologically alive in terms of its reticular activity.[57]
Some halakhic authorities regard a human being, similarly, afflicted,
as being in the same category. Thus a priest and nazirite, who

43

are not permitted under the same roof as a corpse, are enjoined against being under the same roof as a *neveila me-hayyim*, 'since he is imminently a corpse, and is not fit for life'.[58] Prevailing halakhic opinion, however, does not consider human *neveila me-hayyim* as already dead,[59] either because recovery is possible in exceptional cases,[60] or because consciousness in the patient nullifies the other symptoms of the *neveila.*[61]

The human in the final phase of moribundity, is called a *goses*. The major symptom of this final phase is the inability of the patient to swallow his own saliva,[62] which reflects the absence of the gagging reflex and comes close to the medical conception of brainstem death.[63] It is generally held that most patients in this condition cannot recover (*rov gossesim lamitah*)[46] and that death will come within three days.[65]

Some authorities maintain that the legal powers of the *goses* are suspended,[66] but all agree that since he *may r*ecover, his title to life — even to *hayyei sha'ah* — is beyond question.[67] Thus the person buried under a collapsed building is surely a *goses,* but the rules of the Sabbath are suspended in terms of *piku'ah nefesh.*[68] Accordingly, the medical management of the *goses* is conditioned by the obligation to preserve his life, and he is entitled to medical care even in the final phase.

It should be noted that the delineation of a three day survival norm for the *goses* obtains only if there is *no* subsequent evidence of his being alive.[69] As long as he is known to be alive, no time limit is placed upon the treatment to which he is entitled. If he is in pain, a painkilling regimen should be continued or initiated — even if this treatment involved some risk of life, provided that its sole purpose is the relief of the patient's suffering.[70] If necessary, he should be resuscitated, and, if called for, the application of artificial life-supporting devices should be undertaken.[71]

Clearly, no active steps should be taken to hasten the demise of the patient. One should not bind his jaws, annoint him, wash him, stop up his orifices, remove the pillow from under him,[72] place him on the ground, clay or sand, lay a vessel or salt upon his body, shut his eyes (or even place the keys of the synagogue beneath his pillow),[73] since he is compared to 'a flickering flame' which is easily extinguished[74] — and one who hastens his passing is regarded as a murderer.[75]

However, the *halakhah does* make a distinction between prolonging the patient's life — which is mandatory — and prolonging the agony of his death — which is not. In an important gloss on the *Shulhan Arukh,* Rabbi Moses Isserles rules:

> If there is any thing which hinders the departure of the soul, such
> as the presence, near the patient's house, of a knocking noise . . .
> or if there is salt on the patient's tongue, and these hinder the
> departure of the soul, then it is permissible to remove them from
> there, *because there is no act involved in this at all,* but only
> the removal of the impediment.[76]

Indeed, Rabbi Judah Hassid actually *requires* the removal of the
extraneous hindrance.[77]

On the basis of these sources, a good halakhic case can be made
for the discontinuation of non-pain-killing medication (therapeutic
reticence) if the physician is convinced that without such medication
his patient will die within three days, and he is already *goses* in
terms of the above definition of that status.[78] However, discontinuation of medication does *not* include deliberate interruption of intake
of nutriment — which would be tantamount to murder by starvation.[79]

This raises the question of the discontinuation of medication in
a deep and apparently permanent coma, where the patient is
clearly *goses,* but where with continued therapy, he will live more
than three days. Rabinowitz and Konigsberg argue that the
definition of imminent death in this case (*mitah kerovah lavo*) is a
qualitative rather than quantitative one, and regard medication as
an unnecessary external hindrance to dying — on the precedent of
Rabbi Isserles quoted above.[80] This view, however, is convincingly
refuted by Levi both on the grounds that Isserles' precedent is not
applicable, inasmuch as the medication is not an extraneous factor,
and, more especially, since the prognosis of death is not certain.[81]

The same precedents have been invoked for the discontinuation
of artificial life-supporting apparatus in the case of a *goses.*[82] Levi,
however, again argues that the resuscitation apparatus is essential
to the physiological maintenance of the patient, and is not an
extraneous factor inhibiting death. Nevertheless, he suggests another
line of reasoning to justify the deactivation of artificial life-supporting apparatus. The physician may, in fact, merely be simulating
life in a corpse. The question is thus not whether a *goses* requires
resuscitation — he does — but whether the patient is really dead
or alive. Accordingly, he suggests that the machine be switched off
for a few minutes. If, during this time, there is no spontaneous
restoration of life signs (such as an isoelectric EEG, absence of
circulation and respiration), the apparatus need not be reactivated.[83]
This suggestion, it should be noted, is not universally accepted,

since deactivation of a respirator may in fact cause death by asphyxiation.[84]

Also basing himself upon Isserles' ruling, Rabbi Solomon Eger rules that it is forbidden to hinder the departure of the soul by the use of medicine.[85] Although this ruling has been questioned by other authorities,[86] it would seem that the objections relate to medicinal treatment of the condition which has caused the patient to be a *goses*. If he is already a *goses*, however, and his death from the underlying condition is expected within three days, his ruling would appear to warrant therapeutic reticence in dealing with a new complication not directly related to the underlying condition.

V

It is now possible to present the conclusions of the foregoing analysis in summary form: the *goses* has the same title to life as any other living person. His physician is bound to attempt to prolong his life by all available means in terms of the imperative of *piku'ah nefesh* — including the activation of artificial life-supporting aparatus. He is not permitted to hasten his demise actively. However, he is not required to prolong the agony of death through his therapeutic regimen. Accordingly, if the patient is a *goses* and his death can be expected within three days; the physician

1. may discontinue medication for the existing condition,
2. need not initiate treatment of an unrelated and possibly fatal complication.

If the patient is in deep and prolonged coma, the medication should continue. Moreover, strong doubt exists about the deactivation of artificial life-supporting aparatus. It should be noted, in this context, that the *halakhah* does not distinguish between 'heroic' and 'non-heroic' therapeutic regimens. The terms are relative and meaningless, for the moment that a physician decides that his patient is moribund, he is psychologically disposed to define *any* therapy to be initiated as 'heroic'. Obviously, what is 'heroic' in some circumstances is 'non-heroic' in others.[87] In *all* cases, nutriment should be continued and painkillers supplied.

VI

The *halakhah* is not totally permissive. Active euthanasia is forbidden, and even passive euthanasia is severely curtailed.

Sometimes Osler's maxim cannot be translated into practice. Palliative treatment may not work, narcotics may be ineffective, the patient's pain may be unbearable and the course inexorable. Because he cannot cure, relieve or even comfort, the physician may well come to share his patient's agony. By teleological standards, he may be tempted, as a result of his compassion, to resort to euthanasia. The *halakhah,* however, is deontological. It bids the physician to resist this temptation. While it recognizes that the terminally ill patient is a burden on his family and on the doctor, it refuses to allow self interest to be expressed as altruism or idealism. It is aware that teleological motives may, in fact, be the first step on the slippery slope to eugenic euthanasia and to rationalized infanticide. Most important, it recognizes that the ideal of the preservation of life does involve tensions and psychological sacrifices in some cases. In short, it demands that the physician's obligation to preserve life be governed by objective ethical norms, regardless of whether or not they coincide with the norms of contemporary society.[88]

Nevertheless, the *halakhah* is a comfort to the physician. By accepting its deontological standards, his personal tensions *are* relieved. It helps him to recognize that he need not accept the final responsibility for what happens to his patient and that he does not have full control over his patient's sufferings. It assumes that his knowledge may be finite although his desire to help is not. It reminds him that life and death are not his exclusive prerogative, and 'that he is not culpable for the finite limits of medical intervention. Where the epistomological boundary has been reached, he may not function, and he must leave the decision to a higher Power'[89] — who alone understands why His creatures suffer, and prepares for their life beyond the grave.

1. See *inter alia* J. Fletcher, 'Euthanasia: Our Right to Die', *Morals and Medicine,* Princeton, 1954; W. L. Sperry, 'The Prolongation of Life, Euthanasia-Pro and Euthanasia-Con', *The Ethical Basis of Medical Practice,* New York, 1950, chs. 10 - 12; F. Rosner, 'Jewish Attitude to Euthanasia', *Modern Medicine and Jewish Law,* New York, 1972.
2. Phrase derives from a Conference on 'Death Control' on 25 January 1973 at Westminster Cathedral Hall under the patronage of Cardinal Heenan. See Immanuel Jakobovits, 'Recent Statements on Jewish Medical Ethics', *Proceedings of the Associations of Orthodox Jewish Scientists,* **3-4,** New York, 1976, 7.
3. See J. David Bleich, 'Establishing Criteria of Death', *Tradition,* **13,** No. 3, 1973, 108. Immanuel Jakobovits, *Jewish Medical Ethics,* New York, 1967, 121 - 123; Rosner, op. cit., 114.

4. See T. F. Dagi, 'The Paradox of Euthanasia', *Judaism*, **24**, No. 2, Spring 1975, 157.

5. Ibid., 160 - 163.

6. See Rosner, 113, and n. 7, ad loc.

7. See Dagi, 163.

8. See Rosner, 112 - 113.

9. See Dagi, 163.

10. Bleich, 109.

11. Leviticus 18:5.

12. Psalms 118:17.

13. *The Daily Prayer Book,* early morning blessings; *Babylonian Talmud (B.T.) Berakhot* 60a.

14. Cf. Bleich, 108.

15. Jakobovits, 'Recent Statements', 7.

16. *Genesis Rabba* 34:13; *Semahot* 2:1 - 5; Maimonides, *Mishneh Torah, (M.T.) Hilkhot Rotze'ah* 2:3; *Shulhan Arukh (Sh.A), Yoreh Deah (Y.D.)* 345:1. Attempted suicide is punishable by flogging — Maimonides, *Rotze'ah* 11:5; *Sh.A. Hoshen Mishpat (H.M.)* 427:10.

17. Deuteronomy 32:39.

18. Ezekiel 18:14.

19. *Daily Prayer Book.*

20. E.g. *B.T. Sanhedrin* 45a. Although the term corresponds exactly to 'Euthanasia' in its original sense, it is never used in this way in Jewish sources.

21. *B.T. Ketubot* 40a and Rabbi Nissim of Gerondi (RAN) on *B.T. Nedarim* 40a who rules that it is obligatory to pray thus.

22. See W. Hirsch, *Rabbinic Psychology*, London, 1947, *passim*, for a fine presentation of Jewish eschatology.

23. Psalm 118:18. Cf. Jakobovits, 'Euthanasia', *Encyclopaedia Judaica*, Vol. 6, Jerusalem, 1974, 979. Even martyrdom is severely limited by the *halakhah* to exceptional cases.

24. *B.T. Avodah Zarah* 18a.

25. The case of Saul in I Samuel 31:1 - 6 and II Samuel 1:5 - 10 is regarded by Jewish commentators (e.g. Rashi *ad loc.*) as a case of euthanasia, but is justified by the exceptional status accorded to the King and not as normative. See also, Simon Federbush, 'The Problem of Euthanasia in Jewish Tradition,' *Judaism*, **1**, No. 1, 1952, 64 - 68.

26. *B.T. Berakhot* 60a. Maimonides, *M.T. Hil. Nedarim*, legislates that the physician is not purely *permitted* to heal, but that, on the basis of another Scriptural imperative, is, in fact, commanded to do so. Also see Fred Rosner, 'Who Heals the Sick — G-d or Man?', *Modern Medicine and Jewish Law*, 11 - 24.

27. See Abner Weiss, 'The Medical Prolongation of Life: A Jewish View', in G. C. Oosthuizen (ed.), *The Ethics of Tissue Transplantation*, Cape Town, 1972, 103 - 104 and nn. 1 - 7 ad loc.

28. Nahmanides, *Commentary on the Torah,* Leviticus 26:11.

29. For a fascinating discussion of this point, see Bleich, 105 - 106.

30. Ibid., 93.

31. Ibid.

32. Medical opinion is divided on this point. See *inter alia* H. A. Shapiro,

'Criteria for determining that Death has occurred', *Journal of Forensic Medicine*, Johannesburg, January - March 1969, 1 - 3; 'Proposed Criteria for the Determination of Death', op. cit., 4 - 6, noting especially p. 4: 'There is no legal definition of death in the United States today'. Cf. The Report of the Ad Hoc Committee of the Harvard Medical School to examine the definition of brain death, published by Henry K. Beecher, *et al.*, as 'A Definition of Irreversible Coma', *Journal of the American Medical Association*, **205**, No. 6, August 5, 1968, 337 - 340. Beecher's comment in 'Definitions of "Life" and "Death" for Medical Science', *Annals of the New York Academy of Sciences*, **169**, No. 6, 5 August 1968, 471 - 472 (cited by Bleich, 92), is noteworthy. 'Only a very bold man would attempt to define death. I was chairman of a recent *ad hoc* committee at Harvard, composed of members of five faculties of the university who tried to define irreversible coma. We felt we could not define death.' Also see *Report of the Select Committee of the Anatomical Donations of Post Mortem Examinations Bill*, The Government Printer: Cape Town, 1969, 11(40), 21(83), 23(91), and I. Gordon, 'The Biological Definition of Death', *Journal of Forensic Medicine*, Johannesburg, January - March 1968, and the Editorial in the same issue.

33. Bleich, p. 93.
34. The view that death should *not* be defined, expressed by Jakobovits, 'Recent Statements', p. 4, is incomprehensible to the present author.
35. *B.T. Yoma* 85a.
36. Maimonides, *M.T. Hil. Shabbat* 2:19, *Sh.A., O.H.* 329:4.
37. Genesis 7:22. See also *Yalkut Shimoni* on *Lekh Lekha*, 77, and Rabbi Akiva's statement that the nostrils reflect *ikar Hiyyuta* — the essence of life — in *B.T. Sota* 45b.
38. Rabbi Zvi Ashkenazi, *Teshuvot Haham Zvi*, 77; Rabbi Shalom Schwadron, *Teshuvot Maharsham* V, 6, no. 124; Rabbi Moses Sofer, *Hatam Sofer* on *Sh.A. Y.D.* 388. Cf. Gedalya Aharon Rabinowitz and Mordecai Konigsberg, 'Definition of Death and Fixing its Time According to the *Halakhah*' (Hebrew), *Hadorom*, Vol. 32, New York, 1971, 59 - 60.
39. See Maimonides, *Guide of the Perplexed*, 1:42, on this condition in I Samuel 38:37 - 38.
40. *B.T. Arakhin* 7a.
41. *Sh.A. O.H.* 49:11, based upon Maimonides, *M.T. Hil. Shabbat* 2:15.
42. *Sh.A. O.H.* 330:5.
43. Yehiel Michel Tykocinsky, *Gesher ha-Hayyim*, I, 3, 48.
44. Shalom Gagin, *Teshuvot Yismah*, Y.D., 9.
45. *B.T. Semahot*, 8.
46. On *Y.D.* 388.
47. *Teshuvot Hayyim Sha'al*, II, 25.
48. Cf. Bleich, 94.
49. See particularly *Teshuvot Maharsham*, V, 6, no. 124. Rabbi Eliezer Waldenberg, *Ziz Eliezer*, X, 25, 4:5, states that inherent in *Hatam Sofer's* position (see n.38 above) is that where there are other signs of life, breathing *is* present.
50. *Ohalot* 1:6.

51. *Ad loc.*
52. Bleich, 104.
53. *Kreiti U'Pleiti Y.D.* 40:4.
54. See *TAZ* on *Sh.A.*, *Even ha-Ezer* (*E.H.*) 17:44; Rabinowitz and Konigsberg, 74; Maimonides, *M.T. Hil.Roze'ah* 2:5.
55. Maimonides, *H.T. Hil.Roze'ah* 2:5. This applies only if one becomes a *treifah* through natural causes.
56. See Rabinowitz and Konigsberg, 71 - 72, for the primary sources.
57. Ibid. 61, on Maimonides' commentary on *Ohalot* 1:6.
58. *B.T. Nazir* 43a and Rashi ad loc. See *Encyclopaedia Talmudit* (*E.T.*), Vol. V, Jerusalem, 1953, 397.
59. See ibid., n.80 for the sources.
60. For exceptions to the principle *rov gosesim lemitah* (*B.T. Gittin* 28a), ibid., p. 403 *et passim.* Cf. Rabinowitz and Konigsberg, 71 - 72.
61. See the Vilna Gaon, *Eliyahu Rabbo* on *Ohalot* 1:6, and Rabinowitz and Konigsberg, *loc. cit.*
62. *Sh.A., E.H.,* 121:7, *H.M.,* 211:2, gloss. For other symptoms, see *E.T.,* 393 - 394.
63. Dagi, 164 - 165.
64. *E.T.,* 403 *et passim.*
65. Ibid., and *Sh.A., Y.D.* 339:2. See *Perishah Y.D.* 339:5.
66. E.g. in valuations for gifts to the Sanctuary, in legal acquisitions and in divorce. Other authorities disagree, however. See *E.T.,* 399 - 404.
67. *Sh.A. Y.D.* 139:1. He has the full rights of a living person.
68. Tosafot on *B.T. Niddah* 49b: 'In cases of *piku'ah nefesh,* we do not follow the majority principle.' See also *Teshuvot Shevut Ya'akov* 1:3; *Mishnah Berurah* on *Sh.A., O.H.* 329:4. If three days have passed after the collapse of the building, the Sabbath may not be desecrated by removing the debris, for the death of the patient is presumed (*Mahazit ha-Shekel* 329:4).
69. See *E.T.,* 403. Dagi, 164 - 165.
70. Jakobovits, 'Recent Statements', 7; Dagi, 164, based on the precedent of blunting the suffering of a judicially condemned person. (*B.T. Sanhedrin* 43a and 45a).
71. See above, 10.
72. Popular folk-lore believed that feathers prevented the departure of the soul.
73. A popular superstition relating to a quick demise.
74. This catalogue derives mainly from *Semahot* 1:1 - 4, and is codified in *Sh.A. Y.D.* 339 - 1. See commentaries ad loc. Even psychological stress caused by building his coffin is forbidden. See *Tur, Y.D.* 339.
75. Ibid. Cf. Maimonides, *M.T., Hil.Roze'ah* 2:5; *Hil.Avel* 4:5; *B.T. Shabbat* 151b and Rashi ad loc.
76. Isserles on *Sh.A. Y.D.* 339:1.
77. *Sefer Hassidim,* 723.
78. See Jakobovits, *Jewish Medical Ethics,* 124. Cf. Dagi, 165.
79. Maimonides, *M.T., Hil.Roze'ah* 3:10. See also Jakobovits, 'Recent Statements', 7. Also see Ya'akov Levi in *Noam,* XVI, abstracted in *Asia,* pamphlet 8, Nisan, 5733 (1973), 27. The view of Rabinowitz and Konigsberg, p.75, is untenable.

80. Ibid.
81. Levi, 27.
82. Jakobovits, 'Recent Statements', 2 and 7, and *Jewish Medical Ethics,* 125; Rabinowitz and Konigsberg, 73, 75 - 76.
83. Levi, 27.
84. Dagi, 58.
85. *Gilyon Maharsha* on *Sh.A. Y.D.* 339:1, gloss, quoting *Bet Ya'ahov.*
86. See Rosner, 120.
87. Dagi, 165 - 166. It is difficult to understand Jakobovits' repeated recourse to this distinction. See 'Recent Statements', 2 and 7.
88. See Bleich, 107 - 109.
89. Dagi, 166 - 167.

AN ISLAMIC VIEWPOINT

S. Salman Navdi

Since euthanasia is one of those issues which still needs close investigation to bring to light the answers to many unsolved juridical, religious, ethical and also perhaps medical questions, the Islamic answer to this question will not and cannot be a definite one. There is also another aspect to this question. It is that euthanasia is essentially a problem of western origin and is still in the process of exportation to the Muslim world and for that matter also to the oriental countries. Consequently the Muslim world has not yet received the full impact of this question. The Muslim scholars and jurists have not even started to discuss all the pros and cons of euthanasia in an organized manner. It will therefore take a long time before a clear and definite Islamic view regarding the various aspects of euthanasia will emerge. Bearing these preliminary remarks in mind, please note that whatever I am going to say will be of temporary nature. Thus, the views expressed here will change or be modified as answers to various aspects of euthanasia become clearer.

As far as Islam is concerned, the task of finding answers to questions such as abortion, birth control, euthanasia and others is relatively easier than for other religions. This is because Islam has well defined primary sources, the Qur'ān and the Sunnah (the sayings and the practice of Muhammad, the Prophet of Islam), in which the Muslim scholars find solutions to their problems. If one cannot find a clear or definite reference to a certain problem in these primary sources, then a jurist attempts to find an answer in the light of the total attitude of Islam, either by using an analogy to similar questions mentioned in the above sources, or by seeking a consensus of opinion of the jurists. But in both cases the conclusions must not run against the clear injunctions of the Qur'ān and the Sunnah. Since euthanasia is not mentioned either in the Qur'ān or the Sunnah, we shall have to find answers by employing the last two sources, namely analogy or consensus of opinion of the Muslim jurists.

Since euthanasia means 'the action of inducing a quiet and easy death'[1] it is very important for us to know the attitude of Islam towards life and death. Sanctity of human life is the greatest concern of Islam. This is evident from the detailed Qur'ānic verses which forbid the killing of any human being and which prescribe severer punishments for those who violate the sanctity of life.[2] The Qur'ān goes so far as to say that 'whoever kills a person, unless it be for manslaughter or for mischief in the land, it is as though he had killed the whole people, and whoever saves a life, it is as though he had saved the lives of the whole people.'[3] The deep concern Islam attaches to the saving of human life can be determined from the fact that Islam allows Muslims to save their lives if their lives are threatened by starvation, by allowing them to eat or drink even things like pork or alcohol, which are under normal circumstances absolutely forbidden for Muslims.[4] Islam's attitude to death is that it is something which is beyond the control of everybody, except Allāh, and that it will come to everyone no matter who he is and where he is. The Qur'ān says, 'wherever you are death will find you out even if you are in towers built up strong and high.'[5] In Islam both the medical treatment and prayer for recovery are of equal importance. One must try all possible means to save life or cure a disease and the result of these endeavours should then be left in the hands of Allah.

We must now look into the question of euthanasia and all its aspects in the light of what I have said above. If on the one hand we have before us the tragic story of the Quinlans of the USA,[6] we have also on the other hand the happy story of Mrs Dawn Bayer of South Africa, who, having proved medical predictions wrong (that she would be a 'vegetable' and never walk again after a serious car accident), has recently given birth to a child which doctors doubted she could ever have.[7] In the light of these two conflicting events and also in view of the many similar occurrences throughout the world, it is indeed an awesome responsibility for anyone to decide who should live and who should die. When we talk of euthanasia we are actually talking of killing a person, no matter how peacefully we kill him, and no matter how beautiful and attractive the name we give to this act. Someone's life, the only thing he has, is always involved. In this age of transplantations the doctors can transplant human limbs, but can they transplant a human life? The seriousness of the whole question increases tenfold when we do not find definite answers to such common questions as:

Can a patient suffering from terminal cancer or other incurable disease be trusted in his decision, especially when the soundness of his very thinking faculty is in doubt? Can a parent or relatives of a patient decide on his behalf and permit his life to be ended? Shall we or can we authorize one doctor or a team of doctors to perform active and/or passive euthanasia on anyone? If the answers to these questions, and especially to the last one, are in the affirmative, what is the guarantee of protection from the abuse and misuse of this permission? The question of abusing the permission will remain, even if the law grants permission with lots of ifs and buts.

I know a boy of 18 years who is suffering from terminal cancer in an advanced stage. The doctors have told the parents that the boy will die very soon. The boy does not know the doctors' prediction, but the parents who know the diagnosis, and also the tragic result of the diagnosis, have spent and are still spending hundreds of rands to save his life by trying to find a cure for this incurable disease. Now, what advice do you have for this parent and for many more parents in a similar situation? Likewise, arguments are advanced in favour of killing grossly deformed babies or inducing the death of a foetus which has a large head containing pints of fluid, by tapping the head with a needle while the foetus is still in uterus, so that in this way the world may be rid of deformed children. In the same way, passive euthanasia may be performed upon such persons who have no hope of recovery except perhaps as human vegetables simply because they are a burden on society or because they are considered unfit to live. In other words, the law is that only the fittest survives must rule. If this argument is stretched a little further and the process of eliminating 'the unfit to survive' is extended a little more, then old men and people of advanced age should beware because they will soon be considered a liability on society. Those who are young today will be old tomorrow, unless someone decides that people beyond fifty, arbitrarily speaking, must be eliminated. This reminds me of a recent report in a local newspaper which suggested that the dead should be cremated because the city is running out of space. At this stage I should like to ask a sharp but pertinent question: if the world rids itself of all the deformed babies and persons suffering from incurable diseases, then how do we find cures for incurable diseases and for deformity?

The Islamic view regarding turning off the machine which is keeping alive a patient for whom the doctors have no hope of recovery, except perhaps as a human vegetable, will probably be the same as it is in regard to abortion. That is, if the life of a pregnant mother is in danger then an abortion can be performed at any stage of pregnancy. In other words we are choosing the life of the mother over that of the child. This is because in this case the mother is the source of life. The same analogy can be used in the case where a respirator may be removed from a patient for whom the doctors have no hope of recovery except as a human vegetable, and may be used to save the life of a patient whose recovery is sure. Let me hasten to add that the patient from whom a respirator is removed is left to take his own course. Islam may allow this act with lots of 'ifs' and 'buts' and also perhaps allow it only in such a situation where the choice is limited between saving the life of a possible human vegetable and a patient whose survival is a certainty according to all medical progress. Even in this case, the question of guarantee of protection from the misuse and abuse of the permission will have to be solved.

1. *The Oxford University Dictionary,* Oxford, 1955.
2. For instance see the Qur'ānic verses: 6:152; 4:92,93; 2:178,179.
3. Qur'ān, 5:32.
4. Ibid., 2:173; 5:3.
5. Ibid., 4:78 and also see 3:185; 21:35; 29:57; 63:11.
6. *Sunday Times,* Johannesburg, 4 April 1976.
7. *Daily News,* Durban, 18 March 1976.

A HINDU VIEWPOINT

T. P. Mishra

Life is a combination of soul and body. The *Atma,* a particle of Supreme Lord combined with vitality, mind, reason, senses and intelligence is called the soul. It is an immutable substratum in which knowledge inheres. In short it is the conscious agent which uses the senses and body as instruments in producing cognition or doing any action, hence it is responsible for all good and bad deeds.

The body as defined by our sages and philosophers is: a composition of five elements whereof one of these elements is predominant and forms its material cause. The other four elements form only its supportive factors. The body, in fact, is a field within whose bounds the soul has its experiences, and serves as the seat and instrument of its voluntary activities. These experiences are the results of its previous deeds allotted in the body in a measured quantity in the form of weal and woe, at the exhaustion of which the soul forsakes it.

The actions done in a life, once thus starting to bear fruit, continue without break. Once involved in the fetters of actions, a soul cannot escape taking name and form. It continuously assumes these and goes higher than human regions by the force of its meritorious deeds, and lower by committing sins. This is the point on which the idea of reincarnation has been strongly held by the Hindus. The Buddhists, who do not believe in *Atma,* have also adopted the theory of reincarnation in their religion. It is no wonder that some of the inveterately atheistic philosophers, too, have accepted this view. They are inspired by the explanation that as the perpetually recurring transformations of the energy of actions are limited and time is without limit, so a name and form once created must occur again.

The soul being dependent on the results of its deeds, migrates to either divine regions or infernal regions without being a free agent to do any particular act which can be fructuous in any way. Even if a heinous sin or a highly praise-worthy act is committed by it while being anywhere other than in the human body, it is not counted as the moulder of its future. The soul passes again through the human body, only when it deserves it. The effects of its previous deeds become its destiny whereby its human position, tendency, will, action and success in life are shaped.

Man is the best of all living beings, as he only is free to shape his future. He is a rational being in transit to other worlds. The how and when thereof depend on his destiny. Though he is bound in the fetters of his previous actions or hereditary impressions he can never do anything by his independent volition, yet he has to improve his conduct and purify his intelligence. He has to fructify his life, and respond to the spiritual evolution by developing and manifesting the potential divinity of his soul identified with God as prescribed in Hindu Scriptures.

It is strongly stressed in the Scriptures that a man 'doing his duties must desire to live a hundred years'. Moreover, it is ordained to protract the span of healthy life by prescribed means, so that a man may strive to secure a better position in heaven. Nothing is impossible for a man if he discreetly makes use of his inborn intelligence and develops his virile chord of character. He can even free himself from all bondages of actions in a single life if he strongly desires so and endeavours appropriately, otherwise as an ordinary being he forsakes his body as soon as the allotted amount of weal and woe therein are exhausted by experience.

The human body is a spot where the soul has to maintain its positive existence and improve its metaphysical status as it comes nearer to the Supreme Lord. For this reason the life of a human being is the most precious and the most sacred asset to the soul. The Yogis practically confirm this Scriptural statement by proving that the whole universe is centred in a single human physical frame, but requires to be developed by means of yoga-practice.

A practical discrimination as far as worldly business is concerned exists in this world, so that each one can maintain his social and personal status shaped by his destiny and acquired by the efforts in this present life. The self-identifying out-look of *Atma* believing in the unity of all souls is beyond that, confined to the metaphysical world. So we see that people of advanced nature are treated as the support of others, in their respective fields, and help to make the human community run smoothly. A beggar approaches a man of means for alms, a student for education approaches a teacher, likewise a sick man seeks for a medical practitioner to recover his health and so on.

This kind of relationship is termed as 'hopeful relationship' because the man in need hopes that his desires will never be frustrated. But the relationship between a sick and a medical man is sacred too. A man physically afflicted seeks inevitably for the service of a doctor. This means that a patient surrenders his precious life to the mercy and discretion of a physician. He sacrifices most of his happiness and wealth to rid himself of the troubles. He even follows the grim advice he receives, even if it may be against his will and means.

According to the Hindu Scriptures the duty of an honest medical man is first of all, to treat the body of his patient as dearly as he would his own. In all the circumstances he must control his senses and organs and behave righteously thinking that he himself is the patient. Taking the illustration that 'as I am, so my patients are' he should act with extreme compassion. At each step and at each moment he should exert himself to the best of his ability and experience. If he blunders he is deprived of happiness hereafter.

In the ordinary course of affairs a doctor easily decides his duties and acts accordingly. But there are several critical situations to puzzle him even if he be a reputable doctor of legal and philosophical insight. Hindu Scriptures strongly forbid the destruction of a human life. At the same time they draw a line of exceptions to expedite some crucial circumstances. For instance, abortion is a heinous sin, but permitted, if it is meant to save the life of a pregnant woman. Killing of a tender infant is the most objectionable murder, but if a child is being born by transverse presentation impairing the life of its mother, it is openly advised to cut the baby and save the mother. To die or kill in battle-field is a sacred act, and so on.

The greatly responsible doctors who discharge their duties consistently, often find themselves at a loss when they come to treat a sick person suffering severely from an incurable disease causing great pain. The doctors feel that affliction and are moved with compassion. At such a crucial moment the question arises whether euthanasia is practicable or not. In Ancient India there were evidently some prescribed measures in practice to end life at such a stage. Smritis, Puranas and Maha Bharata strongly reprobate suicide, but they also advise the people suffering from irremediable diseases to end their lives by yoga-practice, by fasting to death, by entering the sacred fire and so on. We can easily read the names of many old reputed kings inscribed on stones in India who met their last by one of these prescribed measures.

The passages from the sacred texts such as: 'Do as your pure mind guides. Do as your mental deities please' and so on, are the sources of the Intuitionist Philosophers who opine that in crucial circumstances it is our conscience in the form of mental deity, the supreme authority to decide and prompt us to the right action. This view was appropriately in practice in ancient India when yoga-practice was in vogue to pacify and purify the mind of the saintly authorities whose action was never tainted by human frailties.

It is now obvious from the points given above that at any rate the Hindu Scriptures will not allow euthanasia to be effectuated. It is clearly stated that the soul has to undergo all pleasures and pains allotted to a body in which it resides. So, no medical man has the right to shorten or lengthen the life of anybody. On the contrary, a doctor must show more compassion to the sick man in distress and offer his wholehearted services even if they may be futile and hopeless. Who knows what may be the result afterwards? The world has been for ever witnessing a number of cases where people have recovered from desperately moribund states and have lived for many years; thus euthanasia has no place in the Hindu Scriptures.

A TRADITIONAL AFRICAN VIEWPOINT

Vincent Z. Gitywa

Euthanasia, as an act of merciful killing to relieve the sufferer from the pain and agony of an incurable disease, is a phenomenon unknown to the Xhosa, both in its passive and active forms.

The structure of traditional Xhosa culture was such that the chief was virtually the 'owner' of his tribe. In this capacity, all deaths in the tribe had to be reported to him. Death resulting from the machinations of a witch doctor or sorcerer was punishable by death, plus the confiscation of the perpetrator's stock; murder, in any form, was also punishable, although not always by death. Brownlee (in MacLean: 1858:110) had the following to say about accidental homicide, 'The law acquits the homicide, but the Chief not always'; 'A man is fined for murder, if he kills an adulterer or adulteress in the act although he be the husband of the adulteress'. This he wrote in connection with justifiable homicide. Brownlee (1858:111) further states that 'If a woman procures abortion, with or without the will of her husband, she is fined; likewise the Doctor who caused the abortion. Putting to death the child after birth is punishable as murder, the fine in both cases going to the Chief. It is customary (however) for Chiefs to procure abortion, or to cause the death of supposititious children'. The above citations show clearly the attitude of the Xhosa towards the termination of an individual's life which, in their conception of criminality, is murder.

The report by Warner (MacLean:1858:102) regarding the burial of 'friendless persons' is subject to doubt. He noted that such people were seldom buried, instead that 'They are generally carried away before they are dead, and deposited in some fissure of a bank or rock and left to their fate'. The idea of 'friendless person' among the Xhosa is a strange one since their methods of adoption are wide-ranging. However, the situation noted by Warner was not a case of euthanasia, and from my point of view it was an act prompted by the superstitious fear of death, worse still that of a 'friendless person' who might well be the manifestation of an *impundulu,* the lightning bird, according to their beliefs.

Rather than expedite the death of a sufferer, much care is taken to tend to him until fate takes her own course. Warner (1958:87) writes: 'Sometimes when a person is sick, or some other misfortune has happened to him; or when some calamity has befallen a kraal; the priest declares the cause of such sickness, or other calamity, to be the *umshologu* of one of their ancestors who has taken offence at their neglect, in not supplying him with a sufficient number of sacrifices, and that consequently he is hungry, etc.' When this is the case, a special sacrifice is offered to 'appease the ghost'. The sacrificial portions are conveyed to the hut of the sick person to gratify the appetite of the *umshologu*. The very act of 'appeasing' the *umshologu* (ancestral spirit) is in itself an attempt to prevent the death of the sufferer. When this is compared with Mbiti's (1969:150) account of the Ndebele in more or less similar circumstances, the attitude of the Xhosa stands out clearly. Mbiti wrote : 'If the sick man lingers on in pain, his relatives kill what is known as "the beast of the ancestors". This is generally an ox or a goat (for a poor man), and its killing is believed to hasten death'. We thus see that in the former case it is a matter of supplication for the continued existence of the sufferer, whereas in the latter case it is an expedition (passive) of the termination of the sufferer's life.

It would be appropriate to conclude this evidence on the absence of euthanasia among the Xhosa by quoting from Soga who succinctly put the case as follows:

It is sometimes asserted by historians and writers on Bantu life, that the aged, when they had reached the stage of helpless senility, were taken out to the forest and left to die. If this custom exists as it possibly may among a few degraded tribes, yet it is by no means common to the great majority. Among the AmaXosa the old and decrepit were carefully tended, and their lives supplied with the means of living until nature took control of the final situation. When a Xosa man or woman was no longer able to take the ordinary food an ox or cow was slaughtered, and the inner lining of the skin, the dermis, was peeled off then pegged down to stretch and dry. It was afterwards dressed or curried till soft and pliable, and then sewn into a small bottle-shaped article, open at the one end. This article was called *utwisha*. . . . Into this miniature bottle was poured milk, either curdled or sweet according to taste, and the aged person either fed himself or was fed by someone detailed for that duty, much as a European child is fed with the bottle.   (1931:317)

A DUTCH REFORMED CHURCH VIEWPOINT

G. C. Oosthuizen

Medical power has become a tremendous force in the life of the patient and the balance between medical power and medical limitations has been erased. Medical techniques could be a threat to humane treatment and thus could affect the fundamental human rights and integrity of sick people. Decisions are more and more qualified by medical techniques. The result is that more people who are biological wrecks, 'living corpses', who survive only vegetatively as physiological torsi, who are apersonal, are kept alive. The death of their personalities has taken place although biologically they are alive.

Fundamental human rights and the integrity of sick people are vital issues. Technical equipment and medicines/drugs are responsible for a particularly long prolongation which raises grave issues for the theologian when the cerebral functions of a person have irreversibly ceased. Furthermore, artificial prolongation often means artificial suffering. Medical power has become a moral issue of the first degree.

Today death and dying play a different role than earlier and today the medical aspect dominates. The prevailing definitions in ethics and law have not kept pace with the progress in medical science. When medicine was less effective death came quickly. Earlier, moral and other support was given to a patient by a doctor and in this way he was helped in his suffering but there was relatively little to help him medically; today there is much medical support but so often very little moral support.

It is only since the 1870s that technical and pharmacological progress in medical science in the modern sense commenced. So tremendous has this progress been that it has made its shadow side strongly felt. To this side belongs the fact that too much emphasis is put on the struggle to keep a person alive at all costs no matter how hopeless the end result may be. During the time of medical limitations and inability this was necessary; in an era of medical power matters have changed. People who should have died are kept alive; prolongation of life has become an absolute concept to the exclusion so often of personal dignity and integrity.

Social ethics has to look into the ethical and juridical problems to give criteria to moral decisions to be taken. When is a human being 'humanly dead'? Is it possible to kill a person who is a 'living corpse' but 'humanly dead'?

New definitions of 'life' and 'death' are thus called for. Patients are kept long in an intermediate stage between 'life' and 'death' which touches their personal dignity and integrity; this prolongation of the dying process makes them a burden to themselves and those around them and, one reluctantly mentions the tremendous financial burden to relatives as well. One is reminded here of Karen Quinlan, who at 22 became unconscious and who was kept alive with a thin yellow tube for draining and intravenous feeding which went from her nose and arm, a Bennex MA - 1 respiration machine which helped her *breathing* and which pumped air through a hole in her throat. For the parents it meant nothing but suffering to keep a 'cabbage' alive; they had, too, a hospital bill of 100 dollars a day, before the State took it over. Eventually the Supreme Court removed the possibility of criminal prosecution if the breathing device was removed. Three large church denominations decided this decision was 'not a victory but a just human decision to allow a hopelessly sick girl to die a natural death'. The prosecutor of New Jersey, however, decided that the removal of the machine will be tantamount to murder. This shows the tremendous uncertainty in such cases and the importance that medical men be allowed to act within a certain context on the basis of wisdom and insight. What should be the ethical code in this connection? Must the ethical code of the medical practitioner be reviewed? Should he discontinue specialist treatment in such cases? Is he doing a disservice or service to the patient if he prolongs the patient's life in certain cases? Relief is expressed when a person maimed, and who has received brain damage, passes away. Relief is expressed because of the suffering and pain involved. Even if technically possible the prolongation of life, rather, the prolongation of the dying process, should not be the ultimate aim — medical techniques should not have the ultimate say in 'life' or 'death'. Then it surpasses its limits as a means given by God in the service and to the well-being of man. There is a time when God in His Providence brings an end to life (Ps. 31:15) and then the medical practitioner and his techniques should recede into the background. He has to discontinue such treatment which cannot alleviate suffering but can only prolong the dying process. Man cannot, however, play God — only when God does it, is it good.

Having said this one also has to discuss frankly the implications of death in our modern society. Elisabeth Kübler-Ross, who has done much research on the topic, points out five stages of coping with death: denial, anger, bargaining, depression and acceptance. A patient's moving from acceptance to another reaction is called a 'regression' — regression after acceptance is so often due to an inappropriate handling of the patient. According to Kübler-Ross 'truly religious people with a deep abiding relationship with God have found it easier to face death with equanimity'. When death is seen as a stage in nature's biological rhythms, when it is seen as a natural process, it leads to peace and tranquility. All this could be disturbed by the feverish struggling to keep a patient suffering from a terminal disease alive merely with the aim of prolonging his life. Epictetus already said that death be accepted so 'that the revolution of the universe may be accomplished, for it has need of things present, things future, and things past and done with'. (The Discourses of Epictetus translated by P. E. Matheson, Heritage, 1968, 72.) Marcus Aurelius considered death natural and the fear of it as 'inconsistent with honouring reason'. (The Harvard Classics, II, ed. by Charles W. Eliot, Collier, 1969, 204.)

Of course there is a great difference between the classical naturalistic belief that death is part of a good nature, and the view of 'orthodox Christianity' that death is the result of sin. Historically Christianity considered the continued presence of death a result of the fall from original perfection. Oscar Cullmann in reaction to Kübler-Ross' position, states that Christian doctrine presupposes the Jewish tradition, namely a connection between sin and death. 'Death is a curse, and the whole creation has become involved in the curse' (Oscar Cullmann, 'Immortality of the Soul' in Krister Stendahl, (ed), *Immortality and Resurrection,* MacMillan, 1965, 20). Paul's letter to the Romans is the *locus classicus* for the Christian connection of death with sin and evil. For the Christian, however, resurrection means that 'death is swallowed up in victory' (1 Cor. 15:54 ff). However, Paul remains hostile to it: 'The last enemy to be destroyed is death' (1 Cor. 15:26). John in Revelation states that 'death will be cast into a lake of fire' and 'death will be no more' (Rev. 20:14). On the one hand there is the stoic acceptance of death; on the other hand there is the Christian antagonism to it. Acceptance of death was considered by the Stoics to be the essence of dignity. Cullmann again sees Christ as struggling against the terrifying enemy until the end: 'My God, my God, why hast thou forsaken me'? (Mark 15:34). Christians who see the New Testament governed by a belief in the resurrection will agree with Cullmann that death is no natural phenomenon. But to reveal a morbid fear of death is not the Christian's answer to the dying process. If there is a more constructive attitude to death, raising it to a metaphysical dimension, much of the emphasis on the miracle of medical techniques will be avoided and terminally ill patients will maintain their dignity and be prepared to accept death. Kübler-Ross led virtually an entire nation back to the beds of the dying and this is needed also in our situation.

There are three main types which qualify for medical euthanasia namely:

(a) the newly born with serious deformities;

(b) those who suffer from irreversible brain damage; and

(c) totally unconscious old people with severe basic diseases.

Theological ethics have to give guidance here in a mature manner. The Bible does not give *absolute* value to life and there is no command from God to prolong a life under *all* circumstances. No individual life should be absolutized. The Bible knows about the desire to die; in confidence and in human weakness; a dying as a sacrifice for others. Within the Biblical principle of maturity the ethical consideration will concentrate on the questions as to whether a specific treatment should or must be started or whether a specific treatment should or must be terminated, or whether indirect so-called euthanasia could be justified.

Ethical considerations will prevent all kinds of casuistry. The distinction between passive and active euthanasia has already been made. When the medical practitioner is so often unjustly pictured as an executioner in this connection, when he is portrayed as deciding when a life must be brought to an end or whether a person's life is meaningful or not, one gets a distorted picture of what euthanasia actually implies. The ending of a life by a person who applies active euthanasia raises grave difficulties, such as that man controls life, not only his but those of others. Even the functionalistic question of meaningfulness of a life raises grave problems — idiots, demented old aged, cripples and others come into question. What will the end result be if a society starts to remove these people *ad lib.* from their midst? What then about mercy as a motive in euthanasia? If contemporary medical ethics were to push 'life' into the background in exchange for the criterium to help to relieve suffering, obvious reaction will take place. To kill a person in order to relieve him from pain is unacceptable to theological ethics.

Problems also arise in regard to so-called passive euthanasia, a term which should be dropped as it also gives the impresison that one individual may control the life of another. Where specialized treatment is terminated, it is also an act and spells death. Here a conscious decision is made which is not suicide, because a person other than the subject is involved; neither is it murder because it is not contrary to the will of the patient. To switch off the breathing apparatus in the case of a patient whose brain has died is active, it is an act of commission, but passive in regard to the intention. The term euthanasia should be reserved for what is called active euthanasia. Termination of specialized treatment should not be called euthanasia, not even *passive* euthanasia so as to avoid the idea that one human being could decide on the termination or continuation of the life of another human being. It is in any case very difficult to draw a distinction between active and passive euthanasia — the reason is that the difference between them is difficult to define. Stopping a heart-lung machine in many cases means certain death; so also termination of specialist treatment. But there is a difference, namely, the whole idea of controlling a person's life or death is overruled in so-called passive euthanasia where death takes its course and where it is the patient who 'activates' the dying. A person is then allowed to die with dignity instead of having all kinds of medical techniques applied to him without the hope that it will be meaningful.

Even where treatment could be stopped, great difficulties do arise. A great onus is put on the doctor because he commands the most acceptable means of euthanasia. While the doctor has to venture to save life in all circumstances, he has difficulty in deciding whether he has to do his utmost best to help a person or let him go in a natural way. If the brain has died, the person is dead. But the doctor is not always sure about brain death — there are cases where patients have remained in a coma for a long time. Peter Rish (32) who lay in a coma for six years from 1961 - 1967, was talked out of it by his mother. He died in 1976. The most obvious condition remains that the person's life is really at an end and that treatment be terminated — that he be allowed to die. An irrevocable dying process should be allowed to take its course. A severe disease in the life of an old demented person could be seen as providence of God to bring a merciful end to the life of such a person.

Some have raised the argument of communication — if someone is so deranged that he has no contact, then such a person should not be held especially in life, if no natural cause arises to end his life. Consent and meaningfulness of human life is seen more and more under the criterium of communicability. Theological ethics understands this but will emphasize that a life without communication could have value *coram Deo*. Persons other than unconscious patients cannot communicate — such as retarded ones and idiots — would they too be deprived of specialized treatment? The mandate of medicine is from the community and any community that allows its unfortunate people to be disregarded will eventually degenerate and suffer.

The doctor should in all cases endeavour to prolong life and save it except where he cannot stop dying. New techniques which will not be of value to a cancer sufferer will be withheld as they will only prolong suffering. The medical profession should not be a slave to medical techniques and neither should it enslave patients in these techniques. However, a doctor should be a wise man who acknowledges that the final decisions on life and death do not lie with him. Medical power as a factor should be seriously studied and legislation be called upon to adjust, because non-adaptation in this connection leads to uncertainty and to anarchy.

Legislation may have to provide for cases where persons make a will stipulation that when they are in such a position that they cannot decide about their life and where there is no hope, that they be allowed to die. Social ethics emphasize, because of the increase of irreparably cripple people with brain damage in modern society, that greater attention be given to prevention of such accidents. Furthermore, taking care of those who are terminally ill and permanently handicapped is not only a task of the medical profession but the task of society also. The one-sided task of science must be reletavised. The Church is also against the absolutising of life; the Church itself has a task to think through the questions concerning euthanasia and to make known her standpoint in this connection to all concerned, not to condemn or to accept but to help in the making of responsible decisions, and above all, to be deeply involved also in the dying of its flock.

A FREE CHURCH VIEWPOINT

W. G. M. Abbott

For Christians, and particularly for Protestants, the Bible is the supreme standard of belief. Euthanasia is a modern concept, and as such it is not specifically considered by the Biblical authors. We must therefore look at general principles, both in the Old and the New Testament.

It is clear that the Old Testament prohibits killing. 'Thou shalt not kill' or 'Thou shalt do no murder' is one of the articles of the Decalogue. But it is also clear that there were considerable exceptions to this general rule: First: Judicial punishment. Second: War. Third: The special case of *herem,* where part or the whole of a given population was devoted to death for religious reasons.

Christianity took over the Decalogue as a basis for morality, but was also, and primarily, affected by the teaching of Jesus. In particular, there is a section of the Sermon on the Mount (Matthew 5:21 - 22 and 43 - 48) which is relevant. Note must also be taken of Jesus's summary of the Law in Mark 12:28 - 34. It would seem that these statements would exclude killing of any sort, but in practice Christians continued to allow killing in war, and execution as a judicial punishment. There have always been movements, however, to outlaw war (conscientious objection) and to ban capital punishment.

The suffering of death, rather than its infliction, has also been the subject of Christian thinking. This is partly due to the fact that Jesus himself was put to death, and some understanding had to be found of how this came to be, and what meaning ought to be attached to it. Moreover, particularly in the early days, many Christians were martyred, or put to death for their beliefs. Building on the basis of the Old Testament, particularly of the Psalms and Prophets, Christians came to see that martyrdom, and indeed all suffering, could be seen positively as sharing in the suffering of Christ, and thereby participating in the work of salvation. Jesus himself seems to have been deeply influenced, both in his words and his course of action by Chapter 53 of Isaiah.

The tendency to accept martyrdom as within the will of God was strengthened by the belief in eternal life. The contrast between the Old Testament and the New in this regard is most striking. While there are few and indeed rather uncertain references to life after death to be found in the Old Testament, the whole theme of the New Testament is that of eternal life. This teaching, which must be seen to involve personal continued existence in a life that is richer than our mortal days, must affect the attitude of the Christian to life and death. This lends a new vigour to the belief that the voluntary death of one person may be of advantage (physically or spiritually) to others, and is therefore praiseworthy. On the other hand, the taking of one's own life (suicide) is generally to be regarded as a sin, and may even be considered as destroying the possibility of eternal life.

On this basis, which clearly leaves room for personal interpretation, we turn to look at euthanasia. Looking at it in the widest way, it would seem to allow for at least three possibilities:

1. The putting to death (or allowing to die) of babies born as monsters, or born seriously handicapped.
2. The termination of life of those suffering continued excruciating pain without hope of remission (with or without their consent) (mercy killing).
3. The allowing to die of persons whose life might be maintained by modern machines, but whose brains have been irreparably damaged (again with the possibility of prior consent, or will expressed, or without such agreement).

In connection with this, and as some indication of common thinking on this subject, I quote from a statement of faith known as *The Common Catechism,* drawn up by a group of Dutch Catholic and Protestant theologians (508ff *passim*):

There is no civilization that does not attach a high value to human life at the physical level . . . Hence all civilizations recognize certain exceptions to the prohibition of taking human life. These exceptions range from killing in self-defence or killing in a 'just war', to the exercise of the death penalty or killing someone who is grievously sick on grounds of compassion. But, abstracting from this, human life is universally regarded as sacred and is protected both by laws, and also by religious convictions and taboos. For the Christian, God is the ultimate origin of all life. . . In the last analysis there are the grounds on which faith judges that human life is sacred, and that man has no direct or absolute right of disposal over his own life or over the lives of other men. At the same time, the Christian recognizes . . . that physical life is not man's highest good. The highest good and the highest goal can only be the progressive unfolding of his relationship with God in faith and love, and his relationship with his fellowmen in love and justice. . . From this it follows that even the earthly and physical life of man cannot be his highest good. Situations can arise in which the meaning of human life as a whole can only be fulfilled by man laying down his physical life. . .

The statement goes on to discuss euthanasia in its various forms, and concludes: 'There are two considerations which taken singly or together, may make it easier to decide whether to break off the measures designed to prolong life. Once we have reached the point of questioning the value of continuing such treatment we may ask ourselves first whether it can only be continued at the cost of depriving others of certain vital helps to save their lives, and second whether the life of another could be saved by giving him one of the organs of the dying man which is still sound.'

This statement is obviously only meant as a guideline, and it is somewhat on the conservative side. But it illustrates the kind of thinking that is going on, and leaves room for further constructive thought.

A BUDDHIST VIEWPOINT

Louis H. van Loon

The confusion on the subject of euthanasia is, I think, principally due to the fact that we are attempting to reconcile our primitive religious notions about life and death with an advanced medical technology that can make life flow through plastic tubes and which has reduced death to a horizontal line on the EEG machine. Difficulties arise when our religious assumption that life is a divine 'gift' confronts the medical possibility of its creation in a test tube, combined with the horrifying thought that this 'gift' can be kept trapped almost indefinitely in a corpse. Clearly, our religious concepts and medical acumen must be made to meet on common ground before living and dying can be seen in terms of human experience rather than as specific clinical situations or as arcane and inscrutable metaphysical phenomena. This involves re-assessing our traditional religious interpretation of 'being' as much as it concerns the critical evaluation of 'existence' in the light of modern medical knowledge.

Euthanasia concerns the dilemma whether, in a desperately ill and dying person, life should be terminated or allowed to run out because it has lost its intrinsic meaning and because the suffering involved is inhumanly severe, or whether life must be preserved for its own sake and at all cost, no matter what amount of suffering is involved or how meaningless it may have become, simply because it is precious and sacred — a divine gift. We shall have to determine at what stage life has become religiously meaningless and when, biologically, death has become absolute; whether human existence is to be measured quantitatively — in terms of spontaneous respiration or electric potential in the thalamus — or qualitatively — in terms of the presence of a 'soul' or the ability to be sapient instead of merely vegetative. Buddhism takes a definite stand somewhere between these extreme views. To appreciate this position, an assessment of its view on the nature of suffering and the purpose of life — and death — is necessary.

The non-theistic interpretation of 'life'

Buddhism steers a midway course between mindless materialism and rampant religious speculation. It is neither theistic nor atheistic;

71

it is non-theistic. From its inception 2 500 years ago, it has represented a reaction against the inveterate tendency in all religions and philosophical systems to define the indefinable and concretize the abstract. Consequently, its ethico-philosophical teachings are not enshrined in dogmatic statements, authoritative revelations and institutionalized articles of belief. It has never had to suffer the embarrassment of having serious religious dogmas exposed as mere conceptual fancies, such as for instance, that the earth is the centre of the universe and that creation occurred in 4004 B.C. Similarly, the notion that life is a sacred 'gift' and that man is therefore a unique creation, an embodied 'soul' fulfilling a 'divine' purpose on earth is, in the Buddhist view, equally devoid of truth and just as spiritually shortsighted. Simply because man's intelligence and intuitive imagination is not capable of illuminating and harnessing such problems as initial causation, ultimate purpose, infinity, eternity, etc., this is no excuse to adopt pseudo-solutions in the form of blind religious beliefs or absurd philosophical concepts.

The answer does not lie in burdening our minds, already strained and bewildered under a load of empirical idiosyncrasies, with all manner of notions, speculations and superstitions about problems that are demonstrably outside our immediate range of comprehension and direct experience. They only serve to render our lives even more confounding and perplexing. Concepts that aim to explain such problems as who created the universe and who or what created this Creator, amount to just so much mental acrobatics. In our attempts to solve such enigmas — conceptually — having proved themselves first incapable of logical analysis — we only succeed in concealing and camouflaging them in equally illogical and incomprehensible but religiously respectable articles of faith.

However, this is not the occasion to explain the Buddhist philosophical views at any length. But it is necessary to understand that the Buddhist attitude to euthanasia does not rest on the generally accepted theistic notions. Although a Buddhist considers life to be extremely *precious,* he does not imagine it to be *sacred, divine.* He is therefore not committed to stubbornly preserving a spent, doomed and suffering-ridden life for its own sake and at all cost. For him, there are no 'souls' that can be 'saved' or 'lost' or 'returned' to their Maker.

Is life a quantity or a quality?

To a Buddhist, life should neither be measured merely in terms of basic metabolic functions or elementary brain activity, nor equated with a conceptual supermundane spiritual essence. These interpretations are essentially irreconcilable. After cardiac and respiratory functions have ceased, the brain can still be kept 'alive'; and even after all cerebral activity has stopped, specific organic structures can still remain biologically viable for quite some time. At what stage then, in medical or religious terms, can our 'life' or 'spirit' be said to have lost its grip on its material abode? From ancient times it used to be equated with respiration (spirit <'spirare' = to breathe; 'spiritus' = breath; vigour; soul; life). Are we now to equate it with electrical activity in the brain? Or the organic viability of the skeletal muscles or liver cells?

It is clear that neither the modern medical quantitative measurements of life nor the traditional religious metaphysical parameters, by themselves, or in combination, are likely to give us a satisfactory answer to this problem. There are, for instance, irreversible unconscious patients whose respiration and heart beat nevertheless continue spontaneously. They are 'humanly' dead but are biologically 'alive' simply because machines continue to forcefeed them and drain them of their waste products. Others are semi-conscious but their 'existence' depends totally and permanently on heart-lung machines. Conscious or unconscious, with or without spontaneous or mechanical respiration — where does our 'life' or 'spirit' reside? In our heart, lungs, brain or tissue? In our body or the machine?

The Buddhists have never looked upon 'life' as a single, metaphysical 'ens' — a mysterious spiritual essence, an aspect of a hypothetical transpersonal, individual 'soul'. They consider this notion to be based on faulty reasoning and wishful thinking. It probably had its origin in our primitive past when it was thought that with the expiration of our last breath, our 'spiritus' escaped the body forever to join the almighty Sky God.

Buddhism sums up the empirical totality of our individual experience in five 'heaps' (Skandhas) of psycho-physical activity: a physical framework — the body — through which sensations, perceptions, volitional mental faculties and an integrating consciousness operate. This whole bundle of mental and physical phenomena is held together in a characteristic 'personality' pattern by our ideating consciousness, under strict laws of causality. It is a dynamic flux of interdependent atoms of manifestation and psychic events, even by modern scientific standards. However, man, hemmed in by the narrow scope of his senses and limited by his cramped, survival orientated perceptions, is deluded into thinking of himself as a discrete, stable entity — a distinct 'self'. Ignorantly, he attributes to his composite parts the notion of an 'ego', an everlasting 'soul', to give expression to his sensation of and wish for continuity of identity.

'Souls' and 'divine gifts' have, therefore, no place in Buddhist ethical teachings. However, this has not prevented Buddhism from being one of the most compassionate religions in the world. In fact, the whole structure of Buddhism is based on the Buddha's Four Noble Truths, which deal with Dukkha ('turmoil' or 'suffering') in one way or another. Buddhism is, in fact, unsurpassed in its universal and systematic application of the principles of Ahimsa (Harmlessness), Metta (Loving-kindness) and Karuna (Compassion). It extends these qualities, its reverence of life and its concern to alleviate suffering, to all sentient creatures — to man and ant alike. From the Tibetan monk who will save a drowning fly from his cup of buttertea, to the vegetarian Zen master who cannot conceive of making a meal out of a murdered animal, and the fact that Buddhism has never indulged in animal sacrifices or waged any religious wars — all this is ample evidence that this religion instills a rare and genuine compassion and respect for life in its followers.

It is therefore obvious that a Buddhist would wish to protect life and relieve suffering, probably more so than almost any other religious devotee, with the possible exception of the Jain. Yet, in accordance with his philosophical standards, there are limits beyond which he considers 'life' to have become not only utterly meaningless, but the wilful prolongation of it spiritually criminal.

Volition: The essence of meaningful human existence

Buddhism maintains that man is so entrenched in the banalities of his daily life, that he is doomed to mediocrity. His thoughts are so overshadowed by the anxieties of mere survival, living and dying, that he is barred from ever knowing the real roots of his being. Only meditative introspection, the transcendence of his mediocrity, can lead to a radical transformation of his perceptual world and convert it from one of bewildering appearances and perplexing conceptual notions to one of transpersonal universality.

Introspection is an act of volition; it is the deliberate re-orientation of our consciousness, away from its mundane rut and towards supramundane values. It is this volitional mental faculty in us — one of the five 'heaps' or Skandhaso — that is central to our 'personality'. It represents one's ability to choose and decide, to reflect and intuit, to mould one's actions and control one's reactions. It is the hallmark of true human existence. Without it, life would be a hollow, rudderless affair; man would be 'humanly dead'. It represents our higher cognitive faculties, our sapiency, the operative element of our mind; our only means of truly knowing ourselves. The other 'heaps' — the physical body, sense, impressions, perceptions and awareness — are merely functional channels through which our volitional impulses become conscious experiences and along which they are able to flow into objective manifestation. Indeed, it is this element of volition that represents the meaningful aspect of our 'existence'; the characteristic, functional ingredient of our 'individuality'. Therefore, any question relating to the quality of life should be measured against the degree of volition that is capable of being exercised. In fact, Buddhism emphasizes the need to safeguard life and relieve suffering so much because, by freeing a creature from physical and mental duress we enable it to re-direct its volitional faculties and mobilize its introspective qualities away from its burden of empirical anxieties and towards a transcendental world-view.

The range and limits of euthanasia

The debate on euthanasia concerns the ethics of preserving or prolonging life beyond certain limits of human viability; it involves an assessment of the degree of suffering and distress that may be inflicted or should be endured as a consequence of medical treatment that aims to forestall or delay death. It ranges from cases where patients are no more than mechanically maintained vegetative bundles of protoplasm — irreversibly unconscious and incapable of even the most elementary respiratory functions — to instances of complete idiocy in otherwise physically healthy, but totally helpless, mindless human specimens. It covers patients slowly dying from severely painful illnesses (like cancer with metastases) as well as those who are afflicted with incurable physical disabilities and chronic, unbearable pain but without this necessarily affecting their life expectancy (like crippling rheumatism). It may concern unborn children as well as centenarians. Euthanasia, therefore, spans an enormous range of potential applications and it is clear that definitive standards and limitations should be agreed upon in order that it may be applied with morality and humanity, with confidence and a clear conscience.

Based on the Buddhist view that volition constitutes a man's essential 'beingness', as described above, it should be clear that it is from this standpoint that he judges the desirability or otherwise of all forms of euthanasia. He would, for instance, in principle be in favour of *voluntary* euthanasia, provided it applied within narrowly defined limits. Obviously, we do not want to find ourselves putting down hypochondriacs seeking relief from a toothache, but a dying patient whose ebbing life is artificially prolonged and sustained through tubes, catheters and electrodes, and whose consciousness is totally overshadowed by physical distress and mental anguish, has no independent personal volition left to carry on living meaningfully. Similarly, if incurable, intolerable pain can only be relieved by rendering a patient unconscious (and therefore volitionless) or semi-conscious by the use of life-shortening drugs, then his life has been turned into a macabre and farcical medical spectacle that serves no purpose whatsoever except to demonstrate our ignorance about what life, living and dying is all about. If, indeed, volition is the essence of meaningful human existence, it must surely be allowed to play its part in life's most momentous crisis: death. It is a spiritual crime to prevent a dying man from choosing a painless death in preference to unbearable suffering or artificially maintained, unconscious, vegetative 'existence' by holding him captive in a hospital word, guarded by well-meaning doctors and priests, in the mistaken idea that we are thereby 'preserving' a sacred commodity.

A Buddhist is aware that suffering is never completely profitless. It is never endured uselessly as, in its synergetic interaction with the field of causality that constitutes our characteristic personality pattern (our 'karma'), it antidotes, compensates and moderates adverse karmic tendencies, past or future. But our immediate moral responsibility is the *relief* of suffering, for the reasons already mentioned. Therefore, whether a patient is conscious or unconscious, and expressly requests euthanasia or not, and whether he is already in the process of dying or alive but incurably and painfully handicapped, the general rule should be applied that where a disease or disability — or medical treatment itself — induces in a patient either volitionless, unconscious vegetative existence or an overwhelming awareness of distress, pain and suffering to the exclusion of almost any other sensation or conscious activity — then such a patient should be eased into as 'natural' a death as possible, with a minimum of suffering.

This definition covers what is known as 'passive' euthanasia, but also such borderline cases of active-passive euthanasia as in the case of a patient who can be kept semiconscious but relatively free of chronic agony only on combinations of pain killing and tranquilizing drugs which must, however, be administered in ever larger doses in order to remain effective, finally to become so toxic that they kill the patient. Here, also, our prime responsibility is the relief of suffering to the best of our abilities, even if this inevitably entails killing the patient in the process. In short, we should not forcibly extend a suffering-ridden, doomed or volitionless life simply because it is technologically possible to do so, or in the mistaken idea that we have an obligation to 'preserve' the 'divine gift' of such meaningless life for a few more days, weeks or months.

The 'volition-death' standard

Medical treatment which may initially have been aimed at bringing about a cure and the relief of pain may lead progressively towards a state where the patient is sustained in a persistent vegetative condition. Therefore, the applicability of euthanasia in such cases centres, for the Buddhist, on the exact moment at which life-sustaining devices should be withdrawn. This necessitates defining 'death' in relation to a medical technology that can pump life into virtual corpses almost indefinitely.

The 'Brain Death' standard set up at Harvard Medical School in 1968 was primarily concerned with organ transplant surgery and was meant to determine the point at which there is a total cessation of all biological functions combined with the irretrievable loss of even the most elementary brain activity. However, often long before this technical 'death situation' is reached, a patient has ceased to exist as a person. Such 'personality death' takes place when the higher cognitive functions associated with volitional mentality are irretrievably lost or destroyed beyond repair. 'Life' has then ceased to have any human value; 'existence' has lost all its meaning.

The part of our brain, the cerebrum, that gives us our sapiency, our conscious volitional ability, may have died irreversibly, yet the deeper brain structures may still retain some of their basic functions which often enables spontaneous respiration to continue for longer or shorter periods. Even after this spontaneous respiration has ceased (and has been replaced by mechanical respirators), there may yet remain signs of 'life' in areas like the medulla and the hypothalamus which would indicate that complete 'brain death' has not yet occurred. By then, however, the patient is no more than a biological extension of the machines that keep this inhuman, medical monstrosity going.

To judge the presence of 'life' by the amount of electric potential in the medulla or any other deep-brain structure, is therefore as silly as claiming that a patient is truly dead only when his skeletal muscles have 'died' — which may be a day or so after total brain death. Euthanasia requires a new definition of *human death,* not in terms of the cessation of all electrical potential in obscure parts of the brain — for this gives rise to such grotesque situations as the Karen Ann Quinlan case — but in terms of human viability, judged by the absence or presence of volitional mentality. Moreover, the reliability of the Brain Death Standard itself has recently come under criticism. It has been found that the life-sustaining devices attached to a dying — or dead — person can themselves produce apparent brain activity where there is, in fact, none. The cruel irony of this is that a long-dead patient may be kept 'alive' on the basis of 'evidence' generated by the life support apparatus itself. In fact, it is possible to elicit such 'proof' of life from a bowl of strawberry jelly, once it is hooked up to a respirator and an electroencephalograph.

The death of the human being occurs when he is volitionally dead; when his cerebrum has permanently lost its viability — not when the last traces of electricity have left his basal brain cells. It may however, not be possible to define 'Volition Death' as an exact clinical situation. It may involve a number of parameters and may require a period of observation sufficiently long to ensure that an irreversible 'a-cerebral' condition has, in fact, occurred. Indeed, 'Volition Death' may proceed along a patch of 'grey' twilight existence, between the 'white' of life and the 'black' of total biological death. But it should be possible to establish an area where this grey positively shades into black, which would then unmistakingly signify the death of the volitional personality, the 'human' being. This would avoid situations where patients are kept artificially 'alive' well into the black area of their death. In the case of Karen Ann Quinlan, for instance, there is unanimous agreement amongst her doctors that she suffered the equivalent of a 'Volition Death' some time ago. They are all convinced that she is in a 'persistent vegetative state, without higher mental functions and no hope of recovery . . . to a cognitive, sapient state'. Yet, because her deeper brain structures still contain remnants of electric potential, she is considered 'alive' by today's standards of assessing death.

Clearly, there is an urgent need to re-define, in human terms, what really constitutes 'life' and 'death'. Our present standards suffer from two excesses — the one medical and the other religious, although each influences the other. Because life, any sign of life — however irrelevant to real human existence — is conceived as a sacred metaphysical entity, a divine gift, there is extreme reluctance to draw a dividing line between life and death anywhere except where there is a total absence of any life symptoms.

This attitude not only causes us to turn patients into animated cadavers by keeping them strapped to 'intensive care' machinery long after they have died a human death; it also makes us preserve lives that have become utterly meaningless and are not worth living because they have turned into nightmares of suffering. Instead, the Buddhist would like to see death defined as the stage where a patient has died a 'volition death' — when he has ceased to exist as a human person, which generally occurs upon the irreversable failure of his cerebrum.

A Buddhist considers life, in its human context, to be meaningful only when the higher cognitive, sapient faculties associated with volitional mentality are capable of being exercised. Above all, he maintains that it is as immoral to inflict unwarranted pain and suffering on an ill and dying person as it is on a healthy, living one.

Sociological and Economical Aspects of Euthanasia

THE SOCIAL WORKER AND EUTHANASIA

F. C. Shaw

Although social workers have encountered and been working with dying patients and their families since the beginning of the twentieth century, they have not connected themselves with euthanasia or the euthanasia movement as such. Unquestionably, as part of their function, they would wish for each patient 'a quiet and easy death',[1] but no professional platform has been used for the reform of existing legislation, although there may have been queries in private about the responsibilities involved in either negative or positive euthanasia.

Part of the answer to the question of the lack of an overt platform for euthanasia must lie in the fact that when social workers practice in the field of medicine they operate in what can be termed a secondary setting. That is, their responsibility is as a member of the medical team of which the doctor or medical practitioner is customarily the head. I would hypothesize, however, that the desire for status in the medical setting has militated against any direct involvement against campaigns for practices which are essentially the direct responsibility of the medical practitioner.

The second answer to this question may lie in the slow development which there has been in the field of prevention. Prevention is essentially the province of the community organization method of social work.

To move backwards now, it seems important that we see social work in its correct perspective. It is in essence a part of the whole area of social welfare and social service and is the way in which the impairment and restoration of social functioning and the prevention of social malfunctioning can take place in communities, groups and individuals. In order to achieve this broad social purpose the activities of social work have been confined within certain fields and subject to a certain methodology. My view in relation to methodology is a traditional one. I have taken this stance as for purposes of this paper the traditional methodology seemed to underline a facet of the question of euthanasia which could be developed in a manner that fitted in with the mainstream of my thought.

The three main methods of social work are casework, group work and community organization, with ancillary methods of administration, research and supervision.

It is in the sphere of community organization and research that the question of primary prevention lies, and it is from this starting-point that I wish to look at the rôle social work may have in the attainment of a 'quiet and easy death'.

This hope may appear Utopian, but it seems to be one step in the direction towards looking at a legal and ethical problem in possibly a preventive fashion. We all have to die. It is the one reality of which we can be certain. Even Sir Thomas More in his Utopia says:

The sick they see with great affection, and let nothing at all pass concerning either physic or good diet whereby they may be restored again to their health. Such as be sick of incurable diseases they comfort with sitting by them, with talking with them, and to be short with all manner of helps that there be. But if the disease *be not only incurable* but also full of incurable pain and anguish, then the priests and the magistrates exhort the man, seeing he is not able to do any duty by life, and by overliving his life is noisome and irksome to others and grievous to himself, that he will determine with himself no longer to cherish that pestilent and painful disease, and seeing his life is to him but a torment, that he will not be unwilling to die, but rather take a good hope to him and either despatch him out of that painful life, as out of a prison or a rack of torment, or else suffer himself willingly to be rid of it by other. And in so doing they tell him that he shall do wisely, seeing by his own death he shall loose no commodity, but end his pain. And because in that act he shall follow the counsel of the priests, that is to say the interpreters of God's will and pleasure, they show him that he shall do like a godly and virtuous man. They that be thus persuaded to finish their lives willingly, either with hunger or else die in their sleep without any feeling of death. But they cause none to die against their will, nor they use no less diligence and attendance about him, believing this to be an honourable death. Else he that killeth himself before that the priests and the council have allowed him the cause of his death, him as unworthy either to be buried or with fire to be consumed, they cast unburied into some stinking marsh.[2]

Thus it seems to me in the sphere of community organization and research, social workers have a method which, when located in the field of health, can be used as one way of preventing the incidence of incurable disease. We have a responsibility in our contact with the community and the hospital, not only to be aware of the severity of incurable disease and the impact which it has on the lives of the persons around the patient, but we have the responsibility to agitate for services which, whilst health-orientated, have a welfare base and which can in the realms of our knowledge prevent disease, pain and suffering.

Possibly the illness which is uppermost in the lay mind is that of cancer. Research and epidemiological studies into the incidence of the development of different types of cancer, the establishment of clinics and preventive services, lie within the sphere of social work and the social worker involved in community organization. Obviously, whilst the social worker cannot prevent ultimate death, he can, through vigilance, assure that those cancers for which preventive knowledge is available, have services properly provided for their attention, and placed in a community which appears from relevant research to be at risk.

Family planning services, whilst a health responsibility, fall also into the social welfare field. Prevention of large families, with possible overcrowding, under-nourishment and the painful diseases associated with malnutrition, can prevent illness which in its last stages may be painful and costly. Prevention is not dramatic, but the insurance by the social worker that community immunization campaigns are adequately planned, that clinics are set up in areas readily available to communities at risk, and that adequate publicity is carried out, promotes a positive rather than a negative attitude to health.

The social worker has increasingly assumed an important role in genetic and abortion counselling, which may in its turn prevent the birth of malformed and malnourished children — children who might in their later years require extensive and expensive hospitalization and care, and who may be a drain on other more positive health services. The appointment of social workers, or community liaison officers as they are called, as part of the Municipal Health team in cities, gives great hope for the prevention of needless ill-health.

Apart from this multi-disciplinary research and the provision of services in the field of health, there are other aspects which are important for social workers and which are within the sphere of their knowledge and competence.

More in his Utopia comments on the whole question of dying:

'Such as be sick of incurable diseases they comfort by sitting with them, with talking with them and to be short with all manner of helps that there be'.[3]

Whilst this statement might on first reading appear to refer only to the individual help which is given to dying persons, its implication can stretch further to the area of research and the pooling of information about the attitudes of and toward the dying and of those in attendance on them. Research of this nature is of great importance if we (social workers and other members of the health team) are to understand the feelings of those about to die and to enable them in some small way to have a 'quiet and easy death'.

Kübler-Ross,[4] of whom you must have heard, and Saunders, have acted on research which has been of prime importance in the field of what has now become known as thanatology. Kübler-Ross, as a result of lengthy research with dying patients, consolidated information about the attitudes which dying people have. This research in its consolidated form can now be of use to those who work with the dying patient. It is of interest that Kübler-Ross's work, which took place a little less than ten years ago, was met with such hostility that she was initially refused permission to undertake the required interviews. Kübler-Ross distinguishes five stages which are exhibited by dying patients. These stages are:

a. Denial
b. Anger
c. Bargaining (usually with God)
d. Depression
e. Acceptance.

This effort (that is Kübler-Ross's) towards intellectualization of the problem is admirable; at the same time it is true that what has been most influential in alleviating the loneliness of the dying is the warmth of Dr Ross's sympathy and the intensity of the dedication of her effort. This research, it is hoped, will enable us to break the barrier between the dying patient and those around him and to overcome the frequently commented upon loneliness of death mentioned, for example, by great writers such as Tolstoy[5] and Solzhenitsyn.[6]

Hinton[7] in his studies found that whilst research into the attitudes of the dying was extremely difficult, observations from many disciplines were imperative in order that an unbiased view of the subject might be obtained.

Knowledge such as this enables the helping professions to come to grips not only with the stages through which the patient passes in dying, but with the feelings which the people who work with the dying have towards their patients. Professionals and relatives may often feel rejected by what they may consider the unaccountable 'anger' of the patient they are helping or visiting. Such knowledge as we now have allows us to see that this anger is only a stage in the dying process. Further, patients themselves who are extremely ill are often distressed by the way in which they feel doctors and sometimes nurses reject them when they have great needs. The reaction of the helpers may now also be understood in terms of recent research.

Research into bereavement, loss and separation has been the sphere of the social worker, psychologist and psychiatrist for many years. The research began not only as a result of work with the dying, but with the concern of social workers and psychologists about the behaviour resulting from the removal of a child from his own home to either institutional or foster care. Such observations and research have been taking place over a period of more than thirty years. The behaviour of the child suddenly separated from his own home and parents is similar to that shown by bereaved adults. Research regarding bereavement is of value in assisting those who have suffered loss in order to help them to regain their identity and to function adequately in the community.

Studies on separation and grief by writers such as Bowlby[8] and Lindemann,[9] as well as Parad and Caplan,[10] have shown that bereavement and death have, in psychological parlance, come to be considered as the maturational and situational crises which may be handled within the limits of this theoretical approach. Research of this kind, too, does help the social worker in assisting administrators to introduce into institutions, either for children or for the ill, more humane procedures, so that the trauma which is suffered in crisis situations can be lessened by a favourable environment.

Lindemann[11] from an empirical study, has considered that there is a certain symotomatology associated with loss, and that in order for any equilibrium to be restored 'grief work' must be undertaken by the bereaved. He arranges the symptoms that follow grief under the following five headings:
a. Somatic distress
b. Preoccupation with the image of the deceased
c. Guilt
d. Hostile reactions to the deceased and others
e. The loss of patterns of conduct and social and psychological

disorientation.

Smith,[12] a social worker, has indicated that she considers this theory too person-centred, and does not take fully into account the functioning of the individual in his social environment and the societal pressures that are brought to bear upon the individual in his bereavement. 'A phenomenological and existential understanding of the individual in relation to his social world provides a comprehensive picture of the complex process at work'.[13]

Smith posits further that there will be three processes accompanying bereavement. The first is that of denial, when the dead person, virtually, is still present. The second is that of disorganization and meaninglessness, and the third, the development of a new identity or role and consequently a new place in society.

It is (just) a matter of listening and prompting. The client is encouraged all the time to live out the grief and by talking about it . . . slowly they come to accept it and go on with their lives. Thus the person must be helped to relinquish the last object and to build a new world after the reality of the destruction of the old can be observed.[14]

What of course is interesting in comparing these theories is their similarity. There is a close relationship between the sequence of events passed through by a dying person and the bereaved.

The dying person experiences:	*The bereaved person experiences*:
denial	denial and pre-occupation with the image of the deceased
anger	
bargaining	guilt and hostile reactions
depression	disorganization
acceptance	the development of a new identity. (This appears to me to be very similar to the acceptance which is a facet of the process of the dying.)

The only real difference in these two schemata lies in the absence of bargaining in the process of bereavement. Otherwise the similarities seem to indicate an opening for new thought and explorations about the ways in which similar types of service might be developed for the dying and the distressed.

Research, however, is not only concerned with attitudes, feelings and the provision of services, but also with the provision of manpower. From the outset I have indicated that a social worker is essentially, when we consider this topic, allied to the medical profession. More, however, in his Utopia, calls for persons who will comfort the dying by sitting with them and talking with them. Who are these people who will sit and talk with the dying? They are, of course, the doctor who is in attendance, the relatives, the friends, the social worker in either the hospital or the community who is carrying out what is known as 'individual or family casework'. However, do we have enough of these people that we can call upon to help those who are dying or are in distress?

An article[15] in the *Scientific American* shows that the general practitioner is the only speciality in medicine which is not at the present time replacing itself. The general practitioner in fact appears to be the member of a dying profession. This is indeed a serious matter, for a knowledge of the home, the family, and all its strengths and weaknesses assists a specialist in helping to decide what is best for the patient. Nowadays home visits by the general practitioner and the form of close interaction which he had with the family are becoming more rare. In fact social workers are in some instances being employed in general practice and in hospitals to observe the social interactions and relationships which occur in families, and are required to pass this information on to the doctor. It is, I feel, of great significance, if any programme of euthanasia is to be planned, and if one is to rely on the judgement of the general practitioner, that we are aware of his increasingly limited role within the family.

Organizational research, a knowledge of the structure of bureaucratic organizations, the delivery of health care systems, form part of the social worker's knowledge in the health field of his understanding of the way in which society does or could make provision for the sick and dying. This knowledge can aid the social worker in helping patients to accept some of the more complex hospital procedures, which are often difficult to understand.

A study of 'Dying'[16] showed that in England, for example, approximately fifty per cent of people die in hospitals and some forty per cent in their own homes.

Table 1 shows clearly the kinds of deaths which took place in England in 1968 - 69. In Table 2 it is very clearly indicated that certain classes of people have different types of assistance to call upon when they are ill. Contrary to one's impressions, people who are less well off have wider and closer family ties than the middle class, who are called upon to consult friends and neighbours at a time of crisis. Such a finding would of course

TABLE 1
PLACE OF DEATH IN RELATION TO NO. AND SEX OF LIVING
CHILDREN

Place of death	One son	One daughter	Sons only	Daughters only	Sons and daughters	Any children	No children
	%	%	%	%	%	%	%
Hospital	55	42	63	37	41	45	47
Other institution	2	1	2	2	—	1	6
Person's own home	40	54	28	59	52	48	39
Other person's home	3	3	5	2	3	3	5
Elsewhere	—	—	2	—	4	3	3
No. of deaths*	63	90	60	49	230	492	144

* Excluding those who had been in hospital or other institution for a
year or more before they died and those who died inexpectedly.

indicate that welfare services perhaps in hospitals and in the community should be geared to the middle class rather than the lower
income range, a somewhat revolutionary thought.

The article ends, however, with a depressing statement, namely
that the people who care for the dying are doctors whose training
insufficiently emphasizes the skills and emotional problems involved;
district nurses and home helps, who are often unable to spend as
much time as is needed with them; and relatives, many old

TABLE 2
NO. OF RELATIVES AND FRIENDS WHO HELPED THE DYING

Relationship of people who helped to the person who died	Middle Class people who died	Working Class people who died
	%	%
Husband or wife	16	16
Daughter	14	21
Son	9	14
Daughter-in-law	3	5
Son-in-law	3	5
Other relative	23	21
Friend or neighbour	28	17
Other person	4	1
No. of helpers	509	1 246

Note: Class was determined from the death certificate by the occupation
of the person who died, if a man or single woman, or by the occupation of
the husband if a married or widowed woman. Non-manual occupations
have been classified as middle class, and manual occupations as working
class.

themselves, who have to look after people in poor housing conditions and with inadequate material support from community services. In connection with South Africa's White aged population this is a problem which is causing considerable concern.

From the community organization and specifically research-orientated statements made previously I think it is obvious that in the field of prevention itself the social worker has an important rôle in influencing the community institutions and in providing needed community services for the ill and dying.

There are, however, two other methods of social work to which I have not yet referred and which are of importance in practice with the ill and the dying. These are casework and group work.

Social workers have been employed in hospitals since the late nineteenth century: In England since 1895, in the United States since 1906, in Australia since 1917 and in South Africa since 1938. Many articles have shown that social workers are frequently dissatisfied with their status in the medical hierarchy and complain that they are being improperly used. So often one reads the phrase that the medical social workers were seen and used by the medical staff solely as disposal officers, clearers of beds, and arrangers of practical help. The social worker, like many other professionals today (university professors included), find that they are doing things which a clerk could do. Whilst the social worker does undoubtedly have a knowledge of community resources, he also has skills which he can utilize to help the patient and relatives bear short and terminal illness with some degree of equanimity. The social worker can be the support in times of stress and crisis, and use his skills to help the bereaved find a new way of living.

For the doctor who is encapsulated in the hospital the social worker can, from his visits to patients' homes and his knowledge of community resources enable the doctor to see the stresses and strains and the strengths and weaknesses apparent in the home situation itself. Through contact with employers the social worker can enable employment to be prolonged, although there may be periods of deteriorating health.

Chambers,[17] in her article 'Aspects of Social Work on a Cancer Research and Treatment Unit in a London Teaching Hospital', gives a careful picture of the way in which the social worker was an integral part of the medical team and how she was able to demonstrate her truly professional role. The social worker screened all patients and families admitted to the unit. She dealt with the patient's material, physical and emotional problems. She dealt with the problems of relatives. There was regular communication amongst all members of staff regarding the patient's problem and state of health. In fact the doctors realized the social worker needed to be up to date with medical progress and expected her to be present at weekly clinical meetings. The social worker further provided the team with information regarding the patient's practical situations and emotional problems. Of her, the consultant, who appreciated the emotional problems of his patients, but expressed the view that he did not wish to be over-involved in this aspect of the work as his sphere was oriented to research in the laboratory, said that the social worker defined areas of special emotional stress between the patient and his milieu. A senior registrar commented on the social worker's ability to discuss the patient's attitude to illness and hospitalization, on her work with the family and her help in aiding them to deal with crisis.

In a study[18] done some years ago in a psychiatric hospital I found that there was a more positive outcome in cases (despite negative diagnoses) where there was a close teamwork relationship between psychiatrist and social work staff. In group work the social worker may work in groups with patients for whom the prognosis is poor and where they are able to ventilate their feelings in a group so that they may share common feelings and distress in a therapeutic way. In another way the social worker has been used to work with inter-disciplinary professional groups in the hospital regarding their feelings about working with the dying and how they are enabled to remain emotionally intact in this process.[19]

If euthanasia, either positive or negative, were to become a reality I would see that the social worker could offer skills in research about attitudes towards the subject, objective social, economic and familial information to the doctor and comfort to the dying and the bereaved. In this paper I have attempted to outline the significant role which I consider the social worker has in relation to the sick, and more particularly to the dying patient. Whilst I have from the outset posited the view that euthanasia is to a great extent the sphere of the doctor, I have indicated that the social worker has a knowledge of social functioning which is of significant use in taking a decision about a patient's future.

1. *The Shorter Oxford English Dictionary*, 1959, Clarendon Press, Oxford, 640.
2. More, Thomas 'Euthanasia in Utopia', *Child and Family*, **11**, No. 1, 1972, 86.
3. Ibid., 86.

4. Morison, R. S., 'Dying', *Scientific American*, **229**, No. 3, 57.

5. Tolstoy, quoted in *Scientific American*.

6. Solzhenitsyn, A., *Cancer Ward*, quoted in Chambers, M., 'Aspects of Social Work on a Cancer Research and Treatment Unit in a London Hospital', *British Journal of Social Work*, **4**, No. 2, 143.

7. Hinton, J., 'Assessing the Views of the Dying', *Social Science and Medicine*, **5**, No. 1, 37.

8. Bowlby, J., quoted in Smith, C. R., 'Bereavement', *British Journal of Social Work*, **5**, No. 1, 78.

9. Lindemann, E., ibid., *British Journal of Social Work*, **5**, No. 1, 77.

10. Parad, H.; G. Kaplan, quoted in Goldberg, S. B., 'Family Tasks and Reactions in the Crisis of Death', *Journal of Social Case Work*, July 398.

11. Lindemann, E., op. cit., 77.

12. Smith, C. R., 'Bereavement', *British Journal of Social Work*, **5**, No. 1, 89.

13. Ibid., 90.

14. Ibid., 89.

15. Ebert, Romert H., 'The Medical School', *Scientific American*, **229**, No. 3, 141.

16. Cartwright, A.; Anderson, J. L., 'Help for the Dying', *New Society*, **24**, No. 559, 680.

17. Chambers, M., 'Aspects of Social Work on a Cancer Research and Treatment Unit in a London Teaching Hospital', *British Journal of Social Work*, **4**, No. 2, 143.

18. Shaw, F. C., MSW Thesis, 'Psychiatric Social Work with Single Women', McGill, 1949.

19. Heyman, D. A., 'Discussions meet needs of the Dying Patients', *Hospital*, **48** (14), 57 - 58.

SOCIOLOGICAL AND SOCIO-PSYCHOLOGICAL PERSPECTIVES ON EUTHANASIA

L. and H. Schlemmer

I

Euthanasia as an issue of topical debate is obviously the consequence of advanced medical technology. Prior to our relatively recent advances in medical science, mankind was helpless in the face of terminal disease — helpless to delay death or to hasten it, short of acts which most cultures in history would have regarded as barbaric. Today the possibilities of both lie in cool, clinical pharmaceutical or medical procedures.

Indeed, in less advanced societies (medically and nutritionally), the lack of medical knowledge in many instances probably removed much of the suffering and prolonged anguish which we fear so much today and which is a central consideration in arguments for euthanasia. In earlier times complications like pneumonia or other conditions could be counted on to reduce the length of suffering. In any case, life expectancy was so low and living conditions were such as to reduce the relative incidence of our terrifying diseases of advanced age like cancer, strokes, emphysema, progressive neural deterioration, etc. Hence among people of our age perceptions have been shifted towards an increasing emphasis on the quality of dying — the pre-terminal period — and it is within this context that euthanasia assumes the importance it has.

Therefore, the problem of euthanasia is essentially an issue of our cultural-technological era. From a 'sociological' perspective, this observation is important, since it shows that an analysis of the normative aspects of euthanasia must be essentially contemporary. It is significant that unlike suicide, infanticide, abortion and, obviously, homicide, euthanasia poses very new moral problems for religion, philosophy, ethics, law and medicine.

Moral issues surrounding euthanasia must be seen against a background particularly of contemporary technological values. In this regard one may even go so far as to speak of the technological ethos having become akin to a latent ideology. The pervasive technical-rational ethos in many ways has created widespread acceptance that technologically-based action is intrinsically right. If a process is 'advanced' and 'complicated' it is often unquestionably accepted as right and correct. Hence, we must be alert to the possibility of widespread assumptions that medical personnel have a moral right, as it were, to deploy their advanced techniques in postponing death, notwithstanding the human costs.

The issue of euthanasia falls naturally within the province of the disciplines of law, medicine and religion. Social science, apart from the observation of the technological, cultural and moral changes which have brought this issue to the fore, has no clearly-defined or academically well-trodden approach to the topic. In considering various possible approaches we have decided that what may perhaps be most useful is to consider some of the hidden or latent implications of euthanasia in contemporary urban society, that may be overlooked by professional people who tend to have more narrowly-focused outlooks on the problem.

II

Responsible acceptance of a formal social policy of euthanasia in a society would require that at least substantial proportions of both patients and relatives are able to face death reasonably rationally, and able to take responsibility for the decisions involved, or at least accept the notion of the legitimacy of human intervention in dying. The reasons for this will hopefully become clearer presently.

One of the difficulties in assessing the implications of euthanasia in our society, however, lies in the fact that we are aware of relatively little in the way of research about responses to death in our culture, and what we do know suggests that there is no one typical perception of death and dying. In regard to research on attitudes towards death, Riley observes that 'Great obstacles to research are posed by people's reluctance to discuss so private a matter, as well as by their underlying ambivalence itself'.[1]

It is very well known that perceptions of death are closely connected with perceptions of an after-life and it is equally well-known by now that traditional Eastern and Western concepts are greatly dissimilar. As Riley puts it, for the Eastern traditional person, the route to salvation tended to be either contemplative or mystical, whereas for many modern Westerners it is said to be ascetic and 'active' in the sense that death is seen as the termination of a completed life-cycle of achievement; something to be accepted rationally and with self-control, where grief and mourning are limited to a small circle and involve a minimum of disruption in social life.[2] Talcott Parsons, who gives this characterization, also mentions what he views as a 'deviant' response in American society, in which the reality of death is denied and attitudes are regressive and fatalistic. Riley, however, makes the point that some regard the Parsonian 'deviant' response as the dominant one in our society.[3] There is much to suggest that death is a taboo for large proportions of people in Western society; the *primary* repression, surrounded by deep and pervasive manifestations of 'anger'.[4]

This points to the major unresolved problem concerning interpretation of death in our society. Is death accepted, perceived as inevitable and consciously taken into account in formulating choices in regard to living and dying, or is death repressed, a source of unarticulated anxiety, denied in everyday life and in bereavement, and where conceptualized at all, approached as an event of great uncertainty and anxious mystery? Darnton[5] in a review article on changing attitudes towards death in our history, draws from the work of Aries the following broad stages in the history of our culture's responses to death. In the first 1 000 years of Christianity, men saw it as a collective destiny leading to Paradise for all with the Second Coming, and responses to death were collective, involving larger numbers of family, friends and neighbours in mourning and bereavement. In the next 750 years, as the conjugal family started emerging, death became more and more personal, sharpening the individual's sense of self and representing the supreme moment in a personal journey towards salvation or damnation. By the 19th century, death had come to be charged with great emotionality as a consequence of extremely close conjugal family bonds, and became almost a family obsession. Bereavement could plunge people into prolonged states of depression and irrationality. In the last few decades death, according to Aries, has become indicted, forbidden and denied; an event to be hidden as much as possible.

Whether this outline of the historical changes is true or not need not be considered here. What one can say, however, is that if we take the entire spectrum of sub-cultural differences in Western society, from poverty ghetto to small rural town, to the suburbs, each one of the historic characterizations can surely be found. Is there a modal death in our society? We are sure that there is not, but Parsons' 'deviant' response may be more typical than his analysis would suggest.

Weisman's observations are that death is very generally viewed as 'the embodiment of every form of human evil, failure, disgrace, disaster and corruption'. He also says that 'our common belief, augmented by cultural bias, is that death is a deplorable, evil, unnecessary and premature event'. Weisman goes so far as to say, after Freud, that death is a primary paradox, 'while man recognizes that death is universal, he cannot imagine his own death'.[6] Hinton, in a wide-ranging assessment of death and dying reaches much the same conclusion as Weisman but adds the fairly obvious conclusions that attempts to deny death seldom succeed completely, that distress is thereby heightened very considerably, and that the relative infrequency of death in our times makes it easier for society to attempt to hide and deny death.[7] In our society great emphasis is laid on mastery and control of the environment, of natural events and of disease. Part of the inclination to hide death may result from the perception that death represents our one notable failure in control and mastery.

Interpreting broadly from Hinton it would seem that the higher the level of education in a group, the higher the level of achievement in life, the less negative is the image of death and the more active and rational is the adaptation to death, suggesting that Parsons' 'active' death may be a phenomenon of the upper-middle status group.

Variation in anxiety regarding death among people with differing commitment to religious belief can be expected, yet findings are generally inconclusive.[8] One study quoted by Hinton suggests that anxiety may be least among the very religious or the totally non-religious; 'the tepid believers . . . were more anxious to a significant extent'.[9] Belief in an after-life is no guarantee of lowered anxiety regarding death and, in any event, fewer and fewer people have this belief in the West.[10]

More relevantly for our purposes, it would seem that death is more readily accepted, and more realistically and less anxiously perceived among the aged, and particularly among the aged sick.[11]

Our conclusion to this assessment of attitudes toward death must be that few confident generalizations can be made. Among the most relevant group, the aged sick, an adaptive response to the inevitability of death may be fairly common. However, one certainly cannot count on a widespread rational acceptance of death among populations at large. There are obviously great sensitivities and unresolved conflicts about death. A point to consider is that unresolved fears concerning death, or tendencies to deny it, may perhaps reinforce the value placed on postponing and delaying death through the employment of advanced technology.

III

The reader may well ask what the purpose is of an assessment of attitudes toward death in a paper on euthanasia. The purpose is this: it would be pointless to suggest a general policy of euthanasia if many people, because of complex attitudes to death, were to be unable to confront or reflect on the issue of their dying and take responsible decisions. Furthermore, it would also be wrong to suggest a policy of euthanasia if it were an issue with strong negative symbolic meaning. What might one conclude? In this section we shall briefly offer comments on euthanasia and the individual patient.

On the evidence available to us it would seem that a policy of voluntary euthanasia might meet the needs of many elderly sick patients, since substantial proportions appear to accept death realistically and without unduly complicated emotional responses.

We should add one qualification, however. Hinton, a medical man himself, discusses at some length the great need among patients with incurable diseases for complete faith and trust in their doctors.[12] Obviously this need for faith and trust becomes greatly augmented where it has been agreed to use euthanasia. Patient-doctor communication is not infrequently a source of great anxiety, and the attitudes toward death among doctors may themselves be complicated.[13]

If a policy of voluntary euthanasia is introduced, special skills may have to be imparted to medical practitioners who will find themselves in the position of human agents in a situation previously seen to be governed by divine agency or fate (or perhaps still perceived that way). Obviously the dominant area of skill will be technical-professional, but communication skills and an ability to assess the terminal patient's emotional needs and needs for an appropriate, honourable death will also be important. In this sense it would seem to us that the role of 'taker of life' would pose great challenges for the medical profession.

The description by Kübler-Ross of various fairly typical stages in the response to the knowledge of death is important in this context. The doctor would have to recognize the various signs of the stages of *denial, anger,* the *bargaining* stage, *depression* and finally *acceptance;* helping the patient to work through the various stages and awaiting the final acceptance before raising the issue of euthanasia with the patient.[14]

The terminal patient and the doctor are not the only players in the drama of death. Perhaps the most complicated issues arise in a consideration of the responses of family members and friends. This would be particularly true if close family members were to be involved in decisions regarding euthanasia.

The discussion in Section II should alert us to the fact that tendencies to deny the inevitability of death may be encountered, or at least that many people may not feel inclined to confront or discuss the dark, perhaps even dirty reality of death as they see it. This would be true, more particularly among less well-educated families, where problems of doctor-family communication are very great to start with.

Several potential problems can be noted. Where family members' responses to death are non-rational, the possibility may exist that they refuse to accept fully the inevitability of death and cling to a non-articulated notion of miraculous recovery. Euthanasia under such circumstances is not only problematic but can produce extreme reactions of guilt and/or hostility towards the doctor after the event.[15] (We recall that similar reaction can be observed in some cases of abortion.)

In regard to families we must bear in mind that our culture is relatively unsupportive of bereaved relatives. Riley quotes Gorer as saying of Britain that 'the majority of the population lacks common patterns of ritual to deal with bereavement',[16] and Habenstein observes that 'the loss will trigger off emotional responses that can overflow the channels for appropriate mortuary behaviour provided by the culture'.[17] We are dealing with a situation of potential instability for which it is extremely difficult to make generalizations.

Fulton and Fulton make a distinction between 'high grief-potential' and low 'grief-potential deaths'.[18] Normally the death of an aged relative or even a child after a long illness has been preceded by anticipatory grief and the bereavement is characteristic of a low grief-potential death. However, we can find no literature bearing on the possible effect of euthanasia on grief and we would suggest that the topic warrants careful study. Since Freud onwards, numerous psychologists and sociologists have pointed out that a range of specific responses are involved in the grief syndrome, among which hostility, guilt and remorse can occur.[19] Will euthanasia exacerbate such guilt where it exists, or will it redirect guilt-derived hostility on to the doctor or hospital? Such questions remain to be answered. In this context we might add that one response to the threat of disease in a relative can take the form of adaptive emotional withdrawal, emotional rejection or perhaps even revulsion (the famous short story of Kafka called 'Metamorphosis' springs to mind here). Such patterns may make acceptance of euthanasia easy before the event, but there may also be a very strong guilt reaction after the event, focused on the euthanasia but deriving more basically from the preceding hostility or emotional withdrawal from the patient.[20]

The persistence in some Western societies, like the U.S.A. and including South Africa, of elaborate funeral rites accompanied by superficial religious imagery (which Riley typifies as a regressive response to death)[21] should alert us to the possibility that an unreflective and sentimental popular theology may play a fairly important part in bereavement patterns. What the effect of euthanasia on this would be is difficult to tell and here again research is required. The danger is that popular notions of an honourable or godly death may be sullied or made impossible by euthanasia.

In contrast to the thoughts offered above, we should also observe that there are strong indications that euthanasia may secure for many people what they desire most for their relatives — a quick, peaceful and painless end. Note the great frequency of obituary notices and tombstone inscriptions which read 'passed away peacefully'. It is totally inappropriate to our modern humanistic ethos to have to live with the memory of a relative who died in agony.[22]

V

Having considered some of the possible implications of a policy of euthanasia for individual patients and families, it is necessary to venture a few observations about the implications for society. Our remarks here will of necessity be speculative because very little guidance is available in the literature.

It is possible to make some fairly alarmist predictions about the effects of widespread euthanasia on society. Crude functionalism would suggest that if you tamper with norms regarding death you risk far-reaching effects on norms and values applicable to the living. For example, it could be argued that while religion has the function of consecrating death, protecting society from its impact, and of offering meaning, security and identity in the face of threats of annihilation and meaninglessness, death in turn reinforces and sustains religion because it represents one of the few remaining areas of mystery and uncertainty in a world increasingly understood and explained by science. With the possibility that man may before long create artificial life, a policy of widespread euthanasia, it might be argued, could make man both the creator and taker of life; developments which could shatter the transcendent belief-systems of Western religions, and undermine their other functions in society. Such arguments, however, are probably over-extended. Living itself provides sufficient anxiety, dread and identity threats to sustain the need for religious belief-systems, quite apart from the intrinsic value of the belief-systems themselves.

It has also been suggested that a general policy of euthanasia would serve to legitimate suicide — a process one might term 'moral contagion'. Hinton touches on this in dealing with the related problem of requests for euthanasia coming from people who are chronically ill and at the same time depressed and apologetic about the burden they are on their families and on society.[23] Once again, this argument is probably far-fetched. It is difficult to imagine euthanasia being tolerated outside of situations of terminal illness (see later, however). Furthermore, most suicides tend to occur when individuals are in a state of emotional withdrawal from the rewards and sanctions of society. It is difficult to imagine a general policy of euthanasia, *linked solely to terminal illness,* affecting suicide-prone individuals one way or the other.

Another danger mentioned by Hinton and also by Kluge[24] is that euthanasia sets a dangerous precedent, instituting a practice which is open to political and socio-ideological misuse. Visions of 'mercy killing' of mentally ill, mentally feeble and other disabled people are aroused, reminiscent of the horrors of Nazi Germany. We would not make light of such arguments. Just as Nazi ideology won Germany default so could our own societies lapse into inhumanity in the face of economic and social stress and disintegration, and therefore any practices which may provide ready justification for legalized murder must be viewed very cautiously. It seems essential, therefore, to consider an alternative term to euthanasia; one which denotes the very specific circumstances of terminal illness — illness which will inevitably lead to death or would cause death if life-sustaining technology were removed. We should add very quickly that where technology can sustain a person in a state of conscious-ness and ability to interact with the world, without unbearable discomfort for reasonably long periods, euthanasia should also not be considered, even remotely.

Less we end on too negative a note, there is one argument in favour of voluntary choice of time of death in terminal illness which resonates very deeply in our concepts of humane society. In the words of Hinton: 'the dying person will probably wish others to let him depart in some dignity and not in a welter of failed last measures'.[25] Kluge also advances cogent arguments for euthanasia from the standpoint of personal dignity.[26] Provided that it is voluntary (or agreed to by relatives in the case of a person who is unconscious — and we mean unconscious as opposed to incoherent or irrational) it is essential for our own concept of ourselves and our society that advances in medical technology should not increasingly prolong helpless suffering. Just as there are dangers in euthanasia for society, so equally are there opposite dangers of prolonging painful terminal illness, because they will set a norm, a threshold, of suffering which may blunt the collective sensibilities of the medical enterprise. May writes: 'if the mere fact of perpetuating life is the ultimate goal, we have to some extent lost the distinguishing qualities of being human'.[27] The argument from mercy *and* personal dignity relates to the very ground assumptions of a humane society.

1. Riley, J. W. Jr., 'Death and Bereavement', in *Encyclopaedia of the Social Sciences*, London and New York, MacMillan, 1968, **4**, 23.
2. Talcott Parsons, 'Death in American Society: A Brief Working Paper', *American Behavioral Scientist*, **6**, 1963, 61 - 65.
3. Riley, J. W., op cit., 22.
4. Cameron, J. M., 'Surviving Death', *The New York Review of Books*, **XXI**, No. 17, 1974, 6 - 8.
5. Darnton, R., 'Death's Checkered Past', *The New York Review of Books*, **XXI**, No. 10, 1974, 11 - 14.
6. Weisman, A. D., *On Dying and Denying: A Psychiatric Study of Terminality*, New York, Behavioral Publications, 1972, 13, 16, 28.
7. Hinton, J., *Dying*, Harmondsworth, Penguin Books (Pelican), 1967, 8. On page 64 Hinton observes that death rates may be further reduced in years to come and individual death deferred even longer. This, of course, emphasizes the importance of the point made.
8. Riley, J. W., op. cit., 23.
9. Hinton, J., op. cit., 83.
10. Ibid., 37 - 40.
11. A number of studies are quoted by Weisman, A. D. and Kastenbaum, R., *The Psychological Autopsy: A Study of the Terminal Phase of Life*, Monograph No. 4, Community Mental Health Journal, New York, Behavioral Publications, 1968, 33 - 35. See also Hinton, J., op. cit., 44.
12. Hinton, J., op. cit., 115 - 120.

13. Ibid., 13, 14. Morison, R. S., 'Dying', *Scientific American*, No. 229, 1973, 54 - 62. See also Feifel, H., 'The Functions of Attitudes Towards Death', in *Death and Dying: Attitudes of Patient and Doctor,* Symposium No. 11, Group for the Advancement of Psychiatry, 1965, 632 - 641. Feifel reports on a study among 40 physicians in the U.S.A. as follows: '. . . though they think *less* about death than do two control groups of patients and one of non-professionals, they are *more afraid* of death than any of the control groups'. 634.
    Hinton quotes a study showing that a much higher proportion of patients desire to be told of incurable disease than the proportion of doctors who felt it appropriate to inform patients (Hinton, 129).
14. Kübler-Ross, E., *On Death and Dying,* London: Tavistock, 1969. Hinton (op. cit., 46, 103) and Hertzberg (Hertzberg, L. J., 'Cancer and the Dying Patient', *American Journal of Psychiatry,* **128,** 1972, 806 - 810) provide supportive evidence on the fact that various stages of response to the prospect of death are observable, including the stage of acceptance. The latter author notes that there is no linear progression through the stages, however, and that remission occurs, placing even greater responsibility on the inter-personal skills of the doctor.
15. The observations of Kübler-Ross, E., op. cit., 149 - 150 are important. She observes that families of incurably ill patients, when informed, not infrequently display marked hostility towards the doctor, express remorse as regards the patient, and often fail to communicate adequately among themselves about the problem.
16. Riley, J. W., op. cit., 22.
17. Habenstein, R. W., 'The Social Organization of Death' in *Encyclopaedia of the Social Sciences,* op. cit., 27.
18. Fulton, R. and Fulton, J., 'Anticipatory Grief: A Psychosocial Aspect of Terminal Care' in Schoenberg, B., et al., *Psychosocial Aspects of Terminal Care,* New York/London, Columbia University Press, 1972, 226 - 242.
19. See Kübler-Ross, E., op. cit., and Hinton, op. cit., 169.
20. Hinton, J., op. cit., 86, 87, notes this and terms it the 'bereavement of the dying'.
21. Riley, J. W., op. cit., 22.
22. Hinton, J., op. cit., 73, 140; Weisman and Kastenbaum, op. cit. 36.
23. Hinton, J., op. cit., 144 - 146.
24. Kluge, E. H. W., *The Practice of Death,* New Haven, Yale University Press, 1975, 149, 150 *passim.*
25. Hinton, J., op. cit., 140.
26. Kluge, op. cit., 154, 155.
27. May, R., 'Existentialism, Psychotherapy and the Problem of Death' in Shin, R. L., *Restless Adventure: Essays on Contemporary Expressions of Existentialism,* New York: Scribner and Sons, 1968, 182 - 217.

GENERAL ASPECTS OF EUTHANASIA

B. Robinson

Euthanasia is, then, killing with the object of being merciful to the person being killed. It poses very painful questions to the patient and his family, society and to many religions, philosophies, branches of medicine, sociology and the law.

A dying patient may fight tenaciously for his life or he may genuinely want to die. It is not uncommon for a very sick person to feel he has had enough of the battle to stay afloat. His sick, painful, hideously distorted world can't sustain him in the real world of cut and thrust. His body may be outraged by a mass of tubes and, above all, his spirit can be worn down under the abrasive trivia of everyday nursing, the dreary love life of the junior staff, of being spoken about by doctors as though absent and of no account, and the like. The temptation to wish a plague on the whole lot of these well-meaning people is strong; overwhelmingly powerful at times is the desire to have it all end, not so much by a positive act, as by wishing at times to slip away quietly for good.

That is the essence, of course, 'at times'.

Death in its inevitability is faced by everyone, a reality occurring only once. None of us can say what our reaction to it will be or how we will meet it. To a Catholic like myself, death, like birth and life, is part of the same human condition. One is born in order to live and eventually to die, having made the very best one could of all three conditions in one continuing totality. Death comes at the end of life so that one may go forward and meet God in fullness having completed that life. That is the ideal.

Some time ago, we were born, lived and died exercising great faith but little control over these events. I remember looking at a medieval register of British plague deaths which also recorded deaths from remarkably casual causes. Teeth trouble, gripes, falling down dead were recorded as cause of death, and in addition two were recorded as having died 'suddenly'. The deaths were casual and direct and were so recorded.

Up to recent times the dying were not deemed to be of this world, so the way they died did not really matter, as long as they were not murdered. Now we have another set of circumstances.

104

For the first time we have masses of people who not only appear to have no moral or spiritual guidelines but who do not seem to feel the lack. Religious impulses, important for setting behaviour checks in the past, have now largely disappeared. In the last decade it has also become apparent that a body that has recently died can recover life. Consequently, the line dividing an irretrievable life and one that *is* retrievable is becoming thinner and thinner. Human hearts can be stopped, a human brain can be frozen to require less oxygen when under operation, human breathing can be maintained by machines for years, skin, tissue, arteries, eyes, can all be stored — in principle for centuries — and then made to function again in another body. A whole range of aids, machinery and medicine, are now at the doctor's disposal for reviving the apparently dead or for keeping the dying alive.

Thus, it seems, dying is now by no means always simple or direct. When a person is dying, other people control his destiny. An area which seemed once to be between him and the priest on the one hand, and him and God on the other — or of all three inter-acting together — is now peopled by men and women carrying tubes, pills, legal tomes. Nothing we can do, certainly no over-simplistic insistence on death that has become increasingly less natural, is going to rid us of them. They seem to have become the middlemen of death and indeed it seems they are going to increase and multiply.

People must insist, however, on their public accountability. Abuse could develop in this time of helplessness, when the patient cannot respond at all, the family is distraught and time is often of the essence. Religious, medical and legal men, all of whom occasionally make such a fuss about ethics that one would think they invented them, must act for the people who depend on them for protection in so many ways.

The question now is, of course, whether the process of killing with a merciful intent should in future become legal as some people wish, and whether it is moral. Until now some developed countries have refused to discontinue treatment or medicine which may be keeping a human being alive who would otherwise die (passive euthanasia), but most people, including myself, see no possible moral objection to it. However, if it should become legal or moral to take positive steps to bring to an end the life of a person whose life has become insupportable to himself or others (active euthanasia), the problem is large and the repercussions many.

I would have profound sympathy for a person seeking peace

and an end to abominable suffering through active euthanasia, but would have to say that his oblivion, bought in such a way, would have a very high price indeed. Death in such a case would only occur if someone were induced to kill. Thus the price of that oblivion is that someone has killed.

If the purpose of euthanasia is to protect human dignity then this dignity must be protected at all stages of human life, including birth and during life itself, not simply at death. It is wrong, I think, to reject life at its initial stages (abortion), or by injustice inhibit the life of a person, and then, as many protagonists of euthanasia do, demand an acquired death through active euthanasia on grounds of 'dignity'. Human dignity should be applied at all stages of life, including birth and life itself; life is precious in all its phases, not only one.

As far as passive euthanasia is concerned, if in the opinion of competent doctors the life of a person has gone beyond the point where it could normally be restored, then surely that life may go. I can think of very few people who would not be grateful to accept such aid with a free conscience.

With these few words, of course, I come to the fringe of all the real problems of euthanasia — the socio-legal, psychological, religious and philosophical consequences of introducing killing for mercy as an acceptable moral and legal norm. The public needs a great mass of information about this whole area of thought; it needs more statistics and data which will tell them how many people young and old, sick and well, find their lives insupportable and whether the cause is not rather the structure of society than the thought of imminent death. Much more information is also needed about death itself, when it occurs, and about the effect on the quality of the life of the person of the current revival procedures now in use.

As an example of a few of the very minor problems which may occur in everyday life I quote a few superficial questions about euthanasia which must occur to anyone:

— What happens when a trusted physician has begun to appear to elderly or youthful terminally-sick patients as a potential executioner?
— What about elderly people with cancer phobia or other phobias — will they come for treatment at all?
— Who is going to evaluate terminal illness and how accurate will the diagnosis be?
— If, after a mercy-killing, a post-mortem shows mistaken

diagnosis who would be accountable? Would it be the doctor?

— Who is going to evaluate the state of a person's mind when he gives his consent to be killed? And so on . . .

The British Medical Association has expressed fears that pressure to carry out euthanasia might be put on doctors by the relatives of patient. This was no phantom fear, the BMA said. Such pressure by friends and relatives was already familiar to doctors in connection with certificates of incapacity for work and unjustifiable requests for abortion.

Some elderly people do feel they have outlived their usefulness and have become a burden to others, hoping 'that death will not be long delayed', the BMA said. But 'what is needed here is not a change in the law but a change in the attitude of people towards their dying relatives and friends'.

For my part, I think that attitudes to death are conditioned by society. Large, impersonal cities and the breakdown of the family result in the condition that young and old, joint victims of poverty, loneliness and distress, suffer to the point that they desire extinction. I am of the opinion like so many others that a very great deal of work remains to be done in this field.

AN ECONOMIC INTERPRETATION
OF EUTHANASIA

G. C. K. Fölscher

An interdisciplinary or at least a multidisciplinary approach to an inquiry into social phenomena is an accepted principle today. It is also agreed that uni-disciplinary conclusions and suggestions based on such a one-sided approach can lead to wrong policies when evaluated against the overall objectives of society. This must be so because the multiplicity of human behaviour cannot be compartmentalized at the operational level. However, when I, as an economist, was invited to express some thoughts, my first reaction was that this is a phenomenon where economics can contribute nothing towards formulating a policy. Second thoughts indicated quite the contrary. Economic considerations can certainly not claim some preferred position in the vertical arrangement of the factors which are considered. But then again I suggest that we should not think in terms of a vertical arrangement but rather in terms of an horizontal arrangement of the determining factors when we are formulating policies dealing with social problems in general, and in this case also when formulating policy on euthanasia.

Be that as it may, it must be pointed out that economics is not a normative science and therefore cannot express value judgments. At best it can identify the possible economic effects of alternative policies and behaviour. This then is the basic approach followed in this short paper.

I am in the both envious and difficult position of being unaware of another economic approach to the problem of euthanasia and in fact I doubt whether any exists. However, the economic implications of the loss of human life are not unknown in economic studies.[1] Economists will be the first to admit the difficulties in exhaustive quantification of the costs and benefits that are involved. Little and Mirrlees[2] also readily admit that ultimately there are qualitative cost and benefits which can only be mentioned, because they defy plausible quantification.

Thus whoever is responsible for formulating policy (not the economist) must either put his own money value on such costs and benefits or use some preselected weighted index in arriving at meaningful conclusions. In the final analysis the problem in hand calls for a cost/benefit analysis of performing euthanasia in general and, if required, in a specific case.

Without having investigated the phenomenon empirically the suggestions that follow can at best be regarded as economic arguments based on logical economic reasoning. To clear the air about what we are debating, it should be stated that from the economist's viewpoint it will have to be accepted that the medical scientist has the knowledge to determine whether the patient can recover from the condition he is in at the moment a decision is taken to discontinue further treatment and thereby to end his life. This approach broadens the scope for applying euthanasia because it would include cases where the patient, through natural ill health and other handicaps has an unexpired natural life, but where medical evidence can prove beyond doubt that recovery is not possible. It must be added that the patient will be physically and mentally immobile and endure pain and suffering which can only be checked artificially.

Direct costs and benefits of human life

This wider interpretation of the condition of the patient is necessary in an economic argument, because from the economist's viewpoint the value of every human life is measured in terms of its potential contribution to output, that is, the quantifiable net benefits of maintaining human life is its earning capacity. Mishan[3] regards this as nothing else but the discounted value of all estimated future earnings. At a particular point in the life of each individual this value will be determined by the estimated expected earnings on a cash flow basis over the unexpired lifespan. Naturally it is the net benefit or net value which concerns us, so that the costs such as physical and medical care, educational and training expenditure must be set against the gross benefits. If this net value is positive the maintenance of life is economically justifiable, if negative it is not. Such an oversimplified approach will show a negative economic value for a substantially large number of people, and as Mishan[4] pointed out, may lead to absurd and dangerous conclusions. We can think of a considerable number of aged, mentally and physically handicapped and many others excluding the patients in question, who are affected by this oversimplification. What is significant then is that society will have to identify other qualitative benefits if lives which have a direct net negative economic value are to be maintained. The mere fact that society does not approve of the termination of the lives of these individuals must be taken as proof that such qualitative benefits do exist.

To move closer to the problem under inquiry it is suggested that when medical evidence shows that there is a likelihood that the patient can recover and that life in some artificial form accompanied by physical and mental immobility is the only contribution that such treatment can make, then it must be accepted that the future gross economic contribution is zero. From this must be deducted the direct costs involved in maintaining such life so that the net benefit is negative. The treatment is therefore not economically justified.

So far in this discussion the net direct costs and benefits have been considered; cost/benefit analysis must, however, also include the indirect costs and benefits of prolonging life under these conditions. Without being too technical about the differences between private and social costs and benefits, it should be mentioned that if it is accepted (as has been suggested by De Wet[5]) that the cost and the revenue concerned be valued at market prices to express the social value as against private value, then it is the inclusion of indirect costs and benefits which would distinguish (social) cost/benefit analysis from private cost/revenue analysis.

Indirect costs

Here again Halbach[6] has distinguished between those indirect costs which can be quantitatively expressed in money values, those which are quantitatively measurable but cannot be expressed in money values, and purely qualitative costs.

It would seem that the indirect monetary costs from society's viewpoint are the positive net values sacrificed by allocating physical and human resources to the maintenance of life with a negative direct net value. An example will illustrate the point. When the physical and human resources could perhaps be used to save a life which still has a positive direct net value item, this value is the indirect monetary cost involved in maintaining the life in question. Whether there are quantifiable indirect costs with no money values is not quite clear to me and these are therefore disregarded.

Finally there are qualitative indirect costs involved, such as the suffering of pain and other discomforts experienced by the patient himself, as well as the agony and mental suffering of the family. Against these costs must be set the indirect benefits which again can be classified in the same categories as the indirect costs.

Quantifiable indirect benefits with a money value

In this regard too economics studies the money value of the contribution rendered by research and development activity in a variety of fields.

It is suggested that the maintenance of a life with a negative direct-net value may have some considerable value both in the study of medical treatment in general and in the development of medical engineering; both these could possibly have remedial effects in cases other than the patient in question. The medical specialists at this conference will be able to say whether such results have been achieved in the past and whether they may still occur in the future. When such effects have been identified it should be possible to determine their monetary values in order to calculate the indirect benefits.

Indirect quantifiable benefits without money values

Under this heading I cannot think of examples, except perhaps that of an increase in the confidence inspired by the medical profession of the country in question compared with other countries. I think that the achievement of Professor Chris Barnard and his Groote Schuur team, although at a different level, is a case in point.

Qualitative benefits

Finally we are left with qualitative benefits. Examples of these are not easy to find in cases where euthanasia is contemplated, but we can imagine the psychological relief of relatives who are unable to bear the experience. It is not uncommon for either the husband or wife to terminate both their lives if one is suffering from a terminal disease, especially after the condition has reached a critical level. Maintaining a life in these circumstances would then create negative indirect benefit to the other party involved. On the other hand, religious convictions and other psychological considerations may benefit from maintaining life even when medical

111

evidence suggests beyond doubt that a return to an un-artificial life, not necessarily a natural life, is impossible. From a purely economic point of view then, all direct and indirect costs and benefits have to be valued and added together. If a positive net social value (costs minus benefits) results, euthanasia is not in the economic interest of society. If the end result is negative the opposite is true.

The indirect costs and benefits which cannot be expressed in money terms must be added to this result before a decision can be reached regarding whether euthanasia is in the economic *and* social interest of society. Until an individual or group of individuals comes forward and places an acceptable money value on such costs and benefits (or devises an acceptable weighting index), economics cannot contribute anything more to solving the problem.

1. Examples of these are (a) Grosse, R. N., 'Cost-Benefit analysis in disease control programs' in *Cost-Benefit Analysis* edited by Kendall, M. G., English University Press, London, 1971; (b) Mishan, E. J., *Cost-Benefit Analysis,* Allen and Unwin, London, 1971, 153 - 74.
2. Little, I. M. D. and Mirrlees, J. A., *Manual of Industrial Project Analysis in Developing Countries,* **II,** Development Centre of the Organisation for Economic Co-operation and Development, Paris, 1967, 219.
3. Op. cit., 153.
4. Op. cit., 156.
5. De Wet, G. L., *Evaluering van die Stand van Koste-voordeel-analise in die Ekonomiese Teorie,* unpublished thesis, University of Pretoria, 1974.
6. Halbach von Axel, J., *Theorie und Praxis der Evaluering von Prosekten in Entwicklungsländen,* I.F.O. — Institut für Wirtschaftsforschung, 8 München 19, 1972.

Legal and Criminological Aspects of Euthanasia

EUTHANASIA AND THE LAW

J. D. van der Vyver

1 Jurisprudential remarks

The prevailing legal idea of our time — that is, the current notion of what the law ought to be — can perhaps be characterized in view of the urge of contemporary juridical opinion-entrepreneurs to maintain certain basic principles, commonly known as human rights and fundamental freedoms, in all legal systems of the world. This idea finds expression in a concept of justice which requires the equal treatment of all individuals according to their respective and different merits, and in the need to secure a private enclave of individual rights and freedoms, each with its appropriate and precisely defined limits and exceptions, against state interference.

Much good has come from the post-World War II idea of human rights and fundamental freedoms; and I may also remark in passing that South Africa may very well benefit from taking more careful note of the moral principles it entails. The practical application of this idea has, however, on the other hand, demonstrated a series of vital problems, which arose out of a conflict between the very human values that the doctrine of human rights was destined to serve on an equal footing, and which now necessitate a choice to be made of one's ethical preferences.

To be more concrete, let me by means of a single practical example demonstrate the type of moral conflict I have in mind. The increasing plea for the unconditional legalization of abortions has been inspired, *inter alia,* by the need felt by exponents of libertarian ideals to combat the problem of overpopulation in order to secure the comforts of a prosperous life for the benefit of every living human person. In the United States of America unconditionally legalized abortions are also allegedly being justified in view of a so-called right to privacy, which has been interpreted by some to include the competency of women to choose for themselves whether or not, in the appropriate instances, they wish to remain pregnant. The conflict between the necessity to combat over-population of the world and to secure the comforts of the individual on the one hand and the right to life of a foetus on the

115

other hand, underlines the problem of determining precisely the moment when life really starts and also emphasizes the need for a reappraisal of the pre-natal interests of man.

The problem of euthanasia presents a similar conflict situation. On the one hand one is inclined to approve of all means that may serve to reduce, and if possible to altogether exclude, human suffering at all costs, but on the other hand one finds oneself confronted by a mass of moral and theological dictates advocating the superior worth of life as such. These moral and theological imperatives are fundamental to the jumble of juridical obstacles in the way of legitimate mercy-killing.

If I may add a religious touch to my preliminary observations, I should like to point out that this type of conflict situation, having been caused by the fall of man, is a necessary feature of our temporal earthly existence. The idea of utopia, that would imply *inter alia* the completely harmonious prevalence on earth of all moral and religious virtues, is contrary to Christian teaching, whereby human society has been doomed to everlasting imperfection resulting from man's sin and natural sinfulness, and whereby man is called upon to seek his final destiny beyond the temporal structure of our earthly existence. But the Scriptural incompatibility of the idea of a heaven on earth ought not to prevent Christians from seeking a better life. God, in fact, instructed man to subdue the earth and to rule over all living things (Genesis 1:28), and he bestowed upon man excellent talents for the purpose of improving the world in which we live. The problem of euthanasia presents us with such a challenge — to seek the golden mean between the apparently conflicting values and interests involved, in order to improve the fate of man so that the Glory of God may also be praised.

By its very nature the law is destined to harmonize conflicting interests by seeking and enforcing what its makers believe to be the just appraisal of a given situation; I hasten to add that a juridical choice of values does not always rate the preservation of life first and foremost. In the course of history the law has in many instances in fact sanctioned the taking of lives. In South Africa the law has taken it upon itself to command killing by means of capital punishment, and has also legalized the taking of the lives of others in cases of necessity and self-defence. In International Law mass killings in the course of warfare are still regarded as an acceptable means of retribution. The United Nations Organization, which is supposed to be the international citadel of human rights and fundamental freedoms, actually makes provision for legitimate armed conflicts as part of its implementation machinery[1] and in cases of liberation belligerency.[2] In order to lessen the sting of its bite, International Law has also developed a set of rules, known as humanitarian law, by virtue whereof belligerents are instructed to kill one another — so to speak — gently and with dignity.

When one considers the moral and religious feasibility of euthanasia, the fact that the law sanctions the taking of lives in the relevant instances ought to remain besides the point. Killing of people as a method of punishment or to preserve one's own life or property, or the life or property of others; or in the course of one's belligerent endeavours to maintain or to gain political self-determination, are not necessarily on the same level as the hastening of a person's death in order to end his suffering. Nor ought one's rejection of any or all of the instances of legalized killings to be decisive in the present regard; for in law — as in mathematics — two wrongs do not add up to a right.

2 Prohibition of euthanasia in South African law

In order to find one's way through the hugger-mugger of legal stipulations that may have a bearing on the problem of euthanasia, one must first of all acquaint oneself with the inevitable linguistic differentiations that have become an essential part of a lawyer's communication make-up. Euthanasia with consent can be distinguished from euthanasia without consent; and positive or active euthanasia must not be confused with negative or passive euthanasia.

Interesting though it may be, I need not burden you with detailed particulars of the intricacies of the juridical meaning and impact of 'consent', because the doctrine of *volenti non fit iniuria* simply does not apply in cases of mercy-killing. The law as it applies to-day has been stated concisely by Van Winsen J in the case of *S* v. *Hartmann*[3] as follows: '. . . the fact that the deceased wished to be killed does not exclude the criminal responsibility of him who gratifies the deceased's wish.'[4] It is accordingly beyond the power of an individual to consent, for whatever reason, to be killed.[5] It is equally beyond dispute that euthanasia by means of a positive act constitutes a crime.

The South African law is confused in relation to the question of whether or not a person can be held criminally liable for a mere omission. In this regard simple issues are obscured by two elementary inexactitudes in our courts' reasoning. On the one hand the courts are inclined to confuse negligence and an omission — negligence being constituted by one failure to act reasonably, and an omission being the failure to do anything at all. On the other hand the courts seem to be quite irresolute as to whether or not criminal liability should result from an omission only if the accused has indulged in what has become known as 'prior conduct'. The suggestion in *S* v. *Russell*[6] that an accused could be held criminally liable for a mere omission, that is, an omission unattended by any prior conduct,[7] was completely obscured by Fanin J, who incidentally concurred in the judgment pronounced by Henning J in *Russell's* case, when he later explained the *Russell* opinion as 'an illustration of the variety of circumstances in which a man may find himself, *through some prior conduct* on his part, under a duty to act'.[8] I may add that the distinction between commissions and omissions can in any event become quite superficial. As was said by F. P. van den Heever:[9] 'The difference between acts of commission and those of omission is frequently more apparent than real and the one may be expressed in terms of the other'. If, for instance, a motorist is being prosecuted for having disregarded a stop sign on a public road, it would prove to be immaterial whether the charge is based upon the fact that he failed to stop (that is for an omission) or upon the fact that he kept on driving (that is for a commission).[10]

The popular notion still remains that, as a general rule, a criminal act must consist in doing something — that is in a positive act or an act of commission — and that an omisssion will entail criminal liability only when there is a legal duty upon the accused to perform a positive act.[11] The situations in which such a duty has been constructed are of a great variety, but include one set of circumstances that may be relevant in cases of passive euthanasia.

Those circumstances arise when one person stands in a protective relationship towards another, either naturally or by virtue of his having assumed the responsibility of protecting the other person against harm or death.[12] The rule was stated by Briggs F J in *R* v. *Chenjere*[13] as follows: 'To cause death by inaction may be criminal if there is a positive duty to preserve the life of the person in question. The duty arises where the potential victim is helpless through infancy, senility or illness and the potential killer stands, either naturally or through a deliberate acceptance of responsibility, in a protective relationship to the victim'. Section 130 of the Transkeian Penal Code[14] contains a similar provision in terms of which one person can be held liable for the death of another if the accused has had charge of the deceased 'by reason of detention, age, sickness, insanity, or any other cause' and the deceased's death has been caused by the failure of the accused to supply him with 'the necessaries of life'.

If, therefore, a medical doctor has accepted the responsibility of treating a patient against illness, his failure to supply the medical and/or technical aids necessary to prolong the patient's life may well be taken to constitute an act, in the juridical sense, for purposes of criminal liability. There are, of course, other factors that may frustrate a prosecution in such circumstances, for instance the problem of proving that the doctor's inaction has actually caused or hastened the patient's death. In principle passive euthanasia can, however, in the appropriate circumstances, give rise to a prosecution for, and possible conviction of, murder.

It should be noted that if a medical practitioner had given, and subsequently withheld, medical treatment, the case would clearly fall within the category of omissions following prior conduct; and if death of the patient results, a conviction for murder may be warranted if it can be shown further that the likelihood of death in the particular circumstances was greater than it would have been if medical treatment had never been commenced.

Finally, I should like to point out that if medical treatment has been withdrawn by means of a positive act, such as pushing buttons or closing taps or disconnecting machines, the problem of criminal liability for omissions would not arise. Such acts are downright acts of commission and can be found criminal responsibility.

The present state of the South African law regarding euthanasia can be summarized as follows:

a. Mercy-killing by means of an act of commission constitutes the crime of murder; and acts of commission would include the withdrawal of medical aid by means of a positive action, such as disconnecting a machine.

b. Where mercy-killing is administered passively, that is, by simply withholding treatment that could prolong the patient's life, criminal responsibility can, in the appropriate circumstances, be founded upon (a) either the protective relationship assumed by a doctor towards his patient, or (b) the prior conduct of the doctor evidenced by initial medical treatment that would increase the likelihood of death, if that particular treatment were to be discontinued.

c. In all instances consent on the part of the deceased is no excuse, though it may, as an extenuating circumstance, have a bearing on the sentence to be imposed by the court.

3 Instances of euthanasia in South Africa

During the last twenty years three instances of euthanasia have come before our courts, as far as can be ascertained.

In 1955 *Davidow* was tried in the Witwatersrand Local Division of the Supreme Court for having shot and killed his mother, to whom he was exceptionally devoted and who had suffered constant pain resulting from an incurable disease.[15] The court found that Davidow fired the shot while in a state of emotional strain to the extent that he was not blameworthy. He was accordingly found not guilty by a jury and acquitted.

In 1968 *De Bellocq,* a young mother and former medical student, appeared before the Transvaal Provincial Division of the Supreme Court on a charge of murder, for having caused the death of her seven-months-old child who had been suffering from, and was mentally affected by, an incurable ailment called toxoplasmosis.[16] De Bellocq was found guilty of murder with extenuating circumstances. She was discharged, in terms of section 349 of the Criminal Procedure Act 56 of 1955, on condition that she entered into recognizances to come up for sentence within the following six months if called upon to do so; which simply means that the accused was not sentenced at all but could be called to be sentenced within a period of six months. In the course of his judgement De Wet JP stated the legal position concisely in the following terms: 'The law does not allow any person to be killed whether that person is an imbecile or very ill. The killing of such a person is an unlawful act and it amounts to murder in law'.

Recently the Cape Provincial Division of the Supreme Court was confronted with the equally tragic events that led to the prosecution and eventual conviction of a medical practitioner, *Dr Hartmann,* on a charge of murder.[17] Dr Hartmann administered a drug that hastened the death of his elderly father, who was critically ill and who had been suffering severe and continuous pain. Having been found guilty of murder with extenuating circumstances, he was sentenced to one year imprisonment but was detained only until the rising of the court, the remainder of the sentence having been suspended conditionally for a period of one year. In the course of his judgement Van Winsen J stated, *inter alia,* that euthanasia constitutes the crime of murder even if all that the accused has done is to hasten the death of a human being who was in any event due to die soon,[18] and that consent on the deceased's part is no defence.[19]

During May 1976 the Medical Council took disciplinary action against Dr Hartmann and struck his name off the medical roll.[20]

4 Concluding remarks

I intend to conclude my lecture by briefly pointing out the type of obstacle which, from a lawyer's point of view, will have to be overcome if euthanasia is to be legalized.

The crux of the concern of jurists in the present regard seems to be — as it was summarized by Van Winsen J in *Hartmann's* case[21] 'that to allow mercy-killing even when hedged about with innumerable safeguards would pave the way for abuses which would be damaging to the community'. Assuming that euthanasia can be justified morally and religiously, the jurist must find a plausible and practicable formula for the expedient administration of euthanasia, which would include (a) a criterion for identifying the cases that would qualify for euthanasia, (b) a panel of competent persons who could be entrusted with the final decisions in this regard, and (c) a humane method for the actual implementation of mercy-killing.

What makes the practical administration of euthanasia particularly complicated is the fact that time would be so much of the essence. If the implementation of euthanasia is to be at all efficacious, decisions will invariably have to be taken rapidly, responsibly, reliably, and without the prospect of review.

Euthanasia has, as everyone knows, serious ethical and religious implications. I regard those aspects of the problem to be beyond my brief, and I am convinced that the panel of speakers at this conference includes names of persons far better trained and equipped than myself to speak with authority on those issues. In conclusion I should, however, like to offer a single contribution in this regard.

Life is perhaps the greatest gift given by God to man and the maintenance of it is probably man's foremost aspiration. Sickness and death are also within God's counsel. It would, however, in my opinion be wrong to suppose that man must passively endure sickness and death. God has equipped the human person with reason and talents to be used by him for the purpose of, *inter alia,* bettering the fate of man to the best of his abilities. The excellent achievements of medical science also serve the Glory of God. The question to be considered to-day is whether man should utilize his talents, scientific discoveries and inventions for the purpose of ending the suffering of a person by means of hastening the death of that particular person.

I believe that man has a sacred right to die peaceably and with dignity, and that a person who is ready to do so ought to be permitted to meet his God at the right time. The artificial perpetuation of the life of a person whose death within the immediate future has become inevitable may, therefore, in particular circumstances infringe the Will of God.

These considerations could, however, at the most justify passive euthanasia in the strict sense, that is, refraining from prolonging a dying patient's life by altogether withholding technical aid. There may also be circumstances in which the death of a dying patient could justifiably be hastened by withdrawing medical treatment that has been commenced in a futile attempt to save the patient's life. But I still entertain serious doubts as to the moral and religious compatibility of effecting euthanasia by means of deliberate action, such as the administering of a drug.

1. Cf. Chapter VII of the UN Charter.
2. Cf. General-Assembly res 3103 (XXVII), 1973.
3. 1975 (3) SA 532 (C) at 534.
4. See also *R v. Peverett*, 1940, AD 213; *S v. Robinson & Others* 1968 (1), SA 666 (A) at 678.
5. Cf. Burchell, E. M.; P. M. A. Hunt, *South African Criminal Law and Procedure* (Cape Town, 1970), I, 310.
6. 1967 (3) SA 739 (N) at 742.
7. Cf. also *King v. Dykes*, 1970 (4), SA 369 (R) at 371.
8. *Quathlamba (Pty) Ltd v. Minister of Forestry*, 1972 (2), SA 783 (N) at 797. The italics are mine.
9. *Aquilian Damages in South African Law* (Cape Town n.d.), 39.
10. Cf. van der Merwe, N. J.; Olivier, P. J. J., *Die Onregmatige Daad in die Suid-Afrikaanse Reg* (Pretoria, 1970), 32.
11. Cf. Burchell, E. M.; P. M. A. Hunt, op. cit., I, 103.
12. Cf. Burchell, E. M.; P. M. A. Hunt, op. cit., I, 104 and II, 346.
13. 1960 (1) SA 473 (FC) at 482.
14. Act 24 of 1886 (C).
15. *S v. Davidow* (unreported) June 1955, WLD; H. P. van Dyk, *Die Davidow-saak*, 1956 THRHR 286.
16. *S v. De Bellocq*, May 1968, TPD; first reported by S. A. Strauss *Onvrywillige Genadedood: 'n Belangwekkende Transvaalse Beslissing* 1969 THRHR 385; now reported at 1975 (3) SA 538.
17. *S v. Hartmann* 1975 (3) SA 532 (C).
18. Idem. 534; *R v. Makali*, 1950 (1), SA 340 (N) at 343 - 4.
19. Idem. 534.
20. Dr Hartmann's name has since been put back on the roll.
21. *S v. Hartmann* 1975 535.

SOME LEGAL ASPECTS OF EUTHANASIA

P. C. Smit

The concept of euthanasia is an elastic one. Three distinctively different types of conduct are grouped under this term:
1. Euthanasia in the more specific or restricted sense of the word.
2. Termination of life-sustaining or life-extending treatment with regard to a person of intact consciousness.
3. Termination of life-sustaining or life-extending treatment with regard to an unconscious, i.e. a comatose, person.

1 Euthanasia in the more specific or restricted sense

Van Till analyses various definitions of euthanasia in the specific sense and reaches the conclusion that it basically entails two actions, namely the administering of life-shortening treatment (active euthanasia) and, alternatively, the omission of life-extending treatment (passive euthanasia).[1] Furthermore it appears from her analysis that the two above-mentioned methods of behaviour are inseparably bound up with two facts or indications, namely that the person with regard to whom the act is committed, suffers from an incurable disease, suffers severe pain and suffers acute discomfort.[2] Following upon this analysis Van Till submits a definition of euthanasia in a more specific sense:

Euthanasia is the bringing about of a gentle, dignified and painless death by deliberate life-shortening medical conduct with regard to an incurably ill and pain-suffering patient

or

Euthanasia is the bringing about of a gentle, dignified and painless death by deliberately abstaining from life-extending medical treatment with regard to an incurably ill and pain-suffering patient.

The former defines active euthanasia and the latter passive euthanasia. The basic aim of or motive with euthanasia in the more restricted sense, i.e. a gentle, painless and dignified death, is attained by the acceleration of the patient's death, although from a medical point of view, it is possible to delay the moment of death. The shortening of life is therefore not the goal, but

123

merely the means to an end.[3]

Suffering or the experiencing of pain to a large extent presupposes a degree of intact consciousness. Euthanasia in the more restricted sense by definition only applies to a conscious patient. Where a patient is comatose there is no indication of suffering, and with that any possible justification of euthanasia in the more restricted sense seems to fall away. As long as a patient is unconscious, a gentle and painless death is always possible.

How does the law view euthanasia in the more restricted sense? Hunt[4] defines the crime of murder as follows:

Murder consists in the unlawful and intentional killing of another person.

Van Till's definition of euthanasia has been mentioned. In essence it amounts to the performing of a life-shortening act in so far as it concerns active euthanasia. This conduct falls squarely within the ambit of murder in South African law. The motive for life-shortening, viz. the alleviation or termination of pain and suffering and at most merit mitigation of punishment.

The crime of murder is not committed when euthanasia in the restricted sense is brought about passively. There is no intentional or deliberate life-shortening conduct, but an abstention from, or omission of, life-extending conduct or treatment. When a doctor abstains from administering life-extending treatment, because the patient refuses or forbids such treatment, no criminal offence is committed. By virtue of his rights of personality any person is entitled to refuse all medical treatment or such treatment as is specified by him.[5] Thus a patient is legally entitled to refuse all life-extending treatment, while he may consent to pain-relieving treatment. Any life-extending medical treatment administered contrary to the patient's wish would technically constitute the crime of assault.[6]

Of greater importance, however, is the question whether a doctor may on his own terminate or refrain from further rendering life-extending treatment to a patient. On this point South African law is by no means clear. A strong case can be made, however, for the assertion that a doctor who on his own initiative terminates life-extending treatment with regard to an incurably ill and pain-suffering patient, does not commit a criminal offence: criminal law only demands positive conduct if the person is bound by a legal duty to act positively.[7] The same principle applies to private law.[8] The duty of a doctor, whether imposed by criminal law or by private law, to treat a patient, arises from his contract with the patient. Such an obligation or duty can also arise from his contract with his employer, e.g. a provincial health department. The latter will especially be the case where the doctor is not in private practice, but employed, for instance, by a provincial hospital.[9]

On analysis of a doctor's contractual duty towards his patient, it is clear that this duty basically entails the duty of healing. Healing or therapy forms the cornerstone of the doctor's duty towards his patient.[10] The doctor undertakes the duties of hearing the patient's complaints, diagnosing the ailment, alleviating the symptoms, and curing the ailment.[11] The doctor does not undertake extending of life for the patient, but to bring about recovery if possible.[12]

Logically, as soon as it becomes impossible for a doctor to fulfil his function of therapy towards the patient, because of the incurable nature of the illness, then his therapeutic duty also falls away. Because circumstances beyond his control make it impossible for him to fulfil his primary contractual duty towards his patient, this duty simply lapses. With regard to this aspect of the doctor's duty or obligation towards his patient, there is now no legal obligation on him to treat the illness, simply because cure is not humanly possible. A doctor is therefore only bound by legal duty to treat a patient if such treatment is of a healing nature. No doctor is under legal obligation to carry out futile and senseless medical treatment. It must, however, be emphasized that only the obligation to cure the incurable disease lapses. The doctor's duty to alleviate the symptoms of this incurable disease, e.g. pain and discomfort, still continues to exist insofar as this is medically possible. To summarize: No doctor is legally bound to extend the life of a patient, or to prolong the dying process of an incurably ill patient.[13]

Neglect and omission of life-extending treatment by a doctor can also be justified by necessity. The doctor is set the choice of either rendering futile treatment with regard to an incurable patient, or of rendering therapeutic treatment to a possible responsive patient. Should the doctor render life-extending treatment with regard to incurably ill patients, or should he render healing treatment with regard to curable patients?

When faced with such a dilemma, the doctor's choice is obvious. He must fulfil his primary and basic duty, namely healing and therapy. Common sense dictates that a doctor should place therapeutic treatment above purely futile treatment. The interests of the patient with no hope of recovery must be weighed against the interests of the patient who can be cured. The fact that the doctor puts the interests of the latter above those of the former — even though the former was first his patient, or even though he terminated the life-extending treatment of the former in order to treat the latter with the consequent shortening of life[14] of the former — does not render the doctor criminally liable[15] for the former's accelerated death.

Where active euthanasia is brought about the argument is that it is justifiable because of the noble motive underlying the action, the motive being the termination of pain and discomfort by the bringing about of a gentle and dignified death. It is even suggested that this motive should also legally justify active euthanasia. This motive is in any case brought strongly to the fore as an extenuating factor.[16]

As far as modern medical science and in particular pharmacology is concerned this is a specious argument. The scientific administration of long-known pain-relieving drugs such as opium and its derivatives eliminates the suffering of pain. Any pain can at any time be alleviated even if it should entail a semi-permanent unconsciousness or coma for the patient being brought about by the operation of the drug. Where a patient does not experience pain and discomfort the rationale and motive for active euthanasia fall away. True, a patient may build up resistance against pain-relieving drugs when they are administered over a long period. It is only against the euphoric effect of a drug that a resistance is built up, and not against the pain-relieving effect of it.[17]

2 Termination of life-extending or life-sustaining treatment in the case of a patient with intact consciousness

The legal position in South Africa regarding termination of life-extending treatment being administered to patients with intact consciousness is relatively clear. If such treatment is being terminated by order of the patient himself, no criminal offence is committed if the patient dies as a direct result of such termination. By virtue of his rights of personality a patient may refuse any type of medical treatment. Should the patient die as a result of his refusal to undergo life-extending medical treatment his death could conceivably be considered as suicide. Suicide, or perhaps it is more correct to say attempted suicide, according to South African law does not constitute a criminal offence.[18]

Where life-extending medical treatment is terminated upon the

126

initiative of his next of kin, the resulting death of the patient would constitute the crime of murder or culpable homicide. This is especially the case where indications for euthanasia in the strict sense are absent. The doctor who positively reacts to a request by the next of kin to terminate treatment is co-principal to their crime.[19] Such termination of treatment may even give rise for an action for damages.[20]

If only the indication of pain-suffering is absent, a different situation arises. Termination of life-extending treatment by a doctor with regard to an incurably ill patient suffering no pain, may be legally justifiable. It has already been shown that the basic duty of a doctor towards his patient is of a therapeutic nature and no doctor is bound to extend life in cases of incurable disease.[21] In theory the stage of progress of an incurable disease should not play any role in this context. However, it is only in an advanced stage of an incurable illness that the assertion can be made that the patient is terminally ill, that there is no hope of recovery, and that further medical treatment will only serve to postpone the final hour of death. Whether termination of life-extending treatment by a doctor in the case of a patient with intact consciousness and suffering no pain or acute discomfort, but for whom there is no hope of recovery, would be ethically justifiable, poses a difficult question — which, fortunately, is not for the jurist to answer.

3 Termination of life-preserving treatment in the case of a patient who is permanently comatose

What is the legal situation in South Africa where life-extending or life-sustaining treatment is terminated in the case of a patient who is in a permanent state of unconsciousness, i.e. an irreversible coma? In this situation the most important indication for euthanasia is in the stricter sense, namely suffering of pain, is absent. One can argue that an irreversible coma in effect amounts to an incurable disease. No doctor, however, can positively state that any disease or coma is beyond reasonable doubt incurable or permanent. Medical science is not yet an absolute and exact science. The most a doctor can or ought to state is that a disease or coma is on a balance of probabilities incurable or permanent.[22]

The question is now whether it would be legally justifiable for a doctor to terminate life-preserving or life-extending treatment acting on his own instance with regard to a patient who in all probability will never regain consciousness. A positive answer seems reasonable. One cannot expect a doctor to give an exact opinion with regard to the permanence of a coma; likewise one cannot expect him to give an opinion, and act accordingly, with regard to the non-permanence of a coma. According to the present state of medical science it would appear that a doctor is entitled to act in accordance with the preponderance of possibilities.

In case a patient is preponderantly likely to remain in an irreversible coma, i.e. when his condition or disease is incurable, the doctor is not legally bound to continue treatment, which in all probability would have no healing effect, but which would only be of a life-prolonging nature, and which in effect would only prolong the dying process.[23] This applies especially to cases where the patient is kept alive biologically by mechanical means, without a shadow of a hope that he will ever be able to do without the mechanical aids, or will ever regain consciousness.

A contentious problem is whether a doctor may or should terminate life-extending treatment in the case of a patient in a permanent coma, when commanded thus by the patient's next of kin.[24] Legal duty as far as treatment is concerned originates with the doctor's contract with his patient. Next of kin are usually 'outsiders' as far as this contract is concerned. It is not for them to say whether this contract has been terminated through impossibility of performance.

Where the patient is a young child, the contract is between parent and doctor. In the event of a doctor employed in a hospital, the contract is between the patient, or his parent in the case of a child, and the hospital authorities. Purely theoretically then, 'outsiders', the parent or hospital authorities, can decide whether the contract has ended or not.

As far as children are concerned, it must be borne in mind that the Supreme Court is the supreme guardian of every child, and may therefore upset any decision taken by the parents if the Court feels that such decision is not in the best interests of the child.[25] Theoretically it is possible for a hospital to order a doctor in its employ to cease life-extending treatment with regard to a patient in an irreversible state of coma. In practice, however, this is hardly conceivable. Hospital authorities usually rely on the decision of the doctor concerned.

Termination of life-sustaining treatment with regard to a patient in an irreversible coma would not constitute a crime or give rise to a civil action if the patient has directed such termination. Here one has to do with the situation where a person who is still conscious and capable of volition gives instructions to the effect that all life-preserving treatment shall be ceased as soon as it is subsequently determined that he is in an irreversible coma. This constitutes the case where a patient conditionally consents to treatment by a doctor; the condition being that treatment has to be terminated as soon as it is no longer therapeutic, but solely life-extending or life-preserving. Should the doctor continue with life-extending treatment contrary to the patient's wish, this would constitute the crime of assault.[26] It is highly questionable though whether a prosecution or civil action would ever be brought in such a situation.

The contract between doctor and patient in the case in question terminates when the patient lapses into a permanent coma. The existence of the contract is also subject to the condition that the doctor's duties under the contract include only healing. When the contract expires, the doctor's claim to remuneration for his services also expires.

Where the patient puts into writing this condition or wish whilst still enjoying good health, and it is brought to the doctor's attention after he has begun with the patient's treatment, and the patient is already in an irreversible coma, the doctor is bound to comply with the wish of his patient. It is even conceivable that he can be legally forced by the next of kin to so comply.

Whether a doctor should accept a patient who requests treatment subject to such a condition is a moot point. By accepting such a patient the doctor forfeits considerable professional initiative and freedom. One can even argue that acceptance of such a patient is contrary to the doctor's Hippocratic Oath.[27]

Conclusion

With regard to euthanasia in general the situation in South African law is not at all clear. There is a case to be made out for the justification of some forms of euthanasia, but a conclusive finding in this connection is difficult. Persons concerned with euthanasia in all its form, viz. doctors, remain in the dark concerning what is legally permissible.

There would be two means of eliminating this legal uncertainty. In the first place a test case could be taken to the Appellate Division, thereby giving the highest court the opportunity of handing down an authoritative judgement. It stands to reason that such a case would be hazardous for the experimental subject or 'guinea pig'. It is also doubtful whether the Appellate Division will pronounce definite legal rules with regard to such a difficult and thorny matter, involving theological, sociological and ethical issues. The Court would probably rather view the matter casuistically, and only pronounce judgement on the very facts before it, refraining from laying down universal rules.

Secondly, the existing legal uncertainty with regard to euthanasia in South Africa can be removed by means of legislation. It would seem, however, that Parliament is not overkeen to pass legislation on issues of an ethical and theological nature. Positive action can only be expected from the Legislature after the implications for society of intended legislation have been explored and after Parliament is convinced that such legislation would not be opposed by society on theological and ethical grounds. A good example of Parliamentary circumspection with regard to legislation with theological and ethical implications is the Abortion and Sterilization Act of 1975. This Act has had a 'gestation-period' of at least ten years.

1. Van Till, H. A. H., d'Aulnis de Bourouill, *Medisch-juridische Aspecten van het Einde van het Menselijk Leven,* Deventer, Kluwer, 1970, 98 - 102.
2. Ibid., 102.
3. Ibid., 103.
4. Hunt, P. M. A., *South African Criminal Law and Procedures,* **II,** 1970, 323.
5. Strauss, S. A.; M. J. Strydom, *Die Suid-Afrikaanse Geneeskundige Reg,* 1967, 175 ff.
6. Ibid., 348 ff. Cf. Hunt, P. M. A., op. cit., 429 ff.
7. Burchell, E. M.; P. M. A. Hunt, *South African Criminal Law and Procedure,* **I,** 1970, 149.
8. Van der Merwe, N. J.; P. J. J. Olivier, *Die Onregmatige Daad in die Suid-Afrikaanse Reg,* 2nd ed., 1970, 116 ff.
9. Strauss, S. A.; M. J. Strydom, op. cit., 105 ff.
10. Lindeboom, G. A., *Medische Ethiek,* Kampen, Kok, 1960, 30 ff.
11. Strauss, S. A.; M. J. Strydom, op. cit., 111 ff and 115 ff.
12. Lindeboom, G. A., op. cit., 26 ff.
13. A doctor's primary duty is to heal, to provide therapy and not to lengthen life. One can compare this to the duty of a lawyer. The lawyer's primary duty is not to win his client's case for him, but to bring the facts to the attention of the court whose task it is to apply the law to the facts before it.
14. Or shortening of the dying process.
15. Burchell, E. M.; P. M. A. Hunt, op. cit., 283 ff and 293 ff.
16. *S* v. *Hartmann,* 1975 (3), SA 532 (C).
17. Lack, S., and Lamerton, R. (eds.), *The Hour of our Death,* 1974,

22 ff and 41; also Lamerton, R., *Care of the Dying,* 1973, 105 ff.

18. Hunt, P. M. A., op. cit., 350.
19. The doctor is legally seen only as an instrument in their hands. Burchell and Hunt, op cit., 350 ff.
20. E.g. for loss of maintenance. Cf. Van der Merwe, N. J.; P. J. J. Olivier, op. cit., 318.
21. *Supra.*
22. Van Till, H. A. H., op. cit., 58 ff. Cf. *The Friend,* 9 April 1975 and *Die Volksblad,* 8 April 1975.
23. *Supra.*
24. E.g. by the parent of a fifteen year old child or by the husband or wife of the patient.
25. Spiro, E., *Law of Parent and Child,* 3rd edn., Juta, Cape Town, 1971, 247.
26. Strauss, S. A.; M. J. Strydom, op. cit., 349.
27. Lindeboom, G. A., op. cit., 37 e.v.

ANOTHER LEGAL VIEW OF EUTHANASIA

B. G. Ranchod

Euthanasia is a term generally used to describe a killing that is prompted by some humanitarian motive. South African law protects the sanctity of human life — the unlawful killing of another is murder regardless of the motive of the perpetrator. A leading text-book on criminal law puts euthanasia in this category. The medical practitioner who causes the death of his patient as an act of mercy with or without his consent is guilty of murder.

In recent years such acts of mercy have troubled theologians, medical practitioners, lawyers and laymen. The question posed is — should euthanasia be legalized? One view is that a person is entitled to ask for an end to overwhelming and helpless pain and that the doctor who provides the relief should be legally absolved from blame. But others contend that there are no circumstances in which it can be right for one person to take the life of another. Apart from the proponents of these two extreme views there are many people who have not given the matter serious consideration. Some consider euthanasia acceptable in circumstances which are clearly defined whilst others argue that the law should remain unchanged, relying on judges to temper justice with mercy when it is appropriate.

This question is a mixed one of morality and law. The function of the law is to protect human values and therefore no change in the law can be contemplated unless there have been changes in morality. The older generation was fond of saying that the best things in life seem to be either carnal, illegal or fattening. But in recent times these attitudes have no doubt changed. So also has morality. Nothing in life is simple anymore, not even the entering of it or the leaving of it. In the last decade there has been a revolution of human values and rights. According to United States Supreme Court Chief Justice, Warren Burger, 'the law always lags behind the most advanced thinking in every area. It must wait until the theologians and the moral leaders and events have created some common ground, some consensus'. Before change in morality can be given the force of law it needs the overwhelming support of the public.

What are the altered circumstances relevant to this question? There are three considerations which have affected our attitude to euthanasia. First, the past decade has seen the evolution of legal rights and duties of patients. The patient has a right to be informed of the nature of his illness and his consent to treatment is essential. This implies that the patient has the right to refuse medical treatment and to undisturbed death if he so wishes. But whether the rights to death can be considered as an inalienable right of personality is debatable. Suicide is not a crime under our law but the question whether an individual has the right to determine his time of death and can lawfully obtain assistance to achieve that end has yet to be answered.

Secondly, there has been an increased concern for the rights of the dying. The illnesses of which people today die have changed from predominantly infectious to chronic degenerative diseases which occur late in life. Cerebral degeneration and cardiovascular disease are common before death. With increased urbanization the location and circumstances under which death takes place has changed. More people, usually old people, are dying in hospitals and nursing homes. The trend of dying in institutions has increased the loneliness of the patient and his estrangement from familiar surroundings.

Thirdly, there are new medical techniques for prolonging life. The doctor has always had to make decisions about his patient who is threatened with death. Now new knowledge and its tools enter in his decision that affect the time and nature of the act of dying.

During the past year the news media have given extensive coverage to a series of dramatic medical stories which have captured the public interest and which illustrate the problem of prolonging life. The doctor now, more than ever, makes decisions regarding dying patients squarely in the public eye.

Assuming for the present that there has been a shift in the moral values of our society towards euthanasia, the question remains whether and to what extent legislation should be introduced so as to leave euthanasia to the discretion of the medical doctor.

Before expressing my own view, I would like to make a few preliminary remarks. Euthanasia is generally associated with the killing of those afflicted by old age or terminal conditions. It may vary with the nature of the act, the status of the actor and the victim and the presence or absence of consent. The act itself may be one of commission or omission. There are essentially three groups against or for whom euthanasia may be committed:

a. persons with painful and terminal diseases such as cancer;
b. defective or degenerate persons including the mentally ill, the retarded, those with grave physical defects. Some are rendered permanently unconscious by disease or accidents and are being kept alive through artificial medical means;
c. infants who suffer from grave physical or mental defects.

For the purposes of this paper I shall limit the discussions to the medical doctor and euthanasia. Our law draws a convenient distinction between acts of commission and omission. In discussing legal liability, the former acts will be classified under active euthanasia and the latter under passive euthanasia.

1 Active euthanasia

Active euthanasia, i.e. the killing of a patient by active measures, is illegal. Consent of the patient does not make the act legal. Thus it is murder for a doctor to kill a person at his request or with his consent but in certain conditions the doctor will get a lenient punishment.[1]

The question arises whether we should not consider if a person has the right to decide whether he should live or not (suicide is not a crime) and whether it is wrong for him to ask a doctor to help him carry out his desire and whether it would be wrong for the doctor to do so. To what extent is it true to say that making active euthanasia legal would create risks of abuse and undermine public confidence in doctors and hospitals?

An eminent English jurist, Professor Glanville Williams, has put the case for legislation with cogency. In his book, *The Sanctity of Life and the Criminal Law* (1957),[2] he proposed that a statute be introduced which provides that

It shall be lawful for a physician, after consultation with another physician, to accelerate by any merciful means the death of a patient who is seriously ill, unless it is proved that the act was not done in good faith with the consent of the patient and for the purpose of saving him from severe pain in an illness believed to be of an incurable and fatal character.

There is merit in this proposal but the opponents to such legislation in England are the doctors who fear that they may be branded as killers. Any changes in the law will have to be preceded by public debate such as we have had on abortion. And as indicated earlier, changes in moral values can only be given legislative effect if they have the overwhelming support of the public. If an analogy may be drawn with abortion — today many more doctors regard abortion as a respectable operation to perform than before the passing of the Abortion and Sterilization Act of 1975.

Whilst on the topic of abortion, it has been forcefully argued by the Dutch jurist Van Till[3] that abortions performed where pregnancy has advanced beyond 20 weeks may be likened to active euthanasia, the only difference being that with abortion the killing takes place before birth and by a different technique. She argues that if legal protection should commence at the stage where the foetus is viable or has brain functions the legislature should take cognizance of this in legislation relating to abortion. Our Abortion and Sterilization Act makes no reference to the latest date on which a pregnancy may be terminated. It is, in fact, not unlikely that a number of abortions are performed well after the 20th week — the strict procedural requirements that have to be complied with causes inevitable delays.

Where treatment is necessary to alleviate pain, a doctor who accelerates an inevitable and imminent death of his patient is in theory guilty of murder. In practice, however, it is unlikely that such a matter will be brought before the courts because it is very difficult to prove that the treatment has exceeded the need to alleviate pain.

2 Passive euthanasia

Passive euthanasia is a term for cases where the patient is not given life-sustaining treatment, with the result that he dies earlier than if he had been given this treatment. Although the legal position is uncertain, and has not been tested in the Courts, the propriety of passive euthanasia is widely supported today.

A distinction is drawn between two types of passive euthanasia:
a. not initiating life sustaining treatment;
b. discontinuing such treatment.

With regard to the first form — in practice doctors are not liable for omitting to take steps that could have averted death. But in theory liability will arise if a doctor failed to take necessary steps to save the life of his patient. In other words a doctor is in law not obliged to respond to the call of a stranger who said that he needed help. But where he fails to act, the existence of a doctor-patient relationship will be relevant.

Where treatment is discontinued the doctor may be liable for failing to do that which he is legally obligated to do. However, where the treatment is only to prolong life it is doubtful if liability will arise. For example, a doctor who switches off a respirator where the patient is comatose and has no prospect of recovery does not cause the death but permits death to occur.

In this connection the view expressed by Fletcher[4] is worth noting. He said that

> . . . doctors are in a position to fashion their own law to deal with case of prolongation of life. By establishing customary standards, they may determine the expectations of their patients and thus regulate the understanding and the relationship between doctor and patient. And by regulating that relationship, they may control their legal obligations to render aid to doomed patients.

Thus the medical profession confronts the challenge of developing humane and sensitive customary standards for guiding decisions to prolong the lives of terminal patients. This is not a challenge that the profession may shirk. For the doctor's legal duties to render aid derive from his relationship with the patient. That relationship, along with the expectations implicit in it, is the responsibility of the individual doctor and the individual patient. With respect to problems not commonly discussed by the doctor with his patient, particularly the problems of prolonging life, the responsibility for the patient's expectations lies with the medical profession as a whole.

1. See *S* v. *Hartmann*, 1975 (3), SA 532 (C).
2. At 345.
3. 'Abortus en Actieve Euthanasie', *Nederlands Juristenblad*, 19 April 1975.
4. 'Legal Aspects of the Decision not to Prolong Life', *Journal of the American Medical Association*, **203**, 179 (1968) at 122.

A CRIMINOLOGICAL VIEW OF EUTHANASIA*

M. G. T. Cloete

Introduction

The effort to legalize mercy killing is not something restricted only to our present age. The renewed interest which from time to time arises can be attributed to deliberate instances of euthanasia which come to notice.

Up till 1966 the emphasis was primarily concentrated on obtaining legal permission for adults with a sound mind who may elect to have their lives terminated in the case of an incurable disease. Since 1967 efforts have been extended to include those individuals who, due to clouded minds or brain damage, cannot express their wishes personally and on whose behalf a relative could express certain wishes.

The matter has, however, not yet been settled and the prospects of success in the forseeable future seem rather remote. Only one country legally permits euthanasia while in Switzerland[1] euthanasia is not regarded as murder if the motive is to grant compassionate release from incurable suffering and is justified by the discretion of those dealing with the case. In South Africa no legislation exists to regulate euthanasia and it is dealt with under the existing common law.

What is euthanasia?

Euthanasia[2] may be defined as the theory that when, owing to incurable and painful illness, a person's life has become a burden to him, death should be anticipated through medical intervention by some painless method approved by science, in order to shorten his suffering. This action could follow a discretionary decision by the medical practitioner without the knowledge of the patient (euthanasia) or could result from the expressed desire of the

---

* A criminological analysis of euthanasia is fairly restricted because of the more indirect significance of the phenomenon with the discipline. The discussion will only refer to some aspects which are regarded as of criminological significance.

individual concerned (voluntary euthanasia).

The principal justification for euthanasia is that it would allow some people to escape suffering by merciful death and is based on demands of compassion. The opinion has even been expressed that there is a prima facie duty on society to bring to an end intolerable suffering by legalizing euthanasia.[3]

The definition, as stated above, contains certain elements which require attention, viz.:

    a. Deliberate intervention which may be achieved by direct or indirect methods. It is also referred to as positive and negative euthanasia.

    b. The anticipation of death.

    c. An express and precise statement by the person himself that his life may, under certain circumstances, be terminated. In the case of incapability to do so himself the wish may be expressed by a responsible member of his family.

Deliberate intervention

Deliberate intervention by the medical practitioner to cause euthanasia is an intentional act on his part to accomplish a specific result: death. Such action correlates positively with the applicable elements of common law murder which in our law are:

    a. an act causing death;

    b. the intent to inflict death;

    c. unlawfulness, i.e. the absence of grounds of justification.[4]

Consequently, if a medical practitioner gives a patient a fatal injection with the intention of killing him and the patient dies in consequence, that doctor is strictly speaking a common murderer. The consent of the patient and/or the extremity of the suffering experienced and/or the imminence of death by natural causes nor all these factors combined could not be regarded as a disease.[5] Neither can the doctor rely on the defence that the deceased agreed to the termination of life — a defence of good motive or that the deceased would shortly have died in any event is specifically excluded. Furthermore, the act may also be regarded as an intentional infliction of harm.

The intervention could either be direct (positive) or indirect (negative).

Direct euthanasia, as indicated above, is the direct, deliberate action of mercy-killing to shorten or end life. According to the present state of law this constitutes murder. Courts of law in South

Africa and abroad have up to now acted along these lines when deliberate mercy-killings did occur. Since 1965 three cases of euthanasia came before our courts. The accused were charged with and in two cases convicted of murder.[6] In the latter two cases, the court, however, accepted the surrounding circumstances which motivated the killings as powerful mitigating factors, as was consequently reflected in the sentences. The punishments were of theoretical significance only.

Following a trial in Belgium (1962) at which a mother and a family doctor stood trial for deliberately killing a defective, malformed child, both were acquitted.[7]

Indirect (negative) euthanasia[8] is admittedly practised,[9] and can basically assume three forms which do not present as serious problems as positive euthanasia does, namely:

a. assistance rendered to the terminal patient by administering medicine or treatment that may possibly curtail life;

b. ceasing of treatment aimed at prolonging the patient's life; and

c. withholding of treatment altogether.

With regard to the administering of medicine that may possibly curtail life, the principle of double effect could be raised. In terms thereof the patient receives the minimum dose to relieve his pain but it is at the same time also the minimum dose to kill him. The latter is regarded as of secondary effect and is justified in terms of the doctrine of necessity in the common law — the medical practitioner has to choose between two competing values.

The above situation may arise when a patient develops resistance against morphine or a narcotic of which a small dose could be fatal. Consequently the choice is either to administer a larger dose or leave the patient without any relief. The doctor could then lawfully administer the drug well knowing that the quantities he has to use may sooner or later prove to be fatal. The immediate relief of suffering counterbalances the risk of accelerated death. In such cases it is difficult to determine whether, if at all, there is an unlawful act of euthanasia involved in the progressive administering of drugs. The justification to ignore the risk of drugs as a possible factor that could curtail life because of more violent pain, makes the question of whether the last dose was fatal, extremely artificial.

Williams[10] is of the opinion that, considering the doctrine of necessity, this may be a case where the existing law partially permits euthanasia.

The opposite situation, where the medical doctor anticipates death and administers a double dose in order to save the patient some suffering is, however, not permissible.

Similarly, the law may be regarded as doubtful where the doctor ceases or changes treatment so as to end the patient's suffering. It would be practically impossible to prove euthanasia beyond doubt unless the doctor would cause death in a manner that can be proved.

It appears that there is logically little or no difference between such action and the administering of an overdose of drugs as previously mentioned.

Complete withholding of treatment may pose a somewhat different question. If a patient, at the stage when the doctor acts, is only kept alive artificially and the ceasing of treatment would cause natural death, it may not even raise the possibility of euthanasia. In cases where the doctor withholds treatment at an earlier stage, he may be imperilled by the indiscretion of a third party in which case he may possibly become liable for prosecution.

The establishment of a legal right

Although the question of euthanasia is largely a moral one, it must nevertheless establish a legal right. This legal right depends on legislation but cannot be established unless various related matters can be adequately dealt with. Some of the important matters are:

THE QUALITATIVE NEED

Are the arguments which are raised by the advocates of euthanasia still valid? The fact that life can be prolonged by modern medical techniques and death averted in revolutionary, novel ways raises this crucial question. Both the medical and legal professions must possibly redefine their traditional attitudes toward the problem of euthanasia as a whole.

THE QUANTITATIVE NEED

It would be difficult to determine the actual need and support for euthanasia. It cannot be assumed that all individuals suffering from a terminal disease should or would be candidates for such action.

Organized groups who advocate voluntary euthanasia represent only a limited view and do not reflect public opinion.

The quantitative need for euthanasia will have to be carefully determined before legalization thereof could be considered.

THE ANTICIPATION OF DEATH

The question whether euthanasia should be considered in a particular instance will largely depend on the anticipation of death. The latter will, *inter alia,* be determined by the incurability of the illness, whether the patient is beyond any respite which may come along in his life expectancy, etc.

From a crimino-legal point of view limited life expectancy does not safeguard the physician from prosecution and may only be considered as a mitigating factor.

AN EXPRESSED DESIRE

Indirect euthanasia is admittedly practised and is effected once the physician has discretionately decided on the advisability of it; the patient does not express any wish. Efforts to promote the notion of voluntary euthanasia raise the important aspect of an expressed desire and permission by a specific person to have his life terminated in the case of a terminal disease.

Suitable answers will have to be found to many important questions, some of which are:
— Can the adult patient truly concur to make euthanasia a voluntary act?
— Would the judgement of the patient not be distorted during illness and change his capacity for rational thought?
— Will the patient be given an opportunity and the right to reverse the process?
— Even if voluntary euthanasia were to be legalized the medical doctor may still be walking in the margin of the law and be subject to prosecution if the patient's desire was stated during a variable state of mind.[11] Various safeguards will have to be determined.

Accompanying dangers

If the law were to remove the bar on euthanasia various problems could still arise, some of which are:
  a. Responsibility would be left to the conscience of the

individual. Consequently there will be an inconvertible proposition confronting the patient if according to the doctor who will be legally able to hasten death, he is suffering from an incurable disease. It will render the patient 'too little protection from not-so-necessary or not-so-merciful killing'.[12]

b. Certain individuals may be immunized from the criminal law.

c. It may be dangerous from the point of view of abuse. It would be difficult to define a category which could not be seriously abused.[13]

d. Legalization of euthanasia would undermine the confidence of patients in their doctors; and it would create a new form of distress of aged, sick individuals who would ask themselves whether they should prolong the burden on their families. Making euthanasia legal could reduce the incentive to improve the quality of terminal care and put in its place the concept of assisted suicide.[14]

Conclusion

The problem of euthanasia is complex and introduces various moral, ethical, religious, medical and legal nuances which cannot be easily disregarded. Whether one agrees with the principle largely depends on one's moral and religious convictions irrespective of the question whether it may possibly be justified on medical and legal grounds.

The approach to euthanasia should perhaps be more practical and the endeavour should be to find safeguards against indirect forms of euthanasia in order to protect medical practitioners.

1. Cf. Downing, A. B., *Euthanasia and the Right of Death. The Case for Voluntary Euthanasia,* London, 1969, 22 - 3.
2. The Euthanasia Society, *Merciful Release: The Case for Voluntary Euthanasia,* London, 3.
3. Cf. Matthews, W. R., *Dying,* Pelican, 1967.
4. English law postulates a further element, viz. malice aforethought. Cf. Fletcher, G. P., 'Prolonging of Life and Some Legal Considerations', in Downing, A. B., op. cit., 71 - 3.
5. Cf. Williams, G., *Voluntary Euthanasia. The Next Step,* London, 1955, 1 - 9.
6. In the *Davidow* case the accused was found not guilty by the jury.
7. Downing, A. B., op. cit., 21.
8. Cf. Williams, G., op. cit., 1 - 9.
9. A survey on physicians' attitude toward euthanasia showed that 20 per cent would take either positive or negative action. Reported in *Psychology Today,* September 1974.

10. Cf. Williams, G., op. cit., 5.
11. Cf. Williams, G., *The Sanctity of Life and the Criminal Law,* London, Faber and Faber, 1958, 307.
12. Cf. Kamisar, T., 'Euthanasia Legislation, Some Non-Religious Objections', in Downing, A. B., op. cit., 89.
13. Cf. *Royal Commission on Capital Punishment, Report* 1953, London, 179.
14. 'An Easy Death', *British Medical Journal,* No. 5960, **1,** March 1975, 704.

Medical Aspects of Euthanasia

EUTHANASIA[1]

H. W. Snyman

The middle ages are often referred to the dark ages, implying that the standard of living reached a nadir at that time. History certainly reveals that physical existence then, in comparison with that of the present time, left much to be desired. The standard of health was poor and life expectancy low; great epidemics of infectious diseases, such as the plague and the pox, raged; the wounded of the many wars were badly treated. From word and image of that faraway time, we can deduce with good cause that the ill or injured person remained untended and neglected, that his end must have been a protracted lonely agony. Among those that had to observe all this, the heartfelt desire must have arisen that their ends could be softer and perhaps painless; that is, they hoped for a *mild death.* It is this wish that is embodied in the concept euthanasia, which has belonged in the conscious thought of man since the more prosperous 17th century. As with most concepts, it has been moulded through the needs of circumstances and through the refining of directions of thought, and has gradually been re-formed to the present-day *collective concept,* quite a distance from the original. It is in terms of this collective concept that the various interested parties at this symposium will be presenting their views.

We have not been dealing with the original wish for a mild death, a life's ending which no-one is begrudged, but will move to the contemporary concept, complex interaction between the near to death patient and his attending physician. The point central to the problem of medicine in our society is the *way* in which that inevitable death occurs. Although medicine plays a principal role in the life-death drama, I am convinced that our profession should not have the only or the last word on the subject. This is not only a medical-scientific problem, where a factually won, tested and anno-tated premise is followed by a critically based medical conclusion. By its very nature medicine is directed to and always strives to see man as a whole and medically to serve him in that way. In the case of euthanasia, however, the range reaches far beyond our profession to nearly all the other spiritual facets of our being, from the actual to the transcendental, the physical to the metaphysical,

147

from preceivable existence to faith in an imperceivable life after death. It is therefore something that concerns the entire community and is not related exclusively to medical science. There has been much thought given to the subject in the past century and, especially lately, much has been discussed, considered and even written. Anyone who enters this terrain must, therefore, be thoroughly aware of the fact that he must keep many facets in mind if he wishes to achieve a complete picture regarding his specific community.

Convinced of the need for discussion of this and other related areas of medicine, I have on several occasions suggested to the legal as well as to the medical professions, that a contact committee be formed, consisting of the interested parties, that would meet from time to time to discuss particular related areas. The evident purpose of participating in this well-represented forum is to present the particular medical point of view.

I shall consider euthanasia within a trilateral relationship, namely: patient/doctor/community. The professional relationship between patient and doctor heads the list. Who and what is the patient? The patient is essentially a fellow human being needing medical knowledge and skill to support his life. In discussions about our subject the words 'meaningful 'and 'quality', in relation to the patient's life, are being stressed more and more often. These concepts, to my mind, do carry weight but also involve nuances of meaning and a qualification, all of which must be borne attentively in mind. Having said this, I can supplement my previous statement about the patient, namely: to support his life *meaningfully* and to its *optimal quality*. Certainly, and quite rightly so, the concepts 'meaningful' and 'quality' can be interpreted differently when seen from different viewpoints, because we are contemplating the age-old question of the content and meaning of Life itself. We have to come to some agreement about what the word 'life' encompasses. Albert Schweitzer, the renowned physician, philosopher and musicologist, put the following message over the entrance to his hospital: *Ehrfurcht für das Leben.* His interpretation encompasses all life forms, animal as well as human. I wish to summarize the wide application of medicine in the aphorism: respect for man in his living and in his dying.

The start of a new life is usually greeted with joy and much medical attention. The inevitable end of that life is, however, for many something only to be contemplated unwillingly; hard won acceptance which leads to a balanced and serene attitude to death is seldom encountered. The view of the individual in our care is of the utmost importance in the professional relationship. Behind his view lie the conceptions of his particular community within which his life was shaped and of which he is partly, genetically as well as in regard to his life-style and spiritual norms, a product or expression. Less, or more, consciously lie conceptions of right and rights, good and evil, life and existence, faith and religion, as bases for his viewpoint. As the patient then gives expression to his views, whether clearly or vaguely, the medical profession wishes to respect them and tries to provide for the needs of the particular person.

I want to distinguish three urgent levels of need common to all patients; these are *preservation of life, relief from suffering and softening of death*. These three levels of need are not sharply delineated; they intermingle and may even be conflicting. The relief of suffering and the accompanying softening of death are essentially concurrent. No-one, whichever point of view he holds, can find reason to disagree or can question this. Admittedly, medicine must point out that the ways in which suffering can be relieved can sometimes also involve the preservation of life — in particular, our medicinal capabilities can affect essential life processes such as breathing. Here we enter the area which our legal friends define as *dolus eventualis* and sometimes even *dolus indirectus*.

The first need, namely preservation of life, forms the crux of the question of all the discussions of past years. As regards his own life — now seen in the face of approaching death — certain factors or circumstances exist whereby the patient may wish to, and can, solicit medical assistance, regarding which he would like to make known his wishes or decisions. It is then essential that he has enough insight and his consciousness sufficiently clear to express his wishes lucidly. With a minor and a patient whose mind is clouded, the next of kin have to be consulted. With this predetermined, the patient can therefore do the following in conjunction with his physician: he can

1. make a request of his own accord;
2. approve a possible submission;
3. make no communication;
4. refuse or prohibit certain medical treatment.

The same applies when parents, guardians or next of kin act for the patient.

When, therefore, we consider the physician's actions, we should also pay attention to the needs and expressed wishes. With this I wish to emphasize that the doctor's part in an act of euthanasia should not be seen and judged as a fact on its own.

We turn to the second active participant in the trilateral relationship, namely the doctor. Born of the needs of man, medicine is in essence a science ultimately in the direct service of man seen in his totality and in all the variations of need and service from individual to community. The basic intent or objective of medicine is to have regard for the human being as a whole within his life situation, even though we at times may appear deficient on this score. Requirements for training laid down by the Medical and Dental Council underscore the fact that medicine straddles both the Human Sciences and the Natural Sciences and that the profession is to be shaped by the best from both sources. Often in the past this dual development has found expression in the phrase: 'medicine can be seen as a science and as an art'. Whilst the vast modern medical potential has in the main derived from the thrusting analysis and objective exploitation of the natural sciences, it has been in the field of its compassionate application to the fellow being in need that the doctor has revealed his respect for that life and the professional obligations it brings. He is trained to listen, observe, investigate and construct precisely and critically in order to establish a well-founded diagnosis of this person at this moment in time. His training further entails that he should make himself aware of the background, the setting or life situation of that person in order to add the perignosis to the diagnosis of his patient. Then follows the further demand for a prognosis. From his knowledge of the vast store of medicine and of the natural history of the particular disease process, he attempts to project the defined situation at a moment in time into the future thus to reach a probable prognosis. Naturally both diagnosis and prognosis may have to be amended as further facts are elicited. There is the ever-present danger that we may fall short of the total obligation, by falling into the trap of diagnosing a disease process in terms of an organ or body system. This danger is inherent in our tendency to be objectively scientific and to think and reduce to abstract terms. This is reflected in our terminology, where the disease process is defined in as few words as possible and even standardized internationally in order to convey the same meaning. However well standardized and useful, such terms convey abstract concepts which therefore exist only in our minds. Illnesses have no existence of their own; in reality there are only ill people. However scientifically arrived at, a bare diagnosis; e.g. of bronchial carcinoma,

150

is therefore an incomplete finding for it ignores the whole person and reduces him to the zero value of a case; it is thus 'a case of bronchial carcinoma'. It is only when we have identified John Jones, aged 50, with his personality, dependants and life situation, e.g. in the demanding world of commerce, as suffering from advanced bronchial carcinoma, that we arrive at a meaningful diagnosis and perignosis and can attempt to define his special prognosis.

Having achieved such clarity about my patient John Jones, his individual needs require careful attention. The preservation of his life with medical and supportive measures is my first objective and care. In this instance of advanced bronchial carcinoma, knowing the generally poor prognosis due to our very limited power to cure, *caring becomes more important than curing.* Naturally all other concomitant and curable disease processes from which John Jones may be suffering, or has developed, are combated as effectively as possible.

My second objective is relief of the distressing symptoms which may already be present or rapidly developing and make John's life a protracted agony. The tensions build up in John and me. I see my patient suffering in dyspnoea and pain and become personally involved through that compassion considered a basic ingredient of my profession. Yet, and it is essential, that through repeated discipline, I maintain a professional objectivity in this time of dormant fears and dampened hopes which may at any moment erupt into the very human emotional crises. For perhaps very good reasons John has been informed of the diagnosis and even the tentative prognosis. He may then act in terms of the four possibilities indicated earlier when I considered the patient's role. I mention the fourth one first: He may refuse or even forbid certain, or even all, medical treatment. In such an instance the patient's wishes are to be respected. To force our attention on him would take us beyond our duty and our medical ethic; would negate his free will and our respect for his person; would amount to a transgression which in legal terms could be considered as an assault.

In the absence of such a clear and conscious refusal our prime duty of life preservation prevails with regard to all three other possibilities — where he may be passive, or accede to a suggestion or even actively request. And here I must draw attention to some of the material factors which may help to determine the doctor's decision and action: the availability of or access to sophisticated facilities needed to help preserve or support life functions. It may be professional staff, a hospital bed, expensive apparatus, each of which might be absent or at a premium; each of which might be just as much in demand for another patient and, perhaps a patient with a better prognosis. In addition, the rather sordid but very real factor of cost may arise, especially in the long term. The doctor may thus be confronted with the very thorny problem of priorities and should then consult a colleague. Our second traditional duty, namely relief from suffering — which is not restricted only to the relief of pain — offers no basic problem and is accepted and expected by society. I must, however, repeat an earlier point that, particularly with regard to the relief of pain, the unavoidable side effects of the medicine we use may undermine the life-supporting attempts. This applies e.g. to morphia which *inter alia* may severely depress the life-maintaining respiratory centre and the blood pressure. On these two fronts of duty our attempts normally run parallel and complement each other, but could also come into conflict. This applies particularly at both extremes of life and in the very feeble. The use of such greatly needed and generally accepted measures may well take us onto very thin ice and then become a considered risk, a possible *dolus eventualis.*

It is in our third professional duty, the support of the patient in his mental anguish in the face of inevitable death that we are most troubled and at risk. Here we have to view and accept inevitable death not as the traditional enemy or as a professional failure, but in the broader view, as the awaited goal and natural event in all ecological systems and even perhaps in the mutational evolution of life. It is in this phase that concepts of life and afterlife and the norms of the individual and of society must take precedence. Then comes to mind the call of *Eerbied vir sy sterwe* and 'The right to die in dignity and peace'.

What do we mean by dignity of death? I have had occasion to witness what has been referred to as the *furor therapeuticus* when we, in a frenzy of activity with medicines, machines and monitoring, aggressively project our professional selves and take pride of place as the chief actors in a physical drama of death. The patient is then often relegated to a secondary role, albeit the object of all the activity but in fact reduced to the status of a subject. In all the froth of circumstance and urgency, with all the attempts to allay our professional conscience that we are indeed doing our bounden duty in serving his *physical* functions, we may indeed lose our proper perspective. We have to remind ourselves of the natural history of this particular disease process and of its natural outcome. The service to life may even acquire inhuman features. Our duty, in fact, should include the awareness that at such a moment in the face of death the patient and his *metaphysical* or spiritual needs should receive priority and their due respect. So often the greatest need is for privacy and tranquillity, the quiet presence of an intimate relative or good friend, the comfort of companionship when the awareness of the imminence of the end surfaces into consciousness. There may be greater need for time for discussion, particularly perhaps on religion, time for things of beauty like flowers and music and even laughter. All this I interpret as true euthanasia. Then it is part of our professional duty to keep our mechanized physical support in its proper second place, efficiently but without arrogance. It may well be that our chief professional contribution then lies in the compassionate companionship of dying. But the patient should not suffer from the overzealous compassion of others.

Thirdly in our trilateral relationship of patient, doctor and community, there is the community's viewpoint, especially that of the medical community within the greater communities on earth in all their diversity of emphasis and norms. Euthanasia in the original meaning of the word, i.e. softening of death, is the obvious duty of the physician, a duty from which he may only withdraw if his assistance is needed more urgently elsewhere, Within the present-day interwoven collective concept, we must define the four components which come to the fore in the vast literature of the previous decades. Closest to the original concept is *voluntary passive euthanasia*, a form of dying aid in which the patient indicates that he wishes to die but in which the doctor does not do anything to hasten death.

Then there is the *involuntary passive* form — the patient requests nothing and the doctor does nothing to hasten death. As a corollary to this I wish to add that the physician does not lengthen the inevitable death process in some or other artificial way. In both these main forms of euthanasia, the physician accepts the inevitable conclusion and, irrespective of the patient's request or permission, does nothing to hasten the moment of death, but also halts meaningless aggressive medical attention. His duty is done through personal compassion.

A clear watershed in the physician's possible actions divides the *dolus directus* from the above-mentioned forms of euthanasia. In the third and fourth main forms the focus falls on a conscious contribution by the doctor to hasten death. These forms are *voluntary active euthanasia* — where the patient requests it, or agrees to it — and the *involuntary active* form, where the doctor acts even though the patient had not requested it or agreed to it. The spur for the doctor in this case is his strong compassion with the suffering person.

In our law and all legal systems, the calculated hastening of death is equal to the illegal, deliberate causing of death of another person and is therefore murder, irrespective of the period of time elapsed taken. Wherever the matter has been discussed seriously and has been closely examined, no advocates for involuntary active euthanasia have appeared and it has not proved acceptable to any medical group. The World Medical Association has declared that it is in conflict with the concepts of medical ethics. The Medical and Dental Council, which, as the statutory body in our country determines codes of behaviour for the medical and related professions, has also at the first opportunity at which it was pertinent, disapproved of involuntary active euthanasia as ethically objectionable and as a crime which calls for the highest penalty.

Active hastening of death by the physician remains a basic error that is not acceptable. Strauss and Strydom, amongst others, say: 'Euthanasia on request is illegal'. The approval of any such active behaviour by the doctor is therefore not only in conflict with both medical ethics and the law, but also creates the possibility of abuse by persons whose conscience are lacking or blunted. This is also the dangerous terrain where unbridled compassion on the part of the doctor makes him forget his professional objectivity and act in a manner that he would not consider in lucid moments.

There is a need for order and guidelines for acceptable behaviour in every community. These are manifested on various levels over the course of time. They begin with awareness of the need: the insight or conscious *knowledge* — in French and so in English: 'science'. From this appears the finer determination of right and wrong, good and evil as was described by Socrates in his definition of the concept *conscience,* which is coupled with ethics. In French and so by derivation in English, conscience is the *con*science. As the initially vague traditions gradually crystallized into rules and became generally accepted, so they became defined laws. These laws therefore represent the standards of the community. Social laws and conscience are by no means static concepts and can undergo (and have in fact undergone) dynamic changes or emendations which have also been assimilated into less changeable laws. May I remind you of the early history of euthanasia when Plutarch, Plato and Aristotle pleaded for it; Aristotle even asked that it should be compulsory for malformed children; the Greeks and Romans actually applied it to the aged.

Because of the reasons already given, I am not in favour of a policy of euthanasia through legal determination. We as physicians will of necessity be involved and the faith of the community in the profession could be irreparably harmed if our main purpose of preservation of life and relief of suffering becomes entangled with legal directives. The image of the medical profession as guardian and tender of life should never be debased by any uncertainty about this. The doctor must act within the law, but it is more important that he treats his patient in good conscience.

I referred earlier to the important words 'meaningful' and 'quality' which have occupied our minds so frequently in the recent past. We cannot simply discard these concepts. They deserve careful attention to be meaningful and of value and could, perhaps, with clear knowledge and accepted in conscience, even find a place in our laws.

In this paper on euthanasia I could only touch on some of the most important aspects and have had to omit or be very concise about many others. With our but fleeting life-expectations we should stand humbly and in the best of our knowledge and conscience before this great and far-reaching theme, before the question about the full meaning of the Life of man as it has unfolded over the millenia.

1. Parts of this paper were delivered in Afrikaans and have been translated.

THOUGHTS ON EUTHANASIA

M. Stein

Euthanasia has come to mean different things to different people; it is therefore important to define one's terms. By derivation from the Greek, euthanasia means a gentle and easy death. However, it has come to mean much more than this. It may be defined as a doctrine whereby, in certain circumstances, when life has permanently ceased to be either agreeable or useful, owing to disease, senility, etc., the sufferer should be painlessly killed either by himself or another. It may be distinguished from the extermination of the mentally disordered and also from the uniformly accepted use of sedatives and analgesics such as tranquillizers, cortisone, etc. We might even narrow down the meaning to apply only to people suffering from incurable disease and who have constant excruciating pain. The interpretation of euthanasia may clearly become very elastic. We may, therefore, divide euthanasia into four categories:

a. *Voluntary and direct*

The person decides on death and does so by his own hand, i.e. suicide. Is suicide then wrong under certain conditions of either mental or physical stress? Perhaps suicides have only a temporary derangement of mind, as is often seen when the attempt fails and they never try again. However, they may repeat their attempts until they do succeed.

b. *Voluntary and indirect*

A person has asked in advance (and may even have drawn up a document to this effect) to be killed painlessly under certain specific conditions. This, to my mind, is euthanasia as well as is the next category.

c. *Involuntary and direct*

The patient has not asked to be killed and yet someone decides for him to end his life. This may be termed mercy killing. A person may be in such a mental state that he is not aware of his surroundings and so is not capable of asking; but either the family or the doctors decide that life is no longer meaningful and appeal either to the doctor or to a body appointed by the State to end the life.

Relatives should not be involved in any decisions as they may develop guilt problems and other psychological manifestations then, and for years to come.

d. *Involuntary and indirect or 'Letting the patient go'*

This is a passive or negative approach by simply withholding life-preserving measures such as not treating a complication. For example, pneumonia may occur in a terminally ill person, e.g. a person in extreme pain dying of cancer. The doctors in consultation decide that death is only a short time away and so they withhold intravenous fluids, antibiotics, respirators, etc. This is already practised universally in modern medicine. Clinical decisions are taken every day to discontinue all treatment except for the control of pain, even if the drugs used for this control will hasten the end. Some feel it is just as wrong to adopt this negative attitude as to kill the patient with an overdose of drugs. Not doing anything is doing something and it is a decision to act, just as though we did act. Acts of omission are therefore no different from acts of commission.

The doctor bases his moral and ethical standards on the Hippocratic Oath, so I would like to quote from it. It says nothing about preserving life as such. It merely says: 'So far as power and discernment shall be mine, I will carry out regimen for the benefit of the sick and will keep them from harm and wrong.'

It all depends on how we understand and interpret the terms 'benefit of the sick', harm and wrong. If we regard biological and dehumanized life as harm, then it is quite wrong morally to withhold death. I prefer to use the term euthanasia to describe only the direct ending of life and not the cessation of attempts to prolong life. The moral distinction between the two can be defended as valid and essential. Respect for a dying person may demand that we stop the art of healing so that we help the patient practise the art of dying. In such a case, this is merely the most human way to act, in that we are refusing to attempt to control life and death any further. The Hippocratic Oath undertakes two things: to relieve suffering and to prolong and protect life. Where the patient is in the grip of a fatal and agonizing disease, the two may be in conflict. However, if by relieving suffering with drugs or other means, life is shortened, I do not believe it is the same as shortening life by deliberately killing the patient.

The concept of euthanasia has had a checkered history. Infanticide was a common practice. The Spartans rigidly dispensed with weak infants. Plutarch said that such a child was of no use to itself or the State. Plato had no doubt that intolerable pain was a warrant for suicide. His draft for Utopia was to get rid of frail children and hopeless invalids. Aristotle discouraged the attempt to raise deformed children. Primitive societies have often encouraged infanticide, possibly due to the shortage of food. Robert Louis Stevenson writes of this in the South Sea Islands. An ancient record even tells us that the old men in Sardinia were killed with clubs by their own sons.

In the 1920s and 1930s the whole problem of euthanasia was re-opened, most conspicuously by some of the leading medical practitioners in England, where the Voluntary Euthanasia Legalization Society had been active for many years. In America, too, a Euthanasia Society was formed in 1938.

It is interesting to note who some of these eminent people were Dr C. Killick Millard, M.O.H. for Leicester; Lord Moynihan from Leeds, who was the first President; and Sir Arbuthnot Lane. Amongst the distinguished non-medical sponsors were Sir James Jeans, Julian S. Huxley, Harold J. Laski, George Bernard Shaw, H. G. Wells, the Rev. J. M. Creed, Professor of Divinity at the University of Cambridge, and the Rev. Cannon Harold Anson, Master of the Temple. A petition to the New York Legislature was backed by the signatories of 1 776 physicians in the State. The precise number is significant, as it is the date of the Declaration of Independence.

At the time of the Bill in the House of Lords, both doctors present (Lord Horder and Lord Dawson of Penn) were strongly opposed to it. In spite of all this, there is no solution as yet. Various arguments for euthanasia have been advanced and may be put under different headings. For the sake of comprehensiveness I will include some that I will not discuss at all. These are the first three:

a. *Religious*
b. *Legal*
c. *Scientific*: *the problems of ecology*
d. *Compassionate*: *humanitarianism*

158

Cancer is usually the disease cited in this case as it conjures up in the mind of the layman a person dying horribly, being eaten up by the disease accompanied by shrieking, cursing and groaning. An often quoted example is that of Jonathan Swift, the satirist and Irish clergyman. He ended his life in a distressing and degrading death. His mind crumbled to pieces and it took eight years for him to die while his brain rotted. He would read the Third Chapter of Job on his birthday as long as he could see: 'And Job spake and said, Let the day perish when I was born and the night in which it was said there is a man child conceived.'

The pain in Swift's eye was so acute that it took five men to hold him down to keep him from tearing out his eye with his own hands. For the last three years he sat and drooled. When the end came finally, his fits of convulsions lasted thirty-six hours.

The advance in medical science is such that pain can be controlled more easily and more effectively than in the past. It is therefore no longer valid to put this forward as an argument for euthanasia.

e. *The doctor's point of view*
The lawful availability of euthanasia would raise serious difficulties in the doctor-patient relationship. The fear that the doctor may side with the relatives to persuade the patient to accept euthanasia would be real, as is the fear if the doctor were against it, he would not do all in his power to relieve the patient's suffering. In any case no doctor would like to be known as the doctor who kills.

f. *The curability or otherwise of the disease*
Doctors are not infallible. Mistakes may be made and the responsibility would rest with the medical profession. There is always the hope that a new and remarkable cure may be discovered that will cure the condition from which the patient is dying; but in such a patient it is more than likely that a condition such as metastatic cancer has already destroyed the tissues irreparably and is therefore not compatible with recovery. Diagnosis is not all-important but prognosis is.

g. *Progress*
Opponents of euthanasia are often accused of stifling progress, and are placed in the same category as those who opposed cremation. Is it progress to destroy life?

h. *The thin edge of the wedge*
Euthanasia may start off by being applied only to people riddled with cancer and obviously dying; but it may be extended gradually to include other conditions such as advanced nervous diseases with

paralysis, crippling arthritis, senility, mental disorders, and to justify infanticide. This was well brought out in Nazi Germany.

i. *Ethics*

A medical practitioner is forbidden to destroy life. Nevertheless, abortions are now legal in many parts of the world and legal in most parts under certain conditions. Further, during childbirth the child may be sacrified for the sake of the mother. The utter corruption of medical ethics in Nazi Germany shows how the economic welfare of the State takes priority over the doctors' responsibility to the individual. In Germany, extermination of the physically, mentally and socially unfit was generally accepted. State Hospitals were required to furnish the names of patients who had been ill for five years or more and were unable to work (e.g. chronic heart disease, etc.). Such persons were often liquidated by order of the State. Two hundred and seventy-five thousand persons were put to death in charitable foundations for institutional care. What is terrifying is the relative values of a single concrete individual and the abstract State. One can even foresee an efficiency expert doing a ward round with a Chief of the Ward and deciding who shall live and who shall die. Perhaps this is over-simplification, but it bears consideration. It is a doctor's duty to ease pain and suffering. He must not destroy even a useless, painful life; nor must he prolong such a death.

Summary

Euthanasia conjures up in the popular mind a direct act of killing a patient even though we may use terms like active, passive, direct and indirect. To avoid confusion by the use of these terms, I suggest that the term euthanasia be scrapped and another one found for what we are trying to say, viz. that we withhold extraordinary measures and give pain killers even if these hasten the end in a terminally ill person.

I do not believe that the medical profession wishes to have a law to allow it or another to kill a patient actively, but merely wishes to legalize what is already commonly being done every day.

GENERAL MEDICAL ASPECTS OF EUTHANASIA

H. Grant-Whyte

My views on this subject are based upon information I have gathered in many countries over a considerable period of time. I have had contact with Voluntary Euthanasia Societies and have had the opportunity, through the years, of discussing the subject with theologians, legal authorities, sociologists and the medical profession and have heard views for and against euthanasia; against, because of misinterpretation and misunderstanding as to what the word really denotes.

We in South Africa have only comparatively recently become aware of the importance of euthanasia; and before I proceed I wish to stress the meaning of this word so that there can be no misconception, misunderstanding, or misinterpretation of it.

Euthanasia (derived from the Greek: *eu* = well; *thanatos* = death) mean painless, happy death: an easy and painless death. I emphasize this because the word has been headlined as 'mercy killing', an abhorrent description which should never be used because it savours of murder. This misinterpretation has been responsible for incalculable damage to the cause of humanism which, in fact, is what euthanasia is. I have ardently appealed to the various media to cease using this description.

I am well acquainted with the history of Voluntary Euthanasia Societies in the United Kingdom and the United States, which were founded respectively in 1936 and 1938; I am also acquainted with the Australian Voluntary Euthanasia Society founded just before the South African Voluntary Euthanasia Society, and I am well informed about the situation in Europe, France, Switzerland, Holland, Finland, Denmark, Sweden and Japan, all of which have recently been in the news — and I have visited them all. Everywhere, there has been a complete and striking change of attitude towards euthanasia and there is undoubtedly a world movement in support of voluntary euthanasia.

In the United Kingdom the Society was started in 1936 by Dr K. Millard M.D., D.Sc., and the first President of the Voluntary Euthanasia Society was a world-famous surgeon, Sir Berkeley

Moynihan, K.C.M.G., C.M., D.C.L., L.L.B., also President of the Royal College of Surgeons of England, and other eminent men and women who are active supporters of voluntary euthanasia. I refer particularly to the late Julian and Aldous Huxley and their surviving sister-in-law, Elspeth Huxley, Sir Glanville Williams, Q.C., Sir Herbert Seddon, F.R.C.S., the famous Orthopaedic Surgeon who operated upon Sir Winston Churchill's hip, Baroness Wootton, Lord Platt, Lord Ritchie, and several others in every walk of life, too numerous to mention.

I am well aware of the activities of the Euthanasia Education Council in the U.S.A., and with the Society which was called the Euthanasia Society but is now called the Society with the Right to Die. This change was brought about because of ignorance, confusion and misconception about what the word 'euthanasia' means. This Society was founded in 1938 and its first President was the Reverend Charles Potter, D.D. The present President is Dr Joseph Fletcher, D.D. (Professor of Medical Ethics at the School of Medicine, University of Virginia), a noted theologian and scholar.

More than 750 000 Living Wills have been distributed by the Euthanasia Education Council. Lawyers are requesting it for their clients. Doctors react favourably to it. It is reprinted in textbooks, discussed in newspapers and magazines, talked about on radio and television. The Living Will is an assertion of the individual's right to self-determination over his own body. A patient can decide to refuse treatment and this is no more and no less than informed consent, which it is obligatory for the doctor to obtain. The non-compliance of a doctor with the patient's wishes is culpable, an assault on the patient, and is no more and no less than malpractice for which the doctor can be sued. The Courts must therefore take serious cognizance of informed consent, according to the views of outstanding legal authorities.

In Australia, in September 1974, just before the South African Voluntary Euthanasia Society was founded, the Australian Society came into being. It has had fantastic public and professional support. A world-famous scientist in Australia, Sir MacFarlane Burnet (Nobel laureate and a Fellow of the Royal Society) carries on his person a card on which is typed:

'I request that in view of my age, any prolonged unconsciousness, whether due to accident, heart attack or stroke, should be allowed to take its course without benefit of the Intensive Care Unit or Resuscitation Ward'.

Death in the aged, in these circumstances, he says, should be accepted as something inevitable and sometimes positively desirable. Doctors should not compel the old and incurable to die more than once.

The South African Voluntary Euthanasia Society also issues this type of card for its members.

This Society was founded by Mrs Sylvia Kean on 14 September 1974, at Hilton, Natal, with the assistance of Mrs Mary Morland of Pietermaritzburg.

The Society has progressed rapidly because of the enthusiasm of its founder and, as President of S.A.V.E.S., I am most impressed with the growth of our Society in such a short time and the fact that there are over 1 000 members, 130 of whom are Life Members. This success can be attributed not only to the founder but also to the enthusiasm and dynamism of the secretaries in the various provinces who have done such sterling work in the cause of humanism.

The Living Will which S.A.V.E.S. distributes to its members is based on that of the Voluntary Euthanasia Society of the United Kingdom and also on that used in the U.S.A., where, by July 1975, 750 000 had been applied for to the Euthanasia Educational Council in New York.

I would like at this juncture to state the wording of the Living Will:

To my Family and my Physician

This Declaration is made by me (full name and address) at a time when I am of sound mind and after careful consideration.

If the time comes when I can no longer take part in decisions for my own future, let this Declaration stand as the testament to my wishes:

If there is no reasonable prospect of my recovery from physical illness or impairment expected to cause me severe distress or to render me incapable of rational existence, I request that I be allowed to die and not be kept alive by artificial means, and that I receive whatever quantity of drugs may be required to keep me *free* from pain or distress even if the moment of death is hastened.

This Declaration is signed and dated by me in the presence of the two undermentioned witnesses present at the same time who, at my request, in my presence and in the presence of each other, have hereunto subscribed their names as witnesses.

Signed : ....

Dated : ....
Witnessed by:
Name .... Name ....
Address .... Address ....
 ....
Occupation .... Occupation ....

Note : Witnesses should not be members of the family.

I wish to stress that:

a. The Living Will is entirely voluntary.

b. It must be discussed with those nearest one.

c. A copy must be given to those most likely to be concerned, e.g. family, doctor, clergyman.

d. A copy should be kept readily at hand in case there is use for it — not kept in a safety deposit box.

e. It is a good plan to look over the Will every year and make it clear that one's wishes are unchanged.

f. It is not illegal for a patient to refuse treatment of whatever kind, unless it is a question of an epidemic where he might be a danger to the public if, for example, he refuses to be inoculated.

'No amount of professional skill can justify the substitution of the Will of the Surgeon (or Physician) for that of his patient' (Bennan *v.* Parsonnet (1912) 83.A.948).

g. The Medical Defence Union Booklet on Consent to Treatment (revised in July 1971) should be scrutinized carefully because of its bearing on the subject of informed consent for treatment.

h. The patient has a Bill of Rights. He has, among other rights :
   (i) a right to information necessary to give informed consent before surgery or treatment of any kind;
   (ii) a right to refuse treatment and be informed of the medical consequences.

If he is not *compos mentis* and a Living Will is produced, his next of kin, curator *bonis ad litem* or clergyman must protect him as he requested when he was *compos mentis* and duly signed his Will.

It is interesting that the patient's Bill of Rights has been affirmed by the American Hospital Association, and copies of the complete text are available from the Euthanasia Educational Council in New York. It must be accepted that denial of the right to die with dignity is a violation of an individual's right which neither law, custom, nor practice should be allowed to disregard or curtail.

The aims and objectives of S.A.V.E.S. are clear, explicit,

forthright and humanistic, and in no way complex, confusing, frightening or illegal.

S.A.V.ES.. feels strongly that:

a. Doctors should be not only skilled technicians but also humanists, as Mr Justice Hiemstra stressed in his address on *Aspects of Medical Ethics* to the International Orthopaedic Convention in South Africa.

b. Life-supportive measures, like those used in Resuscitation Wards or Intensive Care Units, should not be used to prolong dying in cases of terminal illness with intractable pain or irreversible brain damage, in other words, mindless humans.

c. Medication should be administered primarily for pain relief and dosage should be so regulated as always to be adequate and effective.

d. Every effort should be made to relieve discomfort, which very often can be worse than pain.

S.A.V.E.S. has an educational function. It promotes open discussion on death and dying and appreciates the assistance of the mass media. It is indeed most anxious to obtain support and assistance in the furtherance of its aims and objectives from all professional bodies and other organizations in the Republic, especially those vitally concerned with human welfare. I refer particularly to the South African Medical and Dental Council, the S.A. Nursing Council, the Medical Association of South Africa, the Churches, the Judiciary, and the various Women's Associations in our country.

The S.A. Medical and Dental Council and the S.A. Nursing Council are concerned, among other matters, with the ethics of their professions and with curricula for training in the fields of Medicine and Nursing. Doctors and nurses, because of their specialized training and experience, must be able to decide if aid should be rendered to the dying. Reports of futile prolongation of life in persons known to be hopelessly and terminally ill appear with frequency in news media and evoke criticism of doctors, nurses and hospitals. What better example to the world of this was the striving of 32 doctors to keep alive the 83-year-old General Franco? Is it any wonder that the new word Franconasia has been coined for such inhumanity? Thus, if the attending doctor in whatever branch of medicine, is of the opinion (his own, or in consultation with a colleague or colleagues) that measures to prolong life are unrealistic and hopeless as far as the patient is concerned, conservative, passive medical care is, without question, the course to be adopted in place of heroic measures in the management of terminal and incurable illness, e.g. Intensive Care (or Resuscitation) Wards with the latest technology, in which the patient is entwined in a tangle of tubes and drains, tied to heart, brain, breathing and kidney apparatus, with needles in veins and tubes in nearly every orifice.

This has been so well described by Professor of Surgery, Roland Stevens, M.D., of the University of Rochester Medical School and the Strong Memorial Hospital, New York. I quote:

Physicians with a broad cultural background, who have an elevating influence on the profession (humanists, in other words) are becoming extinct. In plain truth the effectiveness of medical technology has outstripped the quality of professional conscience which guides it. Under the name 'Intensive Care' a small crowd of highly competent specialists, each with his supporting team of technicians, share the control of a patient's destiny — without anyone running the 'Department of Humane Consideration'.

Prolonging life or delaying death is primarily the responsibility of the medical profession, closely linked with that of the nursing profession.

'Thou shalt not kill, but needst not strive

Officiously to keep alive' (Arthur Hugh Clough, 1819 - 1861).

In these circumstances, doctors, with the help of their sister profession, because of their specialized training and experience, must be able to decide if aid should continue to be rendered to the irreparably destroyed, the dying. This preparation for death is a complicated problem and one for most careful consideration. The care of the dying is a subject which should be considered by the S.A. Medical and Nursing Councils for inclusion in the clinical phase of the training of doctors and nurses. As at this time, there is no provision for this; it is absent from their curricula.

The S.A. Medical and Nursing Associations, that is the practising professions of medicine and nursing, must be concerned with voluntary passive euthanasia. Its members must know what it is and means, and must set about dispelling misconception and misinterpretation, and counter unjustifiable opposition.

These Associations should take active interest in S.A.V.E.S. and should follow the example set by the Canadian Medical Association, which has reaffirmed the right of the physician to write 'No resuscitation' on the chart of a patient with an incurable illness or one whose death is inevitable. Steps, too, have been taken in this direction by branches of the American Medical Association in

166

various states. Voluntary euthanasia, as has been said, is humanism. In a recent poll of doctors in the U.S.A., 80% of those responding agreed that 'people have the right to die' by making their wishes known to their doctors when they are *compos mentis* and before they reach the stage of painful incurability. The medical mandate for voluntary euthanasia world-wide is stronger than ever before and it is fervently hoped that our own medical and nursing professions will obey the wishes of the incurable and dying patients, as set out in the Living Will distributed to members of S.A.V.E.S.

The doctor, in accepting the Living Will from his patient, enhances mutual trust and the patient is assured that his doctor will not allow him to suffer needlessly when dying becomes inevitable.

There is theological acceptance of voluntary passive euthanasia accepted by and large throughout the world by great religious leaders such as Pope Pius XII, Deans of St Pauls (W. R. Matthews and Inge), as also by Methodist, Unitarian, Lutheran and Jewish religious leaders. The Church of England, after a $3\frac{1}{2}$-year long inquiry, has recently issued a report called *On Dying Well,* which gives strong support for voluntary euthanasia. Pope Pius XII, at an International Anaesthetic Convention in Rome on 24 November 1957, pointed out that there was no obligation on the part of the doctor to employ extraordinary means to preserve life where no reasonable hope of benefit existed. He said, 'The task of determining the exact instant of death is that of the physician.' Dean Inge of St Paul's expressed himself as follows: 'I do not think we can assume that God wills the prolongation of suffering and torture for the benefit of the soul of the sufferer'.

The Clergy has taken up a wonderful humanistic attitude: 'To everything there is a season — a time to be born and a time to die' (*Eclesiasticus,* III, 1. 2).

As far as the doctor is concerned, we may take the following example: One of the members of the Working Party of the Church of England Inquiry, Dr Cicely Saunders, *O.B.E.,* M.A., F.R.C.P., S.R.N., and Director of St Christopher's Hospice, Sydenham, London, expressed herself in no uncertain manner when she said: 'It was for the doctor to decide — to treat or not to treat and how to treat', again having obtained informed consent.

The late Lord Horder, famous physician to the King, said: 'Be it observed that the good doctor is aware of the distinction between prolonging life and prolonging the act of dying'.

It will interest this meeting that guidelines sanctioning voluntary

167

euthanasia have been proposed by the Netherlands Government Health Council, the Report of which has been endorsed by the Dutch Royal Society for the Advancement of Medical Science. These guidelines are in keeping with what I have said.

I will not enlarge upon the attitude of the Judiciary to voluntary euthanasia except to refer again to the eminent Judge Hiemstra, who was applauded by an International Convention of Doctors for his humanistic address (published in January 1975 in the South African Medical Journal) in which he referred to voluntary euthanasia. We have one of the most eminent legal luminaries with us, Professor S. A. Strauss, whose thesis on Informed Consent (*Toestemming tot behandeling as verweer in die strafreg en die deliktereg*) is outstanding.

I must, however, also mention the humanism which Judge von Winsen demonstrated in his judgement recently in Cape Town, which was widely acclaimed throughout our own country and also abroad. Sad to say, the South African Medical and Dental Council did not emulate the Court of Law.

MEDICAL ASPECTS OF EUTHANASIA

M. G. H. Mayat

Introduction

'Thou shall not kill' is one of the Ten Commandments, and as a code is universal to all the great religions of the world. Apart from this religious injunction, a doctor's actions are further governed by the Hippocratic oath, which insists that he must apply all his medical knowledge to save life.

Definition

When discussing euthanasia it is necessary to define the term: 'An easy or calm death'. The second definition is somewhat harsh and traumatic in its implication. Gould's Medical Dictionary says, 'The killing of people who are suffering from an incurable or painful disease'. Newspaper editors with a penchant for dramatic sub-headings have employed the term 'mercy killing' as a synonym for euthanasia. Any reference to 'killing' is bound to engage the attention of most people and is used in preference to euthanasia, which is too technical.

Category of patients

There are two main categories of patients for whom euthanasia may be considered.

Firstly, there is the patient in whom the body's vital organs (heart, lungs, kidney and brain) are kept functioning by artificial means. A kidney machine performs the renal function. The respirator assists the lungs and intravenous therapy provides nourishment, replaces body fluid losses and supports the circulatory system. The body soon responds and then the vital organs are able to function independently and all the supportive measures are gradually withdrawn. After a prolonged convalescence the patient may recover completely. In some cases, during this period of artificially sustained life, the delicate brain tissue suffers irreparable damage. If the damage is severe, the patient survives as a human

169

'cabbage' with a vegetable type of existence. Such a person has to be cared for like a child and is fed with or without a naso-gastric tube. He has no control over bladder or rectal functions and depends entirely on relatives who have to resign themselves to dedicated nursing for an indefinite period.

The second group of patients includes those who depend completely on the artificial aids employed to sustain life. These patients cannot be weaned off the machines. Life is prolonged for a variable length of time until the human frame collapses utterly and completely under the hammering of the powerful cardiac stimulant drugs and other artificial aids employed. Whilst on supportive therapy, the patient's condition steadily deteriorates and it soon becomes apparent to the clinician that the case is hopeless and it is only a matter of time before the vital centres cease to function.

The doctor's dilemma

There are a number of circumstances in which the attending doctor is placed in a dilemma. In the two categories of patients referred to, he may be asked to apply euthanasia to a patient who is steadily deteriorating whilst on supportive therapy and when it is apparent that there is no hope of recovery. The following case illustrates the problem:

Mrs A.T., 32 years old, was admitted for severe status asthmaticus. She was 'drowning' in her own pulmonary secretions. The respirator kept her breathing with the aid of an intra-laryngeal tube. She lapsed into coma. In spite of drugs to elevate the blood pressure, the heart was failing. Whenever the respirator was slowed down, she became cyanosed. On the third day it was apparent that there was no hope whatsoever. In circumstances like these, should one not stop treatment? Attempts to prolong life entail a lot of additional cost. This may be a crippling burden with which the family is saddled. I feel that in these circumstances one should not expect the close relatives to guide the physician about what course of treatment to adopt.

In such an emotionally charged atmosphere the relatives will always say, 'Doctor, do your utmost. Don't let the patient die.' In this case I tested out my impression. I asked the relatives (who included the mother and the husband), who were continually in attendance. I told them the true facts and assessment of the three doctors attending the patient. Their answer was as I had expected, 'Doctor, don't let her die'.

Consultation with relatives

This has serious limitations. Under stress, relatives cannot be expected to approach the problem rationally and logically. Then there is the question whether relatives are interested parties in the way of inheritance or whether they seek an escape from the burden of nursing old and debilitated patients who are not likely to recover in any event.

Consultation with patients

Patients fall in two categories. Firstly, there is an intelligent person who is aware of his predicament and requests euthanasia because of the intolerable pain and suffering he is experiencing. In such instances larger and larger doses of morphia are required as the body gets accustomed and resistant to the drug. A person who is heavily drugged has his mental powers reduced and should not be relied upon to give a considered opinion about the desirability of euthanasia. Diseases may have alternate periods of progression and regression. During progression of the illness a patient may feel dejected and forlorn and plead for euthanasia. But soon after, in the phase of regression, the patient regains hope and feels exhilirated. He may then regret wishing for euthanasia, i.e. if his physician did not take him at his word!

In this connection I found interesting the opinion of Trotsky[1] on the subject of euthanasia.

The nature of my illness (and rising high blood pressure) is such as I understand it, that the end must come suddenly, most likely through a brain haemorrhage. This is the best possible end I can wish for. It is possible I am mistaken. If the sclerosis should assume a protracted character and I should be threatened with a long drawn out invalidism, then I reserve the right to determine for myself the time of my death. The 'suicide' (if such a term is appropriate in this connection) will not in any respect be an expression of an outburst of despair or hopelessness. Natasha [Trotsky's wife] and I said more than once that one may arrive at such a physical condition that it would be better to cut short one's own life or, more correctly, the too slow process of dying.

The second group is one in which a doctor performs 'negative' euthanasia by withholding treatment which, in his opinion, will not cure but merely prolong life for a short while.

Mr A.M., aged 74 years, had four sons who were doctors. He

suffered from diabetes and renal failure. The normal blood urea level is 20 - 40 mg%. His was 400 mg%. He lapsed into semi-coma. Should he be placed on a kidney machine? In consultation with his sons, the attending physician decided against this and the patient was permitted to die peacefully at home in the presence of his family.

The new-born child with gross deformities

One of these congenital deformities is hydrocephalus, that is, grossly enlarged head due to excessive fluid in the cranial cavity. The foestus is still *in utero* and alive. The only method of delivery is by caesarean section. Should one needle the head and withdraw a few pints of fluid and thereby enable the foetus to be born vaginally? Such a procedure would most likely cause the foetus to die *in utero*. Is that euthanasia? Occasionally the foetuses are delivered vaginally and are alive but very distressed at birth. Does one administer the full resuscitative measures as for a normal baby or allow the deformed infant to die? If the obstetrician withholds treatment, is that negative euthanasia?

Physician's error

No clinician is exempt from human error. There are cases where patients who were in coma for a long period and were pronounced as beyond recovery, have in fact regained consciousness. Growths which were treated as malignant and regarded as incurable have turned out to be benign and the patient has made a full recovery.

Conclusion

Archbishop Dennis Hurley[2] has summarized what I believe is the general attitude of medical practitioners: 'No positive step should be taken to shorten a life but no extraordinary measures should be taken to prolong a life that seems to be ending.'

1. Carmichael, J., *Leon Trotsky: A Biography,* London, Hodder & Stoughton, 1975, 467.
2. *The Natal Mercury,* 28 February 1975.

NEONATAL EUTHANASIA

T. Jenkins

'The ethical problems of care of the newborn defective are not cut from exactly the same cloth as care of the dying elderly or abortion' (John Fletcher, 1975).

Certain special considerations apply to neonatal euthanasia which do not apply to euthanasia of the adult. There is, for example, no possibility of the individual being consulted or of any of his wishes being taken into consideration when contemplating the act.

Before the birth of a baby many would agree that the total interests of the family take precedence over those of the foetus or new baby. Society has accepted this fact when permitting abortion for the sake of the health of the mother; and when there is a serious risk that the child to be born will suffer from a physical or mental defect of such a nature that he will be irreparably seriously handicapped (Abortion Act, 1975). The acceptance of selective infanticide would to many be a logical extension of selective abortion. If it is not feasible to diagnose a certain disease *in utero,* which disease if it were diagnosable pre-natally would justify abortion, then the diagnosis of the condition at or soon after birth might, it could be argued, morally justify infanticide.

There is in our society a strong abhorrence of infanticide and our Judaeo-Christian traditions require that our actions towards each member of the family of mankind be motivated by considerations of care and protection. If the newborn baby is defective in any way then we are required to show even more consideration to him. 'A society which supports acceptance of defective newborns, where reasonably possible, does more to nurture patterns of acceptance in parents and thus reinforce the child's basic trust in the world's trustworthiness' (Fletcher, 1975). But society has already encouraged attitudes which militate against such idealistic response. Firstly, by condoning abortion to prevent the birth of a defective child society has made it clear that it is sympathetic to parents who are anxious not to have a baby if it suffers from a serious disability. Secondly, cost-benefit studies have been published in the United States which show what a financial burden such a child can be to the parents and to the state. Thirdly, the achiever is undoubtedly more highly praised and valued in our society than is the non-achiever. These and other considerations have already gone a long way to encourage potential parents to expect (and in some cases, to demand) physically and mentally normal children. And the pressures from them will continue to build up. Some ethicists, notably Paul Ramsy, oppose genetically indicated selective abortion for the very reason that it can be equated with infanticide of which they strongly disapprove. Others, notably Joseph Fletcher, approve of both selective abortion and selective euthanasia of the defective newborn in a particular situation. Each situation, they claim, is unique and the human needs which are part of that situation must be considered with compassion and reasonableness; we should be guided by the consequences of our action. A third point of view is put forward by John Fletcher who claims that there are moral differences between the two issues. While approving of selective abortion of defective foetuses he nevertheless strongly disapproves of neonatal euthanasia for three reasons: firstly, the newborn infant is capable of independent physical existence; secondly, there now exists a possibility of therapy being instituted; and, thirdly, parental loyalty to, and the acceptance of, the infant has usually developed by this stage.

Passive neonatal euthanasia is already widely practised in this and other countries. It has been implemented for spina bifida (or 'split spine') and is called the 'judicious management' of the condition. This particularly distressing condition, which is due to a failure of closure of the neural tube during the early weeks of gestation was, prior to 1960, nearly always fatal. The child died from infection which entered the spinal cord through the open lesion over the lower back. During the 1960s active surgical closure of the open lesion, the administration of antibiotics and the insertion of valves in the brain to reduce the increased pressure of the cerebrospinal fluid which usually follows the initial surgical procedure, resulted in the survival of many of these children. I can personally recall in 1962 assisting the Professor of Surgery of the Durban Medical School at many of these operations on little Zulu babies.

In the early 1970s, however, a number of workers (notably Dr John Lorber of Sheffield) set about analyzing the results of this treatment and, to the horror of most, showed that the results as measured by the quality of life enjoyed by these children was deplorably bad. Of the 80 survivors in one series only 5 could walk and had a normal I.Q.; 32 could walk with the aid of calipers but $\frac{1}{3}$ of these had low I.Q.s; 31 were unable to walk, were incontinent of urine and faeces, and most were mentally retarded (5 severely); 12 were confined to wheel chairs, were incontinent of urine and faeces, severely mentally retarded and 2 of the 12 were blind.

Dr Lorber drew up a list of criteria which guided paediatric surgeons in their decision to offer surgical treatment. In consultation with parents, decisions were now made about withholding treatment. If it were decided not to treat a child, he would not be operated upon and would not receive any antibiotics or nutrients other than via the mouth. The success of such 'treatment' was assessed by the time taken for the child to die. In one series of 25 cases not treated 11 were dead by 1 month and all except 2 by 6 months. These died before 9 months.

It is no secret that this approach of 'judicious management' of spina bifida has been followed by many surgeons and I have no doubt that in most cases it is successful. I know of one family, however, in which the child, after discussion with the father, was not treated and the parents advised not to visit the child in hospital. The nursery at home was disbanded and the parents 'mourned' the death of their child. But after 6 weeks the parents received a telephone call from the hospital authorities advising them that the child had done very well, the back lesion had healed spontaneously, and asking them to take the child home because the cot was needed. I need hardly mention the psychological trauma through which this family has gone. And it may not be considered relevant to mention that the child survived for another year and required a number of operations during its short life.

The other case which I wish to mention briefly because it throws, I believe, some light on the complex question of neonatal euthanasia, is the famous Johns Hopkins Hospital case. A baby was born with Down's Syndrome (or 'mongolism'), a chromosomal disease, and, in addition, had duodenal atresia, i.e. an obstruction of the small intestine distal to the stomach. The Down's Syndrome was compatible with life but the atresia was not (at least, it was not unless a relatively simple operation was to be carried out), so the child was allowed to starve to death over the next 11 days. I say 'starve to death' because, without the operation, it was not possible to feed the baby.

Most ethicists and doctors who have commented on this case have arrived at the conclusion that it was morally wrong to have withheld the surgical treatment. And yet this was surely a case of passive euthanasia which is approved by many even though they condemn active euthanasia. The intention of the parents, as well as the doctors concerned, was that the child should die because it was a mongol.

Is there any difference morally between ensuring the death of the infant by withholding treatment and ensuring its death by, say, a lethal injection? The motivation behind both actions is the same — to produce the death of the child. If a sin is involved in the act in the one case it is a sin of commission and in the other it is a sin of omission. I am not aware of any Judaeo-Christian teaching or judgement which would show one to be more acceptable than the other. If the objective of withholding treatment is to hasten the death of the child then, in my opinion, consistency would require that it be achieved as quickly as possible; considerations of humanity would require that it be achieved as expeditiously and as humanely as possible. I believe it is intellectually dishonest to take refuge behind semantic arguments like the 'extraordinary means to save a life' one. It goes something like this: there is no onus on the doctor to resort to extraordinary means to preserve or prolong the life of the child. A Roman Catholic ethicist (R. A. McCormick, S.J.) has written that 'morally speaking, ordinary means are those whose use do not entail grave hardships to the patient. Those that would involve such hardships are extraordinary'. McCormick acknowledges the relativity of these terms but points out that the distinction has had an honoured place in medical ethics and medical practice. It was endorsed by the House of Delegates of the American Medical Association (J.A.M.A. 227: 728, 1974) in these terms: 'The cessation of the employment of *extraordinary means* to prolong the life of the body where there is irrefutable evidence that biological death is imminent is the decision of the patient and/or his immediate family.'

It is my contention that the surgical closure of an open myelomeningocele and the administration of antibiotics could not today be considered extraordinary means to prolong the life of the body. No, what is under consideration is the quality of the life to which that child would be condemned if the treatment were given. 'What kind of life are we saving?' is the question to be asked. And this highlights a 'quality of life' judgement which worries many of us. Nevertheless, we must grapple with it and try to answer it with honesty and compassion.

Brave leaders of medical thought in Britain (with Dr John

Lorber in the van) have been followed by many paediatric surgeons in withholding therapy from these children with the explicit intention that they should die. A legal colleague of mine has told me that in law a doctor who practises this type of passive euthanasia would be just as culpable as another who might resort to active euthanasia. If it is probable that no legal difference exists between withholding treatment so that the child may die, and administering a lethal injection to ensure that the child dies, it seems to me certain that no moral difference exists. Is killing someone morally worse than letting someone die? Rachels (1975) presents two convincing cases to illustrate the non-difference. The two cases are exactly alike except that one involves killing whereas the other involves letting someone die.

In the first, a man who stands to inherit a large fortune if his 6-year old nephew were to die proceeds to drown the little boy while he is taking a bath and makes it appear to have been an accident.

The second man also stands to inherit a large fortune if his 6-year old nephew were to die. He makes his way to the bathroom one evening in order to drown his nephew but when he is just about to enter the bathroom he sees the little boy slip, hit his head on the side of the bath and fall face down in the water. He stands by, ready to push the boy's head back under if it should prove necessary. But it is not necessary and the child drowns as his uncle watches but does nothing. Rachels asks 'Did either man behave better from the moral point of view?' Obviously not. Both men acted from the same motive and both had the same end in view. If the second pleaded in his defence 'I didn't kill him, I only let him die' we would conclude with Rachels that 'such a defence can only be regarded as a grotesque perversion of moral reasoning. Morally speaking it is no defence at all'.

I find the logic behind the argument very compelling indeed. When the doctor lets a patient die for humane reasons he is in the same moral position as if he were to give the patient a lethal injection for humane reasons. The method of carrying out his decision — which is to let the patient die — is not important. When we doctors approve of passive euthanasia but disapprove of active euthanasia we are in effect saying that we didn't kill the patient but his disease did it. The doctor's role was to 'let him die' but this is, in effect, a kind of action and as such can be morally appraised in exactly the same way as any other action. It can be considered right or wrong; wise or unwise; compassionate or sadistic. 'Merely' letting the child die can, I am sure you will agree, be much less humane than giving the child a lethal injection. Once a decision has been made not to try to treat the child then, perhaps, the humane thing to do would be to put it out of its misery. The child with spina bifida who has been 'selected out' is almost certain, if he does not die, to end up with a quality of life which is far, far poorer than if he has been actively treated and that, as I have already indicated, is pretty poor.

I have never thought of myself as an active crusader type: someone who stands on platforms pleading for abortion law reform or, certainly, for euthanasia laws. I have become interested in both subjects out of necessity: many patients have caused me to think about the moral issues surrounding euthanasia, in particular neonatal euthanasia. They have been confronted by practical problems like where to draw the line when it comes to treating a baby with a genetic abnormality when the outlook for that baby's future is very poor indeed.

And I think I can say, in all honesty, that as a Christian the compassion and love (agape) that I have for the family when it has to grapple with the problem of an abnormal newborn baby with a bad prognosis has caused me to arrive at a point of view from which I can see merit in the argument for legalized euthanasia. I can understand why some of my colleagues and most theologians are passionately opposed to euthanasia. What I find extremely difficult to understand is why many of my colleagues are in favour of passive euthanasia but opposed to active euthanasia. I think the view of many, if not the majority, of the doctors in South Africa would coincide with that of the House of Delegates of the American Medical Association which stated a couple of years ago:

> The intentional termination of the life of one human being by another — mercy killing — is contrary to that for which the medical profession stands and is contrary to the policy of the American Medical Association.

Poppycock! Whom are these Delegates trying to convince? How presumptuous of them to claim to speak for the medical profession! Many would argue that merciful killing is preferable to unmerciful keeping alive.

In summary, then, some people oppose prenatal diagnosis and selective abortion because they believe it would represent the thin edge of the wedge. It would, they fear, lead to the acceptance of *selective infanticide*. It would put us on the slippery slope, which would lead to ever more permissive actions.

178

South African law now permits selective abortion. Perhaps the time has come for us to consider seriously legalizing selective infanticide. It is my sincere hope that as a result of this meeting interested members of the legal and medical professions will begin to meet regularly with theologians and ethicists to try to thrash out the problems which surround euthanasia in general, and neonatal euthanasia in particular. Guide lines could be laid down which would help those who are faced with the type of problem I have been discussing. It is my feeling that it might just be easier to make the breakthrough in the field of neonatal euthanasia than in that of adult euthanasia.

A DEFINITION FROM THE VIEWPOINT OF A PHYSICIAN

U. P. Hämmerli

A preliminary note

The following comments represent the personal view of a specialist in internal medicine and Chief of a large department of medicine. They are based not only on my own professional experience, but also on a study in depth of the relevant literature and on the public statements of many professional medical associations. To that extent only, can the statement be regarded as perhaps representing the opinion of a wide section of the medical profession.

1 The present situation

Gigantic technical progress has been made by medicine in our generation. The introduction of reanimation and intensive care units in the early 50s, the development of modern heart, brain and transplant surgery permit spectacular successes. Nowadays it is possible to cure diseases and save lives which only 20 years ago would have been lost.

Not all attempts in this spectacular life-saving are successful. Some failures result in the patient's death, others leave him in a hitherto unknown intermediate stage between life and death. This fact is disturbing for both laymen and doctors. New definitions of the terms 'life' and 'death' are called for. Legislation and, to some extent, ethics have not kept abreast of these modern developments.

1.1 DIRECT RESULTS OF TECHNICAL PROGRESS IN MEDICINE

Things previously impossible can now be done and manipulated in hospitals. It is often possible to prolong life artificially, sometimes for indefinite periods. The new technical possibilities may lead to over-treatment or an excess of therapeutic zeal (*acharnement thérapeutique*). These problems, as yet partially unsolved, have been created by medicine itself. For purely technical reasons, the problems involved in the artificial prolongation of life do not arise in the case of a patient who is treated at home instead of being sent to hospital by his family doctor.

1.2 PSYCHOLOGICAL EFFECTS ON THE POPULATION

The process of dying has been broken down into stages, and more stages are constantly being added, so that, as Helmut Thielicke, the moral theologian, has remarked, what is supposed to be a service to mankind is turned into a terror of humanity.

The artificial prolongation of life can be an artificial prolongation of suffering.

People regard the doctor as 'master over life and death'.

Older patients on the verge of death frequently fear that they will 'fall victim to scientific experimentation' if they are sent to hospital, and visualize an unconscious person with tubes protruding from all the orifices of the body.

The euthanasia societies which have come into being, particularly in the Anglo-Saxon countries, call for the right for each person to decide his own death by making a 'euthanasia will'. A number of Nobel Prize winners support these endeavours.

Those unversed in medicine view euthanasia in terms of 'mercy killing' by a single injection with a syringe, a misunderstanding which is encouraged by the press. Examples are the pictures of a large intravenous syringe lying on the bed of a pretty young woman which appeared on the title page of the German weekly *Der Spiegel* on 10 February 1975, and the similar picture on page 34 of the Belgian weekly *Special* of 14 August 1974.

The doctor thus comes to be seen as a potential executioner rather than a trusted helper.

This is unsettling people. To an increasing extent the press, moral theologians and social moralists are calling for an end to medical action which needlessly prolongs life. In general, doctors support this attitude and also, with few exceptions, categorically reject active euthanasia in the form of killing.

1.3 THE LEGAL DILEMMA

Euthanasia is not mentioned in any national criminal code, apart from killing on request and assistance with suicide.

In the few sensational trials in Europe concerned with euthanasia, the sentence has been mild or even only nominal, the court having been primarily concerned with the motive of the accused.

Specific questions presenting legal difficulty are:

What is the doctor's professional duty?

When is the family doctor no longer bound to send his patient to hospital for action to prolong his life?

When is the hospital doctor no longer bound to take steps to prolong the life of an incurable patient?

When is the hospital doctor no longer bound to continue artificial means to prolong the life of an incurable patient?

Is unlawful homicide necessarily a positive act, or can it also be constituted by omission to act or by suspension of medical action to prolong life artificially?

When is a human being 'humanly dead'? Is it possible in law to kill a person who is 'humanly dead'?

1.4 THE ETHICAL DILEMMA FACING DOCTORS

In medical school and postgraduate training the doctor is taught to *act* (with the scalpel, drugs and machines).

He is not trained in *omitting* to act.

A young doctor feels therefore action to be 'good' and not acting 'bad'.

When acting to prolong life artificially, a young doctor is thus frequently treating his own guilty conscience, not the patient.

Even if the doctor himself is ethically convinced of the correctness of taking no action he may come into conflict with the criminal code.

The development of modern medicine increasingly confronts the doctor with a problem of principle: 'To do or not to do, that is the question'.

2 Prevailing definitions

Prevailing definitions in medicine, ethics and law have not kept pace with progress in medicine and need to be restated.

2.1 The following must be defined for new ethical and legal definitions to be possible:

The duty of the doctor and the task of medicine

The concept of death

The concept of euthanasia.

2.2 These three concepts are inter-related and must be redefined in conjunction with each other.

2.3 Only after redefinition of all three will doctors, moralists and lawyers speak the same language and understand each other.

3 Problems of understanding between doctors and others

3.1 THE COMPREHENSION OF REALITY

A comprehension of reality underlies any creation of definitions. There are two possible processes for grasping reality: cognition and experience.

3.2 COGNITIVE REALITY is arrived at by logical thought processes, based on abstract considerations, of a number of intelligent people. The attempt is made to plan theoretically for all possibilities and incorporate them in the definition of reality. Occasinally this form of cognition is described as 'armchair philosophy'. It has the advantage of producing clear, logical-sounding definitions. Its disadvantage is that only 'black' and 'white' are clearly defined, the intermediate grey area being scarcely touched upon. Border-line and unforseen cases are not covered by such definitions. The grey area is particularly large in medical practice.

Moral theological, social ethics and legislation are mainly based on cognitive reality.

3.3 EXPERIENCED REALITY is based on everyday experience in one's own environment and profession. One 'lives with the problem' and thus experiences it as one's own reality. The advantage of such reality is that it is probably closest to the truth. It is also able to embrace the grey area of border-line cases, since it perceives all aspects of the problem on the spot and so can elaborate them. The disadvantage is that such reality of experience is usually a matter of personal 'feeling' which is seldom consciously expressed in clear words. Indeed, the need for verbal formulation is not actually felt.

Experienced reality gives rise to 'situation ethics'. The situation ethic in a hospital is the 'collective ethic' of the whole medical and para-medical staff (doctors, nurses and social workers).

3.4 THE REALITY OF DEATH

The different reality of death for doctors and nursing staff as opposed to other persons is based on their different reality of experience.

Older doctors (especially hospital doctors) and nurses have

personal experience of the death of thousands of persons.

For the doctor and the nurse, death is something normal, like birth, life, health and disease. Death is part of their everyday professional experience. Ideas such as euthanasia, 'mercy-killing' or 'sub-human life' do not enter a doctor's mind during his daily professional work. Anyone foreign to the medical profession (apart from the clergy) has himself seen very few people die. Formerly, death took place in the family. Today it is almost anonymous, because the dying are taken to hospital, at least in large towns.

The younger generation in particular no longer has any real conception of death. Their idea is influenced by the false image conveyed in films and on television (an accident or disease; a fully conscious patient: a few fine 'last words', the head slumps to one side — death within seconds).

This gives the layman the following false ideas:

The sick and dying person thinks rationally in the same way as when he was in good health.

An old person in a state of mental depression ('If only I could be gone') actually wants to die quickly (to be 'put out of his misery').

3.5 THE EXPERIENCED REALITY OF DIFFERENT CATEGORIES OF DOCTORS

Experienced reality can vary not only between doctors and others but between individual categories of doctors. This difference is very pronounced in how doctors talk about problems of euthanasia. For example:

Organ transplant surgeons speak of the definition of death in the case of the donor of the organ;

Anaesthetists and intensive case unit doctors talk of switching off the breathing apparatus;

Neurosurgeons talk of intensive care units over-crowded with incurable patients whose brains are dead beyond recall;

The internists speak of incurable irreversibly unconscious cases whose respiration and heart beat continue spontaneously;

Paediatric surgeons talk of seriously deformed babies and children;

A doctor who is chronically ill himself speaks in the light of his own problem.

Thus not all statements by doctors are applicable or relevant to the whole medical profession.

4 Definition of the physician's 'duty'

The mission of medicine as an instrument in the service of community health is not necessarily identical with the duty of an individual doctor giving treatment.

Medicine as a whole has a *collective orientation*; it has no direct mandates from patients. In addition to treating disease it is concerned with general health measures such as prophylaxis, hygiene, health education and eugenics.

The individual medical practitioner's orientation is *towards the individual* and he has a contractual relationship with his patient. The collective medical ethic enjoys absolute primacy only in veterinary medicine (selective breeding, race hygiene, destruction of poor specimens and artificial aid to the 'survival of the fittest'). Such absolute primacy is unthinkable in human medicine.

In human medicine the collective ethic can and must be accepted in so far as it supplements and does not restrict the individual-orientated ethic (e.g. smallpox vaccination).

For social and economic reasons it is likely that a conflict will arise in human medicine in the near future between the community and the individual-orientated ethic, because of the spiralling costs of individual medicine in hospitals which can no longer be borne by the community.

4.2 PREVAILING DEFINITIONS OF THE PHYSICIAN'S DUTY

The essence of medicine is an *intervention,* by means of either drugs or the scalpel. Thus the traditional definitions of the doctor's duty always describe an action:

Preserving life
Prolonging life
Preserving and restoring health
Curing
Relieving suffering.

Two problems arise out of such action definitions:

A legal problem: Any intervention (even the administration of a drug) is a form of assault on the patient's body or personal integrity. Accordingly, the doctor must be protected under criminal law by a provision on 'professional duty'.

A medical problem: Nowadays, relieving suffering often means shortening life, either by interrupting treatment which has been begun, by not beginning any treatment, or by administering analgesic drugs in adequately large doses.

4.3 PROPOSAL FOR A NEW DEFINITION OF THE PHYSICIAN'S DUTY

In view of the swift modern development of medicine it is likely to be difficult to lay down firm duties with regard to acting or not acting. In both cases the doctor's *motivation* seems more important. It should be possible to define this, for example as follows:

A doctor must exercise his profession humanely to the best of his knowledge and belief and in his patient's best interests. He must treat his patient in the same way as he would wish his father, mother, wife, child or himself to be treated by another doctor if in the same medical situation as the patient concerned.

4.4 THE DEFINITION OF THE PHYSICIAN'S PROFESSIONAL DUTY GIVEN IN THE HELSINKI DECLARATION

Definitions of the doctor's professional duty on the lines of 'custodian of health' or 'his sole concern is the health of his patients' are deliberately concerned to state that clinical experiments on human beings must not endanger the patients concerned.

5 Definition of death

When medicine had few effective means at its disposal, death occurred relatively quickly. It was enough to regard death as the medically unavoidable end of human life, an end which could not be delayed.

The means available to modern medicine make it possible to prolong life artificially so that for the following reasons new definitions of death are necessary:

'Modern' death is frequently a gradual transition involving a transitional stage of intermediate life.

'Modern' death is a continuous process of dissolution, with a few fixed points which can be medically defined in objective terms (e.g. irreversible cessation of brain function).

Modern medicine creates 'living corpses' (*morts vivants*) which retain partial biological functions.

There is a tendency to distinguish between 'biological or

186

physiological death' (i.e. the final end of all biological life) and the 'death of the human being' or 'death of the personality' (i.e. irreversible cessation of the functions of the brain).

5.1 The old definition: cessation of the heart and circulation

In the past death was defined as the irreversible cessation of heartbeat. This defintion included the death of the brain, since cessation of the heart's activity interrupts the blood circulation and consequently the supply of blood to the brain.

5.2 Newly accepted definition: cerebral death (with collapse of spontaneous respiration)

In 1968 an *ad hoc* committee of the Harvard Medical School established a new and clear definition of cerebral death which has subsequently been adopted verbatim or with few modifications by many national medical associations. This definition is generally accepted but not embodied in legislation.

The new definition was *deliberately* concerned with organ transplant surgery. It made the 'killing' of the donor of an organ (chiefly in the case of kidney transplant operations) for the sake of the recipient of the organ, medically and ethically permissible. 'Killing' for the sake of the recipient normally occurs by switching off the breathing apparatus. As a purely secondary matter the definition permitted switching off the apparatus in the case of other patients whose brains had died but who were not donors of organs. Thus it is not death, or the death of the brain, in general which is defined, but only a specific death situation. The lay press often disregards this fact.

The basic definition refers to total, irreversible central loss of functions or death of the brain, i.e. the cerebrum and the deeper brain centres. Failure of the deeper brain structures implies cessation of spontaneous respiration and frequently of the spontaneous heart and circulation functions. Both these vital functions can today be maintained artificially.

General criteria for applying this basic definition are: Irreversible deep unconsciousness, accompanied by:

Failure to respond to sensory and sensitive stimuli;
Limp extremities, without reflexes;
Large pupils, not reacting to light;

Absence of spontaneous respiration;
A swift fall of blood pressure after removal of the artificial support for the circulation.

All these criteria must be present on repeated examinations, the electroencephalogram being used only as an aid, not as a criterion in itself.

5.3 A DEFINITION NEEDED: BRAIN DEATH WITH CONTINUED SPONTANEOUS RESPIRATION

The definition of brain death with failure of spontaneous respiration hitherto accepted is concerned solely with patients placed in an intensive care unit because of their need for artificial respiration and constant supervision of their heart and circulation function.

Probably more frequent in everyday practice, however, are patients whose brains have died but who have preserved their spontaneous respiration and can be treated in normal wards. In the case of such patients the cerebrum has failed irreversibly, so that they have permanently lost consciousness, although their deeper brain structures are only partially affected and thus spontaneous respiration continues. In their case, too, life has to be preserved artificially, by means of drugs and artificial feeding.

Both categories of cerebrally dead patients (with or without continued spontaneous respiration) have two essential criteria in common:
   a. They have lost consciousness and therefore their personality, irreversibly. They are not only acerebral but apersonal, and survive only vegetatively, as physiological torsi.
   b. Without artificial means of prolonging life they die of their incurable basic disease.

The following questions have to be answered medically and legally:
Can this condition be called 'death'?
Can this condition be called 'life'?

5.4 DEFINITION OF 'IRREVERSIBILITY'

If irreversible loss of brain function is accepted as a definition of human (as opposed to biological) death, the concept of 'irreversibility' acquires the greatest importance. It has to be asked whether the doctor or doctors responsible can make a mistake in diagnosis.

The possibility of such a mistake in the case of dying patients must clearly be considered only in relation to irreversibility and thus to the course of the disease, whereas an error in diagnosing the basic disease of a dying patient may be irrelevant. For example, it is of no importance, when diagnosing irreversible cessation of the heart, whether cessation was due to myocardial infarction or purulent myocarditis. In the case of irreversible failure of brain function due to a 'stroke' it is relatively unimportant whether failure was caused by a massive bleeding in the brain tissues or by complete absence of blood in that part of the brain due to blockage of a vessel of the brain.

What is important when diagnosing irreversibility is an *adequate period of observation of the course of the disease,* which supplements the diagnosis of the primary disease by showing whether the patient recovers or gets worse after the commencement of treatment. An adequate observation period rules out errors of diagnosis with regard to irreversibility.

The length of this observation period always depends on the state of the individual patient concerned:

In the case of heart arrest an observation period of less than an hour is enough.

In the case of failure of brain function of spontaneous respiration, a few days or (very occasionally) weeks are enough.

In the case of failure of the brain function with continued spontaneous respiration, weeks and often months are necessary.

Abandonment of medical action to prolong life artificially followed by immediate biological death (such as the result of switching off breathing apparatus or the heart machine) demands that the doctor must exercise particular care when diagnosing irreversible brain death.

6 Definition of euthanasia

6.1 THE MEANING OF THE WORD 'EUTHANASIA'

The original Greek term meant a 'gentle' or 'good' death. It was used to describe spontaneous, natural death and never meant the killing of one's fellow-men. It is in fact a predominantly philosophical term with little practical application to modern medicine.

At the present time the use of the word euthanasia conceals an *appalling confusion of ideas.* Euthanasia covers practically everything in any way connected with human death from active killing to humane action.

It would be better to drop the term euthanasia entirely and replace it by some objective new terms.

6.2 Forms of euthanasia

What makes the confusion of ideas about euthanasia particularly appalling is that the *motivations* of those who practice it differ completely as between its various forms.

The main, variously motivated, forms of euthanasia are:

Traditional euthanasia before the age of modern medicine: the dying person had the company of the doctor, the clergyman and his family (life was not shortened).

Active euthanasia as practised by the Hitler régime: life which considered to be of no value was destroyed (social killing).

Active euthanasia as proposed by euthanasia societies: the patient who so desires is killed by the doctor (mercy killing).

Passive euthanasia: action is not taken to prolong the lives of patients in whom the death process has already begun and whose life cannot be saved in the present state of medical knowledge.

Relief of pain of dying persons (from the medical viewpoint this is not euthanasia): pain is alleviated by morphine-type drugs which may possibly shorten life as a side-effect, although this is not the aim of treatment.

6.3 Distinction between active and passive euthanasia in the case of dying persons

The confusion of ideas in euthanasia terminology even extends to such a simple and logical sounding distinction as that between active and passive euthanasia.

Patently active euthanasia in the sense of killing is confined to 'social killing' and the 'mercy killing' of patients who will not die of their basic disease (e.g. tetraplegia).

If the overall term euthanasia is *restricted to patients who are bound to die of their basic disease,* then the distinction between active and passive euthanasia may be no more than a play on words. In the case of dying persons the doctor simply has to choose between various forms of treatment (*choix thérapeutique*). He is certainly not the 'master over life and death' in such cases, for medically speaking he is powerless to prevent death where the disease is incurable and progressive. A higher power is 'master over life and death'.

The difficulty of interpretation can be illustrated by the example of the switching off of breathing apparatus in the case of a patient whose brain has died. Whether this is described as active or passive euthanasia depends only upon the definition:

The measure is clearly active if active euthansia is defined as an act of commission by the doctor and passive euthanasia as an act of omission;

It is clearly passive if active euthanasia is taken to mean the deliberate shortening of life as the doctor's primary motivation and passive euthanasia is understood as the omission of interruption of action taken primarily, but without success, to save the patient (abandonment of an attempt to restore the patient's health).

This second pair of definitions corresponds most closely to a doctor's way of thinking.

Legal opinion is that active and passive euthanasia in the case of dying persons can be clearly distinguished if we base our considerations on the *natural, uninfluenced course* of a disease that is medically incurable and leads to death. Active euthanasia is then influence brought to bear artificially on the natural course of the disease in order to induce or hasten death; passive euthanasia is the omission or termination of influence brought to bear artificially on the natural course of the disease where the aim of such influence was to delay death.

With this definition of passive euthanasia, the legal question can be confined to the specific one of the doctor's professional duty to the dying person:

When and in what circumstances is a doctor *no longer bound* to prolong artificially a life which medically speaking is lost, either by refraining from action for its artificial prolongation or by terminating such action that has been introduced but has proved unsuccessful?

When and in what circumstances is a doctor *bound,* in the case of a life which medically speaking is lost, not to take any action to prolong it artificially or to terminate such action that has been introduced but has proved unsuccessful?

6.4 Attempts at a non-terminological classification of the various forms of euthanasia

Table 1 is based on eight typical morbid states where euthanasia in the wide sense could be considered.

Against each such state there is shown on the left the patient's position as regards life expectancy, state of consciousness and power of decision and on the right the motivation of the two parties, doctor and patient, to euthanasia and its ethical and legal interpretations.

The table could be extended to include further examples of disease. What is important about it is that nowhere is it possible to draw a line straight across all the columns. Thus no absolutely reliable terminology is possible.

6.5 THE DOCTOR'S MOTIVATION TO PASSIVE EUTHANASIA

The concept of euthanasia is alien to the doctor in his everyday work and is not used. Laymen are often incapable of understanding this.

With few exceptions, doctors reject active euthanasia, in the sense of killing or assisting with suicide (examples 1 - 5 in the table).

Relief of the suffering of incurably sick persons, such as those suffering from cancer with metastases, and of other grave symptoms, such as difficulty in breathing (example 6 in the table), is not considered by doctors as euthanasia, but as their obvious professional duty. The doctor's view in such cases is in line with the pronouncement made by Pope Pius XII in 1957. Nowadays pain is scarcely ever relieved by means of morphia, but by a combination of pain-killing and tranquilizing drugs, which may result in a state of semi-consciousness in the patient from which it is possible to rouse him. Any 'over-dose' occurs gradually and over a long period. The patient gets used to the drugs in that they are broken down more quickly in his liver. The dose must gradually be increased in order to achieve the same degree of pain relief. Any shortening of life as a result is never the aim but at most an unavoidable side-effect of the treatment. Over-doses of pain-killing drugs by way of 'mercy killing' do not exist for most doctors, despite what laymen imagine.

In the case of termination of action taken to prolong the life of a patient whose brain is dead, i.e. where the personality has died but biological death lags behind (examples 7 and 8 in the table), what is important to the doctor is not his motivation for terminating the action but his primary motivation with regard to the patient. The primary motivation is always a desire to help or cure. Action to prolong life is always begun in the hope that the patient will recover or even be completely restored. Only when it is quite certain that this aim cannot be achieved (irreversible loss of the function of the brain) does the doctor abandon the action he began for the purpose of prolonging life. He does not do this by way of euthanasia, but because of the pointlessness of further therapeutic zeal (*acharnement thérapeutique*), the case being hopeless and it being irrefutably clear to him that no effective help is possible for the basic disease. Lawyers and other persons alien to medicine often find it hard to grasp this concept of pointlessness.

But for the doctor the 'point' of every medical act he performs, is fundamental to his choice of the therapeutic possibilities open to him, even in the case of quite ordinary illnesses where there is no question of euthanasia.

For the doctor there is 'point' in any therapy which seems to him likely to succeed.

Therapy is pointless if it is certain to be unsuccessful (e.g. the choice of an antibiotic to fight bacteria which are resistant to it).

In case of doubt, i.e. when the chances of success are not certain, the doctor's decision is always determined by the patient's welfare and he begins the treatment which he thinks most likely to succeed. But if it is unsuccessful and if no other therapeutic possibilities exist, then the treatment begun clearly becomes pointless.

In the case of patients in whom the process of death has begun and cannot be arrested, it is quite often decided at the beginning not to take any action to prolong life artificially, on the grounds that it would be pointless. This decision is taken by every family doctor who decides not to send an incurable patient to hospital. Strangely enough (from the doctor's viewpoint), this primary decision not to take action to prolong life, i.e. delay death, is completely acceptable to the lawyer, although he may well regard the subsequent abandonment of action once begun to prolong life as legally questionable.

6.6 THE DEMAND OF EUTHANASIA SOCIETIES

Most euthanasia societies very justifiably call upon doctors to spare dying persons unnecessary suffering. But that should be the doctor's obvious professional duty, so that the requests of euthanasia societies would be superflous.

The individual examples published in the general press of inadequate pain relief do not indicate any shortcoming on the

TABLE 1: *Attempt at a Non-Terminological Classification of Various Forms of Euthanasia*

Patient's Condition			Example of Disease	Motivation of Euthanasia		Interpretation of Euthanasia	
Life Expectancy	*Consciousness*	*Power of Decision*		*In Patient*	*In Doctor*	*Ethical*	*Legal*
Patient does not die of basic disease	Conscious	None	1. Complete idiocy (in child or adult)	(Incapable of judgment)	None (relieving the family and nursing staff of a burden)	Social killing: the community takes precedence over the individual	Killing
			2. Severe malformation of central nervous system in child		Sparing the child a future which would be a burden to him	Social or mercy killing	
			3. Severe physical malformation in child (e.g. missing limbs)				
		Normal	4. Tetraplegia after fracture of the cervical vertebrae (total paralysis from the neck downwards)				
		Normal or reduced by senility	5. Severe chronic painful physical suffering without reduction of life expectancy (e.g. crippling rheumatism)	*In individual cases:* Wish for death but inability to commit suicide	To comply with the patient's wish	Mercy killing: sympathy for the individual	Killing or helping to commit suicide
		Normal or reduced by basic illness	6. Severe chronic painful physical suffering in illness leading incurably to death (e.g. cancer with metastases)	Relief of suffering	Relief of suffering	Relief of suffering	Doctor's professional duty
The death process has already begun	Irreversibly unconscious	None	7. Brain death with spontaneous respiration intact	(Incapable of judgment)	Pointlessness of further action to prolong life because of irreversible condition	Abandonment of action primarily taken for the patient's benefit	
			8. Brain death with cessation of spontaneous respiration		Possible donor of an organ		

part of medicine but rather that the individual doctor has failed his own patient. If an incurably sick person suffers unnecessarily, this is poor clinical medicine.

Another demand that is heard far less frequently is that a person who is suffering grievously although not on the point of death, should be killed (examples 4 and 5 in table). These patients' wish to die is a desire to commit suicide which, however, they are physically prevented from doing. In a few cases (tetraplegia in an active sportsman without any other interests) this desire to die is understandable, particularly if it is not due to a passing depression but continues for months or even years. That situation, which is in fact rare (other patients suffering from tetraplegia lead a mentally active life and express no desire to die), certainly calls for discussion in depth by specialists. But it would doubtless be very difficult to legislate for this death wish, particularly in borderline cases. In no circumstances should a doctor be required by law to kill such patients.

7 Legislation of passive euthanasia

7.1 Introduction of the notion of euthanasia into criminal law

Most medical associations and also most professors of criminal law agree that the criminal law in its present form is adequate to deal properly with any criminal charges laid against doctors. The outcome of the sensational euthanasia trials in recent years seems to confirm this point of view. A flexible interpretation of the law to meet the individual situation involved seems sufficient.

Rigid definitions with regard to euthanasia are scarcely possible and are also pointless. The doctor is always treating an individual and his decisions must take account of a large number of factors related to his patient's case history and whole past life. Definitions can be applied only to groups.

7.2 Legal protection for the doctor against inappropriate criminal charges

Doctors and experts in criminal law both regard legal protection for the doctor as urgently necessary.

It should be possible to provide such protection by means of accepted definitions of the doctor's professional duty and of cerebral death. It is for lawyers and legislative authorities to decide whether it is necessary for such definitions to be given a special place in criminal law.

8 Summary

Present-day problems of euthanasia relate mainly to patients whose personalities are irretrievably lost and who are being kept 'alive' artificially, or prevented from dying, with the help of the latest medical and technological aids. These problems have been created by medicine itself.

Objective discussion of euthanasia is possible only if all the professions involved use the same language, i.e. interpret the same words in the same way. This calls for new and clear definitions of the doctor's professional duty and of human death.

Any new definition of the doctor's professional duty should be primarily concerned with his motivation for his professional actions.

The definition of brain death which is currently accepted is correct but too narrow, since it was arrived at solely in connection with donors used in transplant operations. It is confined to patients in intensive care units whose brains have died and who have ceased to breathe spontaneously.

At the present time there is no accepted definition of cerebrally dead patients with retained spontaneous respiration where the personality has died although biological death lags behind. The word euthanasia has given rise to an appalling confusion of ideas. It would be better to abandon the word completely and replace it by some new terms.

It may perhaps not be necessary to give a legal definition of passive euthanasia and make it lawful, provided the doctor's professional duty and human death are clearly defined. A legal definition of the doctor's professional duty should make legal protection for the doctor posssible.

The doctor and nursing staff should be consulted in any discussion of euthanasia and in the establishment of new definitions because of their experience at the sickbed. Their experienced reality should be compared impartially with the cognitive reality of theologians, social moralists, lawyers, politicians and other professions. It is also important to take public opinion into account.

All discussion and any new definitions and conclusions resulting from it should satisfy two simple criteria:
a. Common sense
b. The humanitarian principle.

A CASE FOR EUTHANASIA

C. F. Barnard

Some time ago I was in New York and had a very hectic schedule. I had had a very late night — the next morning I was due to appear on the early morning show, a television show, and I was very late. I rushed out of the hotel, got into a taxi and said to the taxi driver: 'Please hurry up, I have *got* to get to C.B.S. by eight o'clock'. He turned round to me and said, 'Mister, there are only two things you have got to do. You have got to pay your tax and one day you have got to die', and I realized then that in his simple way he spoke a great truth, because if you think about it, death is really life's only certainty. It is the sole indisputable fact of life.

In fact, it is difficult to define life without using the term death, because what is life really? It is that interval between birth and death. So you can understand that without life there can be no death and without death there can be no life, just as without darkness there can be no light, just as without cold there can be no warmth.

If one looks at the problem in a different way, then one recognizes that from the time of conception in the womb, we have a pre-destined life — that diminishes with each moment that passes. In fact, I think we can say now that we are all living, but it is as correct to say that at the moment we are all dying. It is this indisputable truth that makes death the most awesome of all events to be surveyed by the mind.

As a result of this inevitable end to life, I think we all try, during our travels over this earth, to live it up, to have a good life; that is why we say, 'Let us drink and be merry, for tomorrow we die.' We all aim to have a good life but, as I have just said, death is so much a part of life, is it not also important to have a good death? As we are so set in our endeavours to live well, and as life and death are so closely related, surely it is also important for us to have a good death. It is the right of every human being to have a good death. And that is what euthanasia really is.

The word euthanasia comes from the two Greek words *eu* which means good, and *thanatos* which means death, and that is

197

why I am so opposed to talking about mercy killing. It is not mercy killing that we are trying to achieve. We are trying to see that a patient has a good life and progresses to the end of life by having a good death.

I have talked about life, I have talked about death, I have talked about living and I have talked about dying, and I think it is very important that, before we go any further, we clearly define what we mean by these words.

Let us start with the inevitable: death and dying. What do we mean by death? Now it interests me that until I did the first transplant I thought that doctors knew when a patient was dead. I thought that doctors had the capability and they could be trusted to diagnose the moment of death; but as soon as we did the first heart transplant, there were numerous discussions and hundreds and thousands of words have been written about what we mean by death, and how we can define the moment of death, and having listened to all these learned discussions and read all these hundreds of thousands of words, I come to the same conclusions and I have the same idea that I had before I did the first transplant. Do you know when a patient is dead? A patient is dead when the doctor says he is dead. That is the moment of death.

What happens in a hospital today? Let us say, for example, that a man is knocked down by a motorcar in the street. He is picked up in an ambulance and taken to hospital; the ambulance driver thinks that the man is dead, so what does he do? He goes to the hospital and says to the doctor, 'Doctor, I think that this man is dead on arrival'. The doctor opens the ambulance and looks at the man and says, 'You are right, this man is dead' — and after the doctor says that that man is dead, he is dead. There is no question about it: I think that from a legal point of view, from a medical point of view and from the point of view of the layman, that that is the moment of death — when the doctor certifies that a particular patient is dead.

Now you will immediately ask: 'Well, when does the doctor say that that patient is dead? When does he actually feel that patient is dying?' I think it is very important to recognize that death, the diagnosis of death, of the moment of death, is exactly like the diagnosis of pneumonia or acute appendicitis or an acute gall bladder attack. It is a clinical impression. There is no real way to define it; it is a clinical impression and therefore, the moment of death, the diagnosis of the moment of death, depends on the presence of certain symptoms and signs, and we never diagnose the moment of death on a single symptom or a single sign. I am quite sure you would think him a very stupid doctor, who, when you go to see him and you only cough, says you have got pneumonia. He would never diagnose pneumonia solely on one symptom. It is by a whole groups of symptoms and signs which by experience the doctor knows are associated with the clinical condition of pneumonia that he can diagnose the condition.

So, in exactly the same way, death is diagnosed on a certain group of symptoms and signs that are present. So often during my discussions I hear the audience say, when we talk about the moment of death: 'Well, we are not quite sure that you can determine the moment of death, because we know of a patient who has been comatose for six months and after that the patient recovered'; or a patient has had a flat EEG (electro-encephalogram) and even though the flat electro-encephalogram was present the patient recovered. To repeat: we never diagnose the moment of death because a coma is present; we never diagnose the moment of death because there is a flat EEG; it is a whole group of symptoms and signs which we put together and this gives a clinical impression, or the clinical diagnosis, of death.

For hundreds of years the age-old dictum of the English Common Law has been followed, that life does not end until the heart stops beating, until respiration ceases. This we have used for a long time. Now we know that this concept is completely erroneous and that the cessation of the heart beat, and the cessation of respiration, do not mean death, nor does the presence of a heart beat and the continuation of respiration mean that the patient is still alive.

Let me give you an example to prove this point. I recently operated on a man in whom I replaced one of the valves inside the heart. During the period when I was working inside the heart, there was no heat beat; if you had felt for the pulse, there would have been none — the patient was not breathing at all; there was no respiratory effort. Yet, I hope, the patient is alive tonight. Here is a man who had an absence of respiration, and an absence of cardiac activity, and yet this man remains alive. Why is this man alive? It is because during the period that his heart was not beating and he was not breathing, I was keeping his brain alive by using the heart-lung machine, by which means I supplied oxygenated blood to his brain. This is the example of a man with no heart beat, with an absence of respiration and who is alive tonight.

So we know that this can happen, that the age-old symptoms and signs that we followed to diagnose the moment of death are incorrect. You can also have the reverse. You can have a man whose heart is beating and who is breathing, but who is not alive. If you think about the various ways people can die, you will find that the cessation of respiration and the cessation of the heart beat can precede death, or can actually follow death. In most cases, the absence of respiration and the absence of a heart beat are the consequence of death — it is not the moment of death.

Let me give you a few more examples. Let us take the case of a man who has a severe brain injury. As a result of this severe brain injury, his brain is irreparably damaged and the brain has died. What happens next? The brain died, and because the brain died, the patient stopped breathing, because the brain tells the body to breathe; so when the brain dies, respiration stops. As a result of the cessation of respiration, no oxygen enters the blood and as a result of this, the various organs die because they cannot live without blood. One of the first organs that dies after breathing stops, or rather does not die, but stops beating, is the heart.

So you see, in this case, brain death started and the cessation of respiration and the cessation of the heart beat followed brain death.

Let us take the reverse. A man is electrocuted. Often, as a result of electrocution, the heart stops beating. In this case the heart beat stops first and often the patient stops breathing as a result of electrocution. For three minutes that brain is still alive. At that stage (when the heart stops beating and the man stops breathing) he is not yet dead. He only dies three minutes later when his brain dies, resulting from the lack of oxygen to this organ. So you see, it is completely incorrect to say that one can only diagnose death when there is an absence of respiration or an absence of heart beat because, as I have pointed out, the cessation of these two events may precede death or may follow death.

In the case of heart transplantation, the question has often been asked: 'How is it possible for you to remove the heart from a man who is dead and transplant this into another individual and get that heart to start again; surely you have murdered this individual by taking out a heart that is still alive, and why did you not restart the heart in the donor and bring him back to life?'

Those are the arguments being put forward merely because these people do not realize what death really is. I think it is important to look at death in this way (or to look at the brain and brain death in this way), that the brain is the only organ that determines the quality of life; no other organ in the body determines the quality of life, and therefore, once the brain dies there is no further purpose to that life because it can never have any quality again and therefore the need and function of the other organs cease. In other words, the heart, the liver, the kidneys and the lungs are there for one purpose only and that is to keep the brain alive. That is their only function, and when the brain stops functioning, the brain dies; there is no need for those organs any more. It is interesting to note that it is usually the brain that dies first.

The brain is the organ that dies first because, even when the heart stops beating, the heart is not dead; the heart continues to live, but the brain dies three minutes or four minutes later. So the brain is the first organ to die and then after that the other organs die. Let us take the example of a patient who has a severe brain injury. When there is a severe brain injury, then the patient stops breathing. When the patient stops breathing as a result of the lack of oxygen in the blood, the various organs die afterwards. It is interesting to note that the various organs die at various periods and not at the same time. So actually, the total death of the body is by degrees — this continues over many hours. In fact, the heart is probably still alive and can function well two to three hours after the brain has died.

We have had cases recently in the experimental laboratory in which we have transplanted a heart six hours after brain death. We have restarted that same heart again in the body of an experimental animal and have got that animal to live with that heart, six hours after it had been removed from a body that has had a brain death.

The liver probably dies about a half to a full hour earlier than the heart. The skeletal muscles die about six hours later, and the various other organs die even later than the skeletal muscles. So I think this is what we must get quite clear when we talk about death, and that is that the moment of death, there is no doubt about it, is when the brain dies.

I think that if there is a seat of the soul anywhere in the body, it is not in the heart. It will be in the brain because, as I have said, that is the only organ in the body that determines the quality of life; the other organs are there for one reason only and that is to keep the brain alive.

Now let us go from death to life and living; here it is perhaps a little bit more difficult for me to define the terms, life and living. I believe that human life starts with conception. You may disagree with me because immediately you would see that by making this definition, I am totally against abortions at will, because I believe with every abortion a human life is destroyed; nor does it matter when it occurs, whether an hour later, or six weeks later, or three or four months later. Why does life start with conception, you may ask. As soon as the sperm of the male enters the ovum of the female, all the ingredients are present in that fusion for that individual to become alive, because by that fusion all the genetic information to form a living human being is present. The potentials are there, and therefore if you destroy the result of conception, you must destroy a potential human being. What worries me so much about 'abortions on request', is that at that moment, because life is so uncertain, we do not know what we are destroying.

Beethoven may have been aborted if his parents were living to-day. So too may Einstein have been aborted, and therefore, because of this uncertainty, because we do not know what we are destroying after conception takes place, I can never agree with the idea of abortion.

It is interesting that when somebody so mad as to attack a famous masterpiece like the *Nacht Wacht* in Amsterdam or the *Mona Lisa*, actually does so, then everybody is angered and says: 'Now, this stupid idiot, how can he destroy such a masterpiece? It is a fantastic masterpiece, look what he has destroyed.' But when the doctor puts his curette into the uterus and scrapes out the results of conception, he too destroys another masterpiece and nobody worries about it. Nobody cares about it, although the fusion of the ovum and the sperm is another masterpiece, and what is more, it is as unique a masterpiece as the *Nact Wacht* or the *Mona Lisa*, because no two individuals are the same.

When I talk about being able to become alive, I do not mean by simply exhibiting a few vital signs such as respiration or a heart beat. I mean rather that whole conglomeration of sensual experiences that we call 'being alive'. These experiences, by their very complexity and subtlety are unable to be measured or analyzed statistically, but usually they are known to that individual.

He knows what he means by being alive. It is often known to the loved one what is meant by being alive, and it is often known to the doctor.

So that is what I mean by life and by being alive. Life occurs at conception and by being alive we mean that that person has reached the stage where he can experience and he can enjoy those experiences which he associates with being alive.

No, I have defined death, I have defined life and I have defined living, but I have not yet defined dying. What do I mean by dying? By dying I mean that gradual irreversible deterioration in the quality of life which eventually leads to the death of the brain. So I think we now clearly understand what we mean by these various terms.

If you look at life in the way that I have just described, then I think you will all agree with me that life, being alive, can stop long before the heart stops beating and before respiration stops. It can stop when the liver is still metabolizing. I think we all as doctors, and I am quite sure you as laymen, have seen life become unenjoyable, intolerable, long before the heart stops beating and before respiration ceases. It is also important to note that intolerance does not only come to the patient when he feels, 'Life has become intolerable, I cannot stand it any more'. It also comes to the relatives of those patients and to the people who love him. So when we talk about the end of life, we must not only consider the patient, but we must also consider the people who love him and the people who stand around and watch his suffering, because often he is not in a state anymore to recognize that suffering.

If we look at life in this way and we feel that life must only continue while it is enjoyable, while that patient is alive, why should modern medicine try to prolong the process of life when it cannot be enjoyed any more? In fact, we are not prolonging the process of life; in this way we are actually prolonging death.

What clock that can tick but cannot tell the time is preserved and cherished, often at prohibitive financial and emotional cost? What vegetable is given the best of modern medicine and technology, often to keep it for a few more days from rotting? In plain truth, the effectiveness of medical technology has outstripped the quality of the professional conscience that guides it. I think that it is very important to realize this about our medical technology. I can give you many examples where it has been clearly shown that people are kept alive for no other reason but this, not to try to alleviate their suffering, but for reasons that are often unknown to me.

I want to quote to you what Lord Richard Calder said in 1971 at the Annual Health Conference in New York, at the New York Academy of Medicine. 'Medical science has produced an ethical crisis which transcends our conventional ideas of good and evil.'

I think that is a very serious accusation to make about medical science. I can asure you — I speak for myself too — that doctors often apply these herioc treatments for incurable diseases in order to feed their own egos. At medical school and during our practice of medicine, we have been taught to consider ourselves as champions chosen for the sole purpose of preserving life, or rather of preventing death — not to treat the patient and the suffering of the patient — all we must do is prevent death. Insidiously the promotion of this image becomes so sacred that when the death occurs, the doctor feels a sense of guilt and defeat. So, the treatment of this patient is actually due to a selfish attitude on the part of the docor. He does not preserve life because he feels he is helping the patient in this way, but does it mainly to show that he is a good doctor, that he is a better doctor than the next doctor if he can keep the patient alive.

I must honestly admit that I, too, have often stood at a patient's bedside and tried my best to keep the patient alive, I have shouted at the doctors and the nurses working with me, and have made things totally unpleasant for everybody. When I sit down calmly and think about it, what has motivated these actions? I can come to only one conclusion, and that is that if this patient dies my records are spoiled. My mortality rate would be higher if the patient were to die. Now sometimes that may be good, but often it is bad, because all we are doing is continuing the suffering of the patient. I think it is important to realize that the duty of a doctor is not to prolong life; it is only to alleviate suffering, and if by alleviating suffering he prolongs a life as well, he must consider that as a *pasella,* an extra. It is not something for which he is striving; this is not what his goal in life must be. His goal must only be to alleviate the suffering of his patient.

Surely, in his medical practice and in his endeavours the doctor tries to give the patient a good life, an enjoyable life. He takes

204

out the appendix of the patient because acute appendicitis gives pain and vomiting and a temperature, which do not make life very pleasant. So all his treatment is aimed at improving the quality of life. When this is not possible any more, surely the doctor should ensure that his patient has a good death, because death is the certainty of life and, therefore, if his aim is to improve the quality of life, then he must also make certain that the end of life will be without suffering as well.

But what do you find in today's hospitals? There are many intensive care units and doctors standing by with bleepers in their pockets. Whenever a heart stops, there is an emergency call — we call it crash card, call 99, or blue call — and the whole team of doctors is generated into action, supported and backed by a team of technicians. They share one responsibility and that is to control the patient's destiny, because they can allow that heart to restart or to die.

Now that is good, and I agree with it, but what I find disturbing is that the whole team is run without a particle of human consideration. They think only about keeping the patient alive and never think about the consequences of restarting that heart. These intensive care units often lead to some therapeutic endeavours, some financial commitments which can only be described as more heroic than humane.

I want to tell you a story which illustrates this very clearly. It is a story about an old man by the name of Eliah Kahn. At seventy-eight years old he was admitted to a hospital with abdominal pain and vomiting. Having investigated him and taken X-rays, it was quite clear that the patient was suffering from an obstruction of the small bowel. He was a thin, frail man with a weathered face, but had beautifully bright eyes and, as the doctors entered his room, his eyes were fixed on the patient next to him. This man had had an abdominal operation for cancer of the large bowel, and the operation had not gone very well. He now lay there entwined and entangled in drains and tubes, all of which Eliah Kahn was watching.

The doctor introduced himself and Kahn wrenched his gaze away from the man next to him and said to the doctor, 'Doctor, I am dying, I know it, I am dying'. To which the doctor replied, 'Don't be silly'. He said, 'What is silly about dying?' and the doctor replied, 'Nothing, there is nothing silly about dying; but you must remember you are now in the University Hospital and we have got all the modern equipment, we have the latest technology and we simply do not allow patients to die just like that.'

Kahn said to him, 'Doctor, my time must come, I know it.' The doctor said, 'You know, in this University, we measure time differently.' And he said to the doctor, 'You know nothing about time. Wait until you are seventy-eight years old, tired and alone and you have a pain in your belly — then you will know what time is.' And the doctor realized that there was no need to argue with this old man. He had clear ideas about life and death.

On physical examination she realized that he was very ill. He had an erratic pulse beat and a wet lung, his abdomen was distended, his prostrate was enlarged, and he also had severe arthritis. When the examination was over, Kahn said to her, 'You see, doctor, the engine has broken down; it is time for the engineer to abandon it'.

The staff met and discussed the case of Eliah Khan; they suggested that they should decompress the bowel and then do an operation to try to relieve the obstruction in the large bowel. So the doctor came to pass the tube down the nose into Eliah Kahn's stomach. The doctor said, 'We must pass this tube down to decompress the stomach. You have got to get a tube down, like that man there', pointing to the other man who had had his bowel resected and who was now covered with tubes. So the doctor said it was not the same, 'because your tube will only be in for a short time, because then we are going to help you'. So Kahn said to her, 'Doctor, look, you can pass this tube, but I want to ask you one thing. I do not want to die looking like that man. I have been a dignified man in my life; I have never been rich, but I have put my sons through the university, and I have kept my head up high and lived with dignity, and that is the way I want my children to remember me. I do not want to die like that man there with tubes and catheters sticking out everywhere. I am dying now, I am not complaining. But I want you to realize that I do not want to be a vegetable that somebody comes along and waters every now and then. I do not want to be like that man there.'

Anyway, they put the tube down and then the doctor left Kahn. Later on he began to dehydrate because he was not taking in anything and everything was being sucked from his stomach. So the doctor came along and said that it was now necessary to put up an intravenous drip to give the patient fluids. Kahn again objected to this and said he did not want it, but only wanted to die in peace. All he wanted the doctor to do was to make him comfortable, to realize that the end of life had come; but the doctor persuaded him to have the intravenous fluids, and so they put up the drip. Now he had a tube through his nose sucking out the gastric contents and he had a drip in his arm to supply him with fluids.

The next morning the doctor heard there was a call for an emergency — the so-called crash card call — and she rushed to the hospital to find that the patient next to Kahn had had a cardiac arrest — his heart has stopped beating.

The whole team that deals with cardiac arrest was called into action and all were on top of this man. He was naked, lying in a pool of his excretions; some doctor was blowing air into his mouth, another was trying to set a drip up through his vein, yet another was pounding his chest to get his heart beating; fortunately they did not succeed, and eventually the man next to Kahn died.

During all this, Kahn was watching and saw what was happening. When everything was over, he called the doctor and said, 'Doctor, just one minute. I want to ask you one thing. You must promise me one thing, and that is that you will not do that to me. Do not allow that ever to happen to me.' He was absolutely serious about this request, pleading with the doctor never to treat him the way he had just seen the patient next door to him treated; and the doctor promised to do as he asked. After speaking to Kahn the doctor said, 'Look, we must get a post-mortem on the dead man. Please keep the X-rays for the conference. Do not lose his electrocardiogram; I thought I said to put him on anticoagulants, he probably had a pulmonary embolus.'

On the Thursday, Kahn went into congestive cardiac failure, and was having great difficulty in breathing. Swiftly the cardiac failure team swung into action again. They gave him morphine, oxygen, intermittent positive pressure respiration, digitalis and diuretics and eventually decided that as he still had difficulty in breathing they must now put a tube down his windpipe to breathe for him — they must put him on a respirator.

When the anaesthetist came along to put in this tube, Kahn was gasping and he could hardly speak; all he could say was, 'You promised, doctor'. Anyway, they put the tube down and put him on the respirator. He just lay back and stared in a different direction. They attached him to a monitor and a ventilator, and put up the drips, and there he was, lying with the monitor ticking away, the ventilator swooshing away, and the stirring movement of the intragastric suction.

He looked an old frail man then, although he got very adequate medical treatment. Now he was left, having been treated as the doctors thought he should be treated. The doctors thought it was their duty to do what ever they could do for this man. During the night Eliah Kahn woke up and managed to reach across and switch off his ventilator. The nurse came several hours later, and called the doctor to diagnose death, because when she had arrived there had been no rush of air through the ventilator, the monitor was not tracing the heart beat, the suction machine was shut off, and when she shone the light into his eyes she saw big, dilated pupils. Next to his bed she had noticed a note scribbled in Kahn's uneven handwriting. This is what it said: 'Death is not the enemy, Doctor, inhumanity is.'

What role can society play in preventing this inhumanity that occurs every day in big hospitals where patients are treated, not to alleviate their suffering, but because doctors want to prove that they can master death, which they cannot do, because death is a part of life?

I think that society can ask for three things: firstly, that doctors should be humanitarians and not only scientists; secondly, that life-supporting measures and all modern medical technology should not be used where there is no hope for the patient any more and, thirdly, that if the patient is suffering from severe pain, medicine should be given to alleviate pain, even to the extent where this can shorten life.

This is what passive euthanasia will allow the doctor to do, and that is why I plead that we should have total support in this country for passive euthanasia, because all it allows the medical staff to do, is to give the patient a comfortable, dignified death. That is all. We are not trying to kill the patient, we are only allowing him to die in comfort and with dignity.

The age-old argument will immediately come forward, that by doing this we are 'playing God', because only God has the right to decide the end of life. But I want to ask this: have we not perverted the Christian tradition into the belief that biological existence *per se* is of supreme value, and on the basis of that interpretation, have we not been side-tracked into an ethical dilemma of ghastly proportions, in that we believe that a biological existence is life and that it is of supreme importance to have just a vegetable lying there? We believe that it is Christian to preserve that sort of existence and as a result of that we have landed ourselves in a tremendous mess.

Is it not more Christian and more godly or, in a way of God, to allow Nature to take its course in those cases? Because that is really the only thing we are going to do with passive euthanasia. We are merely allowing Nature to take its course; we are not going to interfere with that particular illness and the progress of that illness.

Now let us see how religion views this attitude, if we accept passive euthanasia. One would expect that those most opposed to any sort of hastening death would be the orthodox Jews. I have met the Rabbi Immanuel Jacobowitz, and have read his book on Jewish medical ethics, which he wrote in 1959. The orthodox Jewish view accepts the legality of expediting the death of an incurably ill patient in acute agony, by withholding from him such medicaments as would sustain his continued life by unnatural means. So you see that in the orthodox Jewish teaching there is nothing against passive euthanasia. It agrees that no special treatment and special medicine should be used to continue a life by unnatural means when there is no future for that particular life.

The Roman Catholic view has been clearly stated by Pope Pius XII in a series of addresses in 1950, in which he clarified the Roman Catholic view on many questions regarding medical ethics. He pointed out that there was no absolute obligation on the physician to employ extraordinary means to preserve life; he defined extraordinary means as those means which cannot be used or obtained without undue expense, pain, or other inconvenience, and with often no reasonable hope of providing benefit.

I have not yet seen a really authoritative Prostestant statement, but from what I have heard and read, I feel that even the Protestants would also agree with this idea: that life should not simply be preserved because it is medically feasible to do so. It is interesting, when you read the views of the various churches, that one has the impression that they are more willing to accept the aims of euthanasia than the medical profession is, and that it is more in keeping with religious teaching than it is with medical teaching, to practise this form of treatment of terminally ill patients. The supreme value in our religious heritage is placed on the personhood of man, the person in his wholeness, the person in his freedom, the person in his integrity and in his

209

dignity. When any illness brings a person to a state in which he is less than a free person, less than one with dignity and integrity, then what is most valuable and precious, is gone, and we may well feel that his mere continuation by machine or drug is a violation of him as a person. I think it is very important to realize this.

There are various attitudes that doctors can take to terminally ill patients. For example, there is a doctor who says, 'No, I am not going to stop treatment, I am going to do everything to continue and I will treat this patient to continue his suffering or to continue his life.' This is the way the doctor feels about it, and therefore he keeps on with the treatment. He is completely one hundred per cent anti-euthanasia.

Then there is the doctor who has the qualified 'no' and that means that he will not continue. He will continue with ordinary treatment, but he will abolish extraordinary treatment. For example, the case of a child suffering from a condition in which there is a lack of immunity, that is, a child who cannot live in an environment full of germs. That child's doctor will say, 'I will not put him in a germ-free environment, I will allow him to live in an ordinary environment, because the germ-free environment will be an extraordinary means of keeping him alive,' and he will therefore say 'no' only in those circumstances.

Then there is the third attitude, that of the doctor who declines to start treatment, for example, in a patient who has terminal cancer, who is admitted to hospital with pneumonia. Acute pneumonia can be treated by antibiotics, but the doctor says, 'I will not give antibiotics to this patient; I will refuse to start treatment, and allow the pneumonia to end the patient's life because he is already suffering from incurable cancer'.

There is yet another attitude, a fourth one, and that is that the patient's treatment will only be stopped when the patient consents to have the treatment stopped. For example, the patient who has had both his kidneys removed, or has a kidney disease and is on an artificial kidney to continue life. If the patient says, 'Doctor, I want you to stop the kidney treatment. I do not want to be on an artificial kidney any more', in other words, if the patient asks his doctor to stop the treatment, the doctor will agree to do so.

Then there is the doctor who would stop treatment without consent. For example, a patient who has had a gastrectomy for carcinoma of the stomach; this is followed by a pulmonary embolus, by cardiac arrest, several bouts of resuscitation and eventually the patient's heart stops again and without consent, the doctor says, 'I am not continuing treatment; I am going to stop treating the patient'.

The sixth way concerns the patient who has an incurable disease about which the doctor feels so strongly that he leaves an overdose of a drug with the patient, explaining that if he uses that dose of the drug, he will die.

Then there is the doctor who will agree to terminate the patient's life with prior consent from the patient, i.e. when the patients says to the doctor, 'I want you to end my life, I have cancer, I know I am going to die and I do not want to go on with this. Please give me an overdose of drugs and allow me to die'. Lastly, at the other end of the scale, is the doctor who will end the patient's life actively without prior consent.

Now those are the various attitudes and the various approaches doctors may have to terminal disease. If you consider these, the first one is negative, of course, so that one is not included; but if you look at the other seven, then I think one can clearly divide them into the following: termination of life where the doctor plays only a passive role and termination of life where the doctor plays an active role, in terminating the patient's life. It is very important in my opinion to clarify what we call passive euthanasia, for example deciding not to treat a patient with a terminal disease or deciding to discontinue his recent treatment, because he is dying. In active euthanasia the doctor actually gives the patient a drug, either with or without his consent.

We should distinguish between these two, because in active euthanasia there is a deliberate act by the doctor in taking a human life. Although I feel, even though he feels that society and that particular patient will benefit from this act, and although I fully understand the humanitarian goals of those who support active euthanasia, I do not believe that this can be practised until such time as the necessary safeguards have been developed so that active euthanasia cannot be misused. Therefore, I am in favour of not starting or continuing useless treatment, but I am not in favour of actively taking a patient's life. It is interesting to note that active euthanasia is not a necessary adjunct to the physician in his attempts to alleviate the suffering of the majority of dying patients; it is not necessary for him, if his aim is to alleviate suffering, to actively take that patient's life, because he can use enough drugs, as I have said, to make that patient comfortable, even if the continuation of those drugs may eventually lead to the death of that patient.

I think it is important for us to distinguish clearly between these two, since active euthanasia is repugnant to many. Actively taking a life is against everybody's feelings, and in this country it is illegal; thus there is often confusion amongst physicians and amongst the lay public about euthanasia. That is why I do not like the idea of talking about it as *genadedood* or mercy killing. It is not a *genadedood* and we are not killing the patient. I think we must distinguish between the two, because if we do not, then we shall always have opposition to passive euthanasia, although there is no doubt that passive euthanasia plays an important part in the goal of the doctor to alleviate human suffering. As I have said, that is really what he is there for — not to prolong life, but to alleviate suffering.

the benefit of the present generation and are entitled to enjoy it;

d. persons suffering from incurable diseases;
e. low-grade mental defectives. The parents of defective children cling to them, even to the detriment of the healthy children. This is most probably due to a feeling of guilt. Few parents with such a child will willingly accede to euthanasia;
f. cases fully dependent for a long period for continuation of life on some device or other. A person with a pace-maker or a baby in an incubator, as cases of a similar nature are, of course, excluded.

3 Voluntary or involuntary euthanasia

It is imperative that a decision should be reached whether euthanasia should be voluntary or involuntary.

3.1 *Voluntary*

For a request to be voluntary implies that the individual is completely *compos mentis* and that the implications are understood. The reasons for the request may vary:

a. Unbearable pain. Many of the painful conditions can, however, be controlled in one way or another.
b. Incurable and fulminating disease leading to a morbid depression. Most depressive states are amenable to treatment.
c. The person does not want to be a burden to relatives or the community. This can also be a form of depression.
d. Incapacity.
e. Unsavoury odour as a result of the disease.
f. Inability to bear the changes in appearance and of becoming ugly.
g. A morbid state of depression. In most of these states the patient can usually be treated with good results.
h. Pressure applied by relatives.

It has been shown that most of the above can be overcome in one way or another.

3.2 *Involuntary*

In this respect the following questions will have to be answered:

a. Who should decide that this is a case for euthanasia? The doctor would be the most suitable person because he has the specialized knowledge about prognosis and other circumstances. He has been trained to carry responsibility and to act for the benefit of both the patient and, where necessary,

of the community.
b. The relatives? We may here be on very dangerous ground because they may have ulterior motives as, for instance, an inheritance or the nuisance value of the patient. There should, however, be no reason for ignoring a request from relatives.
c. The State or some specially constituted body?

4 Who is to decide that a case is suitable for euthanasia?

a. A Judge in Chambers?
b. A tribunal:
  (i) with a Judge presiding?
  (ii) with the family doctor as a member?
  (iii) with a family member of the person concerned?
To bring in a member of the family may lead to a lot of unpleasantness. This person's conscience may trouble him with a guilt feeling at a later stage. He may be reproached by the other members of the family. It is not always easy to exclude personal gain which may not necessarily be of a material nature.
  (iv) A person unconnected with any of the above?
c. Two or more doctors, one being the doctor in charge of the case and the other one an independent doctor and not in partnership with the first?
Medical men have been trained to sustain life, to make decisions and carry responsibility. I can assure you that when a doctor commits euthanasia it is only after a lot of consideration. It would be as easy to turn off a machine as to give an overdose to an incurable cancerous patient, but before he does that he has to over-rule his training and come to terms with his own conscience.
Euthanasia has been practised for thousands of years by doctors and I do not think it has ever got out of hand; but once it has become legalized the doctor may feel that he has *carte blanche,* and the weighing up will not play such an important part as would have been the case otherwise. The doctor may now feel that he has become a legalized executioner.
Every doctor who has been in practice for some years can give many instances where he has been called out to see an elderly, debilitated, demented person *in extremis,* just to ease the relatives' conscience and to obtain a death certificate. The doctor knows full well that the relatives have neglected the patient, hoping that he will die and that, if he was not called, the patient would have

218

Psychiatric, Psychological and Nursing Aspects of Euthanasia

EUTHANASIA AND THE PSYCHIATRIST

A. V. Opperman

In this paper I present my personal views on this problem.

1 Introduction

In a discussion on euthanasia it is important to clarify two difficult problems concerning the concepts 'life' and 'death'.

When does human life commence? Is it when the spermatozoon enters the ovum, at the time of the first cell mitosis, or when the foetus can continue living after having become physically separated from the body of the mother?

The most scientific view would be to accept the instant of the first mitosis as the commencement of life. At this stage, however, in spite of the correct number of chromosomes and genes, the embryo can hardly be regarded as human. According to the Talmud the embryo reaches ensoulment only 40 days after fertilization.

The most practical view would be to accept the instant of commencement of life as the moment when the child can continue to live independently, i.e. after having undergone physical separation from the body of the mother.

Where does the premature child fit in?

In practice the incubator has taken over part of the *in utero* function for which the mother was responsible before the child's birth.

When does life come to an end, i.e. when does death occur? Does death occur with cessation of one or more of the vital functions, like breathing and the heartbeat? If one or the other of these two stops first, which one can be accepted as indicative of death? I do not think that any doctor has ever told the relatives that a patient has passed away before both the breathing as well as the heart has stopped beating, in spite of knowing in his own mind that all is over.

The brain tissues are extremely susceptible to oxygen deprivation; therefore it is logical that a patient is dead when the heart beat and the breathing have stopped, and that there is an absence of all brain waves on the electro-encephalogram.

We are dealing with two extremes: being physically alive or physically dead. To be physically alive is a very relative concept with a great variety of possible gradations. Being alive consists of far more than breathing, eating, excreting and functioning of the brain. The same applies in both the objective as well as the subjective sense to being healthy and being ill; being useful and being of no use to the community; being wanted and being unwanted.

There are three ways in which life comes to an end:

a. natural causes;
b. murder;
c. suicide.

The killing of another human being, no matter how it is looked upon and no matter what the circumstances are, is still murder and the State must take cognizance thereof, otherwise chaos would result.

It is right that in practice the circumstances of the killing should be considered, whether a pure accident, in self-defence or other mitigating circumstances. War can be accepted as self-defence.

The old concept of 'self-preservation is the highest law in nature' still holds true. (Self-preservation includes the preservation of the species.)

A person whose request for euthanasia is acceded to, commits suicide and the person who implements the request, commits murder. The question arises whether a person who commits suicide can be looked upon as having been in full possession of all his normal mental facilities.

2 What norms are to be used and which cases will be considered for euthanasia?

The obvious norms and type of case for consideration for euthanasia would be individuals who are physically and/or mentally incapacitated to such an extent that they are a burden to society and/or themselves. Furthermore, they must be incurable in terms of our present knowledge.

The following types of cases come to mind:

a. senile psychotics;
b. chronic deteriorated psychotics;
c. the elderly useless. The argument that there is a world shortage of food and that therefore euthanasia should be used to decimate the number of the 'elderly-useless' does not hold because these people, in their prime, made a contribution to

lingered on for a few days longer. Can he be blamed if he asks himself why they bothered to call him and that they would most likely not have called him if it was not a case of obtaining a death certificate?

As a psychiatrist I am consulted to decide whether a patient would be a fit case for, for example, a kidney transplant, and if I find the patient unsuited, then I feel that I have passed the death sentence on that patient.

Many psychiatrists are upset by legalized abortion and they find it extremely difficult to recommend whether or not a pregnancy should be terminated. It is felt that, amongst other things, the unborn child's future in the community should also receive consideration.

d. A standing committee appointed by the State or Medical Council?

e. By testament? The idea has been expressed that a person should be able to make a will early in his/her life to the effect that he/she would wish euthanasia in particular circumstances. This type of will is illegal in this country and who is going to execute it?

5 The person carrying out euthanasia

It is well and good to have a case fit for euthanasia on your hands, but who is going to be responsible for its implementation:

a. The patient himself by giving him the opportunity of obtaining and taking the substance to carry out euthanasia?

b. The doctor in charge of the case, by giving a lethal dose or stopping or removing a life-continuing device?

c. Somebody appointed by the State or the Medical Council? This would be too much like an official executioner.

d. A relative? This would be foolish in view of the interfamilial developments which may follow, as already mentioned.

6 Who should know?

a. Should it be reported to the State, the Medical Council or some special body? The old professions, of which medicine is one, have always tried to keep their own house in order and are therefore not happy with too much State interference in affairs which they look upon as being their province. They feel that their ethical code, much of which is unwritten, should be sufficient.

The State, however, as with most housekeepers, wants to have everything orderly and legalized. This is understandable because an important function of the State is to look after the common good.

Laws are still necessary for the exception to the rule for those who do not conform.

b. Should the relatives be told? In all fairness to everybody concerned and to minimize after-effects, it is felt that the fewer people who know, the better. The relatives should therefore be left in the dark even if they have requested euthanasia.

7 Recommendations

I recommend that the principle of euthanasia be accepted; that the type of case as well as the norms for consideration should be well defined; that two doctors, who are not in partnership and at least one of whom has been qualified for more than five years, should be sufficient to decide and implement euthanasia; that every case of euthanasia should be reported to a specially constituted body, preferably a standing committee of the Medical Council; that secrecy, even when euthanasia had been requested by relatives, must enjoy the highest priority.

PSYCHIATRY AND EUTHANASIA

M. S. Paterson

In recent months both medical and lay publications have contained articles about modern attitudes to death, a subject which some maintain has replaced sex as the most unmentionable taboo. One hears too the words 'Death with dignity' repeated more and more frequently as people express their feelings of revulsion against extraordinary methods of prolonging life such as in intensive care units, where a person lies naked and lonely with tubes in almost every orifice of the body. Cases like that of Karen Ann Quinlan in America cause not only doctors but the man in the street to pause and to consider the quality of life as opposed to mere existence. Modern technology has done much to prolong life, and where people can live more or less normally this is a boon. Sometimes, however, the mental anguish of patients and their families makes a mockery of dependence on machines.

When we discuss euthanasia, in the current sense of bringing about an easy death, it is important to recognize that psychiatrists are medical doctors whose primary function is to treat patients suffering from diseases of the mind. Because of the nature of his contacts with patients, the psychiatrist is regarded by many people as an arbiter of social behaviour; but this is not and never should be his rôle in the community. This does not mean that there is no place for the psychiatrist in the treatment of the dying patient or in the team which makes decisions about allowing a patient to die because there is no hope that he could ever have a meaningful life again.

Although we have all come to recognize the inevitability of death, it is a strange fact that medical students and nurses are seldom taught very much about it. In spite of arguments which favour frankness with people who are dying, many doctors are reluctant to speak with them of death; and we are all familiar with the type of argument concerning how much a patient should be told and how much his relatives should know about his condition. Often a person does know that his illness is grave and possibly fatal, but he does not know how to discuss it with his medical advisers. It is therefore important to spend time with terminal patients so that one can learn to recognize their fears and anxieties and to discuss them with frankness and understanding.

In addition to the physical suffering found in the dying patient, there is a considerable amount of mental disturbance. The manner in which a man faces his death is bound to be affected by his previous adjustment to life so that there are all grades of courage, fear and emotional disturbance to be seen in the last stages of life.

Any seriously ill patient may be worried about himself and this is equally true when there is no chance of recovery so that anxiety is one of the common emotional disturbances we find in patients who are dying. Anxiety is due to an inherent fear of death and to fear of further suffering. Patients often say that they cannot bear the anticipation of the recurrence of a previously experienced agony. Breathlessness is a potent cause of fear. It is distressing to watch a person struggling to breathe and patients describe the almost unbearable stress and anxiety which accompany respiratory failure.

Sometimes the patient will concentrate his anxiety on some lesser symptom or something in his immediate environment and the apparent pettiness of his complaint may be misunderstood and perhaps treated with unnecessary harshness or lack of understanding which will add to his distress.

Important factors which affect the degree of anxiety found in the dying are religious belief and the age of patients. The man or woman with a strong religious belief has less anxiety than the tepid believers who often experience great fear. Agnostics fall somewhere between these two groups. As might be expected, younger people are more anxious in a terminal illness because they feel that their lives and hopes are being disrupted and they are distressed at leaving their young families.

Commoner than anxiety, however, is depression which may vary in depth from mild unhappiness to utter despair. Suicide is a definite risk because the individual simply cannot face the future. In some cases where the suicide bid fails, the patient is angry and distressed because he wanted to die and to have an end to his suffering.

Severe depression also occurs in patients who have no serious physical illness, and is one of the commonest conditions seen by psychiatrists. It is often an unbearable burden for the patient who feels that it is impossible to continue and who looks for release from his suffering in suicide. These patients, too, often resent the medical expertise which returns them to a life of suffering.

The Church Assembly Board for Social Responsibility in Britain has published a booklet about the problems facing doctors caring for the mortally ill patient. They suggest that the doctor must make his decision about maintaining life in the light of the patient's Christian preparedness for death, and on other factors such as his medical condition and prospects, his own wishes and beliefs as well as the views of his kindred and the wider interests of society. Most doctors faced with the unconscious doomed patient, kept alive by mechanical devices, almost hope for an intercurrent infection which will end the prolonged existence.

If, then, it is permissible to let mortally ill people die, one cannot help asking if it is necessary to wait for a disease to kill them if the life that remains to them is to contain much physical and mental suffering. Are there good reasons to deny patients the right to end their own lives if they come to a firm and reasonable decision that this would be best? Is it possible that the law could be so altered that such people could be helped in their suicides and, from this step, is it not possible to permit euthanasia which could bring urgently needed relief from suffering to many people?

The whole training of doctors emphasizes the treatment of illness and the goal is the cure of illness. After long experience, however, we come to accept the fact that illness is not always curable and our function is to relieve suffering and to comfort our patients always.

While it is true that religious beliefs utterly prevent some people from taking life, there are others who do not feel themselves bound by a code which forbids killing in all circumstances, especially when they see in the world about them killings for reasons which are often hard to justify.

Attempts in Britain to legalize euthanasia, while attracting considerable support, have always failed, mainly because of the religious belief that excludes deliberate killing of the sick, but also because many people fear an irrevocable step, when there might have been a mistaken diagnosis even in those who seem near to death. There are no simple rules and the thought of selecting someone suitable for euthanasia is frightening to many people. What are the limits of disease where euthanasia should or could be considered? Is there some stage in the process of dying which must be reached before it can be contemplated? These and many other problems show the complexities and potential dangers in advocating euthanasia.

It is important in our ethical code not to end life and it is impossible to define by logical argument the exact circumstances in which it is permissible to take life and when it is forbidden.

We believe that our society sets great value on life and that this would be a safeguard against errors and mistakes in applying euthanasia. However, we must always be aware that some people might become careless in its administration. Judgment may be blurred by pity, and we must never forget that there are unstable individuals in all walks of life whose judgment might be unsound because of the influence of feelings they are unaware of or unable to control.

We come then to euthanasia on the request of the dying person. But here, too, we are beset by problems and difficulties. A mere request could not always be regarded as valid because the person would need to be in a sound state of mind for his request for death to be taken seriously. A seriously depressed person may, just for a while, be serious in his wish for death, but he may change his views when his suffering has been relieved by treatment.

Another and unacceptable reason for euthanasia may be a feeling the patient has that it is expected of him because he is a burden to his relatives. We know that many people have been left to die when their usefulness to the community has ceased and they have become a burden to the primarily nomadic tribes to which they belonged; but in our present level of development this should be an unnecessary reason for euthanasia.

In the final analysis one cannot help feeling that if our care of the aged and dying was as good as it could be, and if the suffering in a terminal illness was fully understood and better relieved, there would be less need for euthanasia. Officious efforts to keep people alive, when all hope of a reasonable life style has gone, should be discouraged and, to quote today's cry, death with dignity should be the aim.

It is impossible to say how profoundly guilt feelings would affect both the doctors and the families of people whose lives were terminated by euthanasia. It is easy to use intelligent and intellectual arguments in its favour, but in our society where the preservation of life has been the outstanding aim of medical treatment, there are many factors both conscious and unconscious which might lead to intense suffering, the remorse in those who continue living. Self-doubt and remorse might be the doctor's lot and the patient's kinsfolk may have a tremendous burden of guilt which they may try to minimize by recriminations against the medical profession whose responsibility is, after all, the greatest one in treating all the sick of a community.

A PSYCHOLOGICAL VIEW OF EUTHANASIA

B. A. Balkisson

The shortening of life by suicide or with the assistance of a third party was permitted in antiquity and is not unusual today in non-Christian cultures, according to Eysenck *et al.*[1] (1972). Euthanasia was forbidden by the church but became a subject of discussion again after the publication of More's *Utopia* in 1516. The general tendency for man's life span to be increased has again brought interest to bear on the subject and there is a minor trend to permit euthanasia for patients suffering from incurable, painful illnesses.

While this may be so, an article in the *Atlantic Monthly* (Vol. 199, 1957) claims that there is a new way of dying today. It is the slow passage via modern medicine. If you are very ill, modern medicine can save you. If you are going to die, it can prevent you from doing so for a very long time.

We cannot inquire from the dead what they have felt about this deterrent. As they fight for release from life and are constantly dragged back by modern medicine to try again, is their agony increased? To those who stand and watch, this seems ghastly. Apparently there is no mercy which the family may bestow at such a time. Only in an entirely hopeless situation may doctors desist in their effort to preserve life.

Enter the ward and sit with your beloved, and endure the long watch while this incredible battle between life and medicine takes place. It may continue for weeks, sometimes for months. But the victim is going to die. It is just a question of time. Every new formula, all the latest wonder drugs, the tricks and artificial wizardry, are now prescribed and brought to bear. The dreary dreadful days and nights proceed. 'We are doing all we can,' say the doctors. The patient, however, is too far from us already to tell us in what way he is doing all he can.

A psychological explanation of opposition

There is a curiosity about dying — part is wanting to know; part is dread, or being afraid to know. We can't admit we want to know;

225

we're not supposed to admit it. We live in a state of ambivalence, a mixture of pleasure and fear. There is the fear of the unknown and there is the fear of knowing. It is likely that a projection of this fear or 'terror' as Becker (1973) calls it, urges almost all of us to preserve or prolong life against all odds. In this regard Gregory Zilboorg (1943), a noted psychoanalyst, says that most people think that death fear is absent because it rarely shows its true face; but he argues that underneath all appearances fear of death is universally present.

Keleman (1974) indicates that such a pattern, as with all patterns, does not develop at random. Patterns are built on each individual's interpretation of and responses to prevailing social myths. The two most dominant myths in our culture are modelled around sexual roles. Most males develop patterns around the heroic myth — images of strength, of conflict, of struggling against something threatening or evil. The male is tough, aggressive, never shows feelings and is willing to die bravely and without complaint for his cause. The female is expected to develop patterns around the martyr myth, images of service and sacrifice, giving her life to help her mate and children achieve their goals, always supporting others, easily expressing feelings of love and feelings of loss, permitting her will to be killed for this cause, waiting always to be rescued by a male, always being the doctor's prize.

Such patterns are first learned in the pre-school years. Little boys play soldiers; little girls play with dolls. As one grows older, variations develop. The successful person lives a wise man's myth. Life is as it should be. Death is a sleep, a resignation. Accept it and do all you can to ensure that you live your death. The unsuccessful or frustrated person lives the fool's myth or the morbid defeated myth. For him life is an evil joke, a trap. Dying is meaningless; death is the ultimate insult and is intrinsically evil. Hence the dying one and those around him try to defy death. In so doing such individuals delude themselves into believing that they perform a useful function by prolonging and preserving life whereas we know that it is far better to alleviate suffering. In reality people with such a philosophy preserve and prolong agony and suffering. Euthanasia would only be acceptable to them if they were to alter their own conception of death.

Perhaps our reluctance to accept euthanasia is caused by our denial of the fact that everyone's dying is inevitable. Keleman postulates the view that people fear endings because they must surrender their power in the world. It is quite possible that

opposition to euthanasia is basically a check on the anxiety that
will be generated by acknowledging a surrender of power.

A new philosophy

It is almost always true that with the emotional impact of someone's
death or imminent death we feel that their dying is tragic. We have
the impression that the person's death is an interruption of their
life; it is not how that person's life was supposed to be. However,
tragic and fearful feelings are not a universal response. It is not the
only view regarding death. It is in fact a peculiar cultural notion,
an idea most likely to occur to an impersonal observer, someone
removed from the succession of organismic events through which
the dying person has lived. This concept (that someone's death
need not be an unhappy or tragic events, or an interruption to their
organismic existence, but the logical termination of their process)
gives a wholly different feeling for and image of another's death,
and of your own death. A person's death may be perceived as
socially tragic, in that he died before fulfilling an obvious or
expected destiny. John F. Kennedy is a good example. But of
course the organism does not give social realities the highest
priority. The reverse situation also occurs. Someone's death may
be perceived as relief, or even as a joy, a new freedom. Think of
the reports of ecstasy over the news of Stalin's death. In fact, the
same person may trigger many different responses from grief to
joy.

We live in a time that denies death, that distorts the dying
experience by retaining traditional myths. What we need for a
positive approach to euthanasia is a fresh start, a new myth, a
new vision of maturity and longevity. We are not victims of dying;
death does not victimize us. But we are victims of shallow, distorted
attitudes towards dying, which we conceive as tragic. This, therefore,
negatively influences our attitude to euthanasia.

The time is also ripe for all doctors to change their philosophy
from preserving or prolonging life to one of alleviating suffering.

Some views for and against euthanasia

In the words of Rosenberg, euthanasia is not only wrong from
the ethical, moral and religious point of view, but it is also based
on a wrong and false assumption that doctors know what is a
curable or an incurable disease.

The fact is that doctors still do not know or understand half the diseases that human flesh is heir to; and of the diseases they do understand and can cure, they can never tell with certainty when it is hopeless; and when it is definitely hopeless the patient will soon die anyway, at which stage, ninety-nine times out of a hundred, the patient is not suffering much at all. Besides, medical science has as yet much to gain and far to go to fill all the gaps in its body of knowledge; and doctors have as yet too much to do in order to help prolong and improve human life. Rosenberg adds that doctors can therefore hardly afford to divert their attention to such an unworthy cause and it is equally inglorious for a civilized country to sponsor such a cause.

On the other hand, Morgan in an article in the *British Medical Journal* (3 May 1975) claims that it is right and proper that all those who are dying or likely to die within days or weeks should be helped to do so without suffering, and there is no reason why the appropriate treatment should ever be withheld, given adequate staff with knowledge, sympathy and compassion, and the means to carry this out.

Morgan (1975) continues that to his mind these are not the difficult cases. Take that of a man who is half paralyzed, perhaps with difficulty of speech or part loss of hearing and sight, and perhaps with some incontinence, but with adequate mental capacity to realize that he cannot really improve, in spite of every attention, to a degree which might be tolerable; and that he might live like this for another ten years without being able to take part in any worthwhile activities. He longs to be out of it all, and suicide is either a messy and lonely affair or it is too difficult to achieve for a person in his situation or, as Keleman (1974) claims, we can allow others to take our lives, but we prohibit ourselves from overtly ending ourselves. Why does the law prohibit others from responding? To get pills and find a place where he can consume them without any risk of being discovered and resuscitated is almost impossible. He almost demands 'assisted suicide' in a helpful and comfortable atmosphere and is justified in doing so.

Most suicides are tragedies and occur in fits of depression which are curable. They cause anguish in the family and complete loss of a possibly useful future. The type of case described (and there must be very many of them) is quite different. This man has completed his life's work for good or ill, and deserves to go if he so desires.

The Church Information Office (1975) points out that it is

misleading to confuse euthanasia with a decision by a doctor cease active efforts to treat disease. Good medical care of a pati should include recognition of the moment when it is time to all him to die; and he should be given as good a death as possible.

There may be cases in which active euthanasia is morally justified, emergencies or accidents in war or in the jungle where medical care is lacking but, according to the Anglican Church, they do not provide arguments for a change in the law. Such a change could be justified only if it would clearly remove greater evils than it would cause. Legislation for euthanasia would weaken the confidence of patients in their doctors; and it would create a new form of distress for old, sick individuals who would ask themselves whether they should prolong the burden on their families and attendants. The crucial objection, however, is the change in attitudes it would produce. Care of the dying has been improved in recent years, but it can and should be improved much further. Making euthanasia legal could reduce the incentive to improve the quality of terminal care and put in its place the concept of assisted suicide.

Attitudes of physicians

In a poll reported in a recent issue of *Medical Opinion*, the overwhelming majority of doctors (79%) expressed some belief in the patient's right to have a say about his own death (Rice, 1974).

The magazine sent questionnaires to a random sample of some 3 000 physicians and asked for their reactions to the following proposition: 'People have a right to choose how they die by making their wishes known to their physician before a serious illness strikes'. Of the 933 physicians who responded, representing all major specialties and age groups, 20% agreed totally; 38% agreed in most circumstances; and 21% agreed in some circumstances. About 10% disagreed with possible exceptions, and only 7% completely disagreed.

The physicians' responses did not differ much across specialties but they did vary considerably according to religion. Catholic physicians were least likely to accept the idea of a patient's right to influence the manner of his death, while those doctors with no religious affiliation were most likely to express total agreement with it.

To test the physicians' feelings about euthanasia without actually using that emotionally laden term itself, the questionnaire asked what they would do if a member of their family were suffering from a terminal illness, which they, as physicians, knew carried little or no hope for survival. Nearly two-thirds (61%) of the respondents would take no heroic measures to keep the patient alive, and only one in 10 would do everything possible. Eleven per cent would take positive action to end his or her suffering, and 10% would choose a course of benign or passive neglect, and simply withhold supportive treatment.

Again, Catholics tended to show a preference for supportive action to keep the patient alive. Of the 11% who would bring about death by active means (euthanasia) two-thirds were either Jewish or without religious affiliation. Those who chose euthanasia tended to be younger than the average age of 50. Psychiatrists and internists were most likely to agree to euthanasia, and obstetricians and paediatricians were least likely.

Conclusion

In principle I firmly support the decision to reserve the right to end ourselves independently or with assistance. It is the decision to accept responsibility for our living and our dying.

A NURSE'S POINT OF VIEW ON EUTHANASIA

N. K. Lamond

I wish to share with you a personal evaluation of the nursing rôle in this responsible situation. I do not pretend to be a figurehead for the opinion or philosophy of my nursing colleagues, for indeed, in any discussion, it becomes obvious that so deeply individualized a concept cannot become anything other than a highly contentious issue.

Some six years ago I had an experience that proved to be most enlightening in many ways. Unexpected tragedy struck my family so that in two capacities, both as a registered nurse and as a daughter, I was deeply involved. In the first few days of confused, frightened, lost mourning that followed that incident, my professional, observant, nursing 'self' was constantly bombarded with an awareness that even my best friends were in turmoil. Why? I soon realized that it was because very few of them knew *how* to communicate their very deep sympathy, even although they wanted to, very much indeed. I found my own 'self' assisting them to share with me their desire to come to my comfort. This taught me a most important lesson in communication at times of acute and distressing emergency. It also taught me the reward that always comes in encouraging soul-to-soul communication, however transitory this may be, with one's fellow human beings.

Nurses are indeed privileged people. The greatest rewards of all come, I believe, to a midwife. Having worked with a mother in a most profoundly intimate interaction of soul to soul as she is supported in all spheres, physical, psychological, social and emotional during labour, the midwife receives rewards beyond measure in the joy of that 'Thank you' as the baby is safely delivered. Many of my colleagues experience similar rewards in paediatric, medical or surgical units in our large hospitals. Every one of us as nurses knows the joy of this acknowledgement of our professional selves in the 'Thank you for being here at this time, sister'.

And so I believe we nurses can make it even at the time of dying. As Cooper (1976) states: 'Dying is a part of living. The problem of dealing with death and dying calls for our unqualified acceptance of what is real and true. Above all, it calls for an acceptance of one's own mortality and an ability to talk about it in the same way as one is prepared to chat about other aspects of life.'

How, in this crisis time of my *living,* do I wish to be supported? Do I wish to be abandoned, left dirty and neglected, in pain, lonely and frightened, surrounded by people feeling anxious and perturbed because they consider themselves impotent when faced with my incurable condition? No, of course not.

How can I, as a nurse, therefore, and as an educator of nurses, possibly dare to refrain from making an idealized nursing credo known loud and clear, if in so doing it assists in the development of a more enlightened appraisal of the nursing role and function to assist the patient in all manner in which he is no longer capable of assisting himself in this, the final stage of his living?

Speaking as a nurse, I can do no less than attend to my dying patient's physical needs of cleanliness, warmth, comfort, nutrition as best fitting his present situation. I willingly help him in co-operation with other members of the health team in the relief of his pain.

I try my utmost to make myself a sensitive, perceptive sounding instrument to harmonize my professional, feeling, emotional self to be in tune with his anxiety, fear, denial or whatever his most prevailing emotional need may be. And I do this in full humility to the very best of my ability, knowing all the while that this is the height of 'doing unto others that which I hope one day, somebody will do for me'.

I remember how, when I am stressed, I am so grateful that my supporters help to lessen the distress I am causing there. Thus it follows that I assist my patient in lessening the fear that his condition is arousing both in himself and in those closest to him.

In order to gain grace and strength for the performance of this ultimate service to my patient I do not permit his state of dying and impending death to be a constant reminder of my failure as a nurse. Instead I concentrate my staunch faith in the knowledge that I am a privileged person to be specifically educated, trained and prepared to assist another human being to die with dignity.

This is absolutely essential if I am to remain calm and supportive and enable myself to comply with Elder's (1973) injunction. She writes: 'A major problem arises when goals lie in living and prolonging life rather than those associated with improving the quality of the last days. The justification for prolonging life must be based on the quality of the period of dying.' The last sentence expresses so neatly the motivation that underlies the concept of

232

euthanasia. When the existence remaining to the patient is any less than that of dignity and any modicum at all of fullness of life, surely euthanasia is the gift you and I would request for ourselves.

It is perhaps easier to accept this belief for older folk, irretrievably injured victims of accidents, sufferers of tumours or other grievous circumstances. In younger people, in children and in babies the thought of life seems, somehow, to be so very much more precious. Two thoughts support me in my belief. First, any modicum of human fullness of life that evokes a spark of 'togetherness and sharing' between one human being and another is a reward. Last year I was privileged to be a student psychiatric nurse and I know the joy I gained and gave in 'communicating' even if merely and only on a 'singing-call' with grossly mentally retarded fellow human-beings.

However, the second thought presents the other side of the coin. In that same hospital I nursed people who had no spark of human dignity as far as one could tell at all. Where such people exist requiring no *human* interaction whatsoever, apart from technically skilled physical care, and involving their families in an unceasing burden of guilt and despair, I state with full awareness of the burden of my belief that (paraphrasing Noyes[3]): 'these patients should not be treated as though they were diseases, and that the object of their care should be a painless and peaceful death' when, and this is my addition, basic physical nursing care is insufficient to sustain life.

I go further in my manifesto. Should treatments such as surgery, blood transfusions, medications such as antibiotics be used, or, should grossly deformed and defective newly born babies be resuscitated?

I deny with every fibre of my professional being, the sentiment expressed in Weiseman's statement. He writes: 'Euthanasia is a unilateral decision of survivors who wish to obliterate their own anguish in the presence of another person's secondary suffering.[4]

Suffering to no purpose when no enrichment of anybody's life can possibly be taking place, not within the victim, his family or closest friends, or society, or even a sense of personal or professional fulfilment in the nurse; suffering, long, sustained, and unalleviated, whether physical, mental or on an interactional basis where degradation is actively occurring; such suffering is not obliterated to deny anguish. It is alleviated in a conscious, conscientious, clear-cut, objective, decisive manner as the contribution of the professionals involved to the community.

A time must surely come when circumstances are such that the awe-full, fearsome task of bearing the burden for such a responsible decision as to no longer prolong this individual's life should be entrusted to the members of the health team.

I deplore the sharing of this responsibility with anxious, grief-stricken relatives. Turmoil, guilt and shame should not be added to the burden of those folk who are already so overloaded.

Finally, I believe that we nurses, who are educated to accept the joys and privileges accorded us by our community, should also be prepared to accept this burden of responsibility and accountability that is equally part of our duty.

1. Cooper, H., in 'Death with Dignity', Symposium at Groote Schuur Hospital, February 1976.
2. Elder, R., *Int. J. Nurs. Studies,* 10, 1973, 171.
3. Noyes, R., *Arch. Int. Med.,* 128, 1971, 299.
4. Weisman, A. D., *On Dying and Denying,* New York, Behavioural Publications Ltd, 1972.

SUMMING UP

H. A. Shapiro

Prof. S. A. Strauss demarcated the territory to be explored in an extremely helpful and comprehensive way. He put many questions and we have had answers to some, but not all of these questions; I find particularly interesting the cross-section of religious opinion that was revealed in the very first session.

I have always felt that theologists try to define the indefinable, and I am still of that view. It is like trying to catch a very slippery eel with greased hands.

What has emerged uniformly from the contributions in the religious section, the religious attitude, is that, possibly with the exception of the Anglican contribution made by Rev. Roger Ellis, all condemn active euthanasia. I think the Anglican view, as expressed here, might be interpreted as going along with active euthanasia; but by and large (and I say that because you will recall that significant sentence: 'Lord, we return thy child to thee') there appeared to be nothing incongruous and nothing improper in intervening, even actively, to bring about that end; and this, of course, is rooted in the religious foundation on which the faith rests.

This fairly uniform approach is interesting because, in connection with the Catholic view, a speaker quoted Arthur Hugh Clough's couplet from *The New Deacalogue*:

Thou shall not kill but needst not strive
Officiously to keep alive.

This sums up the general religious view, however it was expressed.

The other point that emerged not only from the contributions to the section on religious aspects but also very clearly from the medical sections, and from several other sections, was that modern medical technology has outstripped virtually all medical limitations. That is how Prof. G. C. Oosthuizen puts it, together with the suggestion that this technological monster must not be allowed to take over and dictate what the ultimate say must be.

Prof. Chris Barnard echoed this view very eloquently in his moving address and, of course, it was echoed in one way or another by almost every speaker.

235

So the consensus that emerges is that we may, and indeed we must, discontinue treatment (in the context we are discussing) of the terminal, incurably ill patient with unrelievable, or almost unrelievable pain; we must discontinue treatment when it can no longer alleviate suffering and only prolong the process of dying.

The Buddhist view, as I understand it from Mr van Loon's presentation, is really a view based on a social code of conduct, but the conclusion reached is the same. I would like, however, to draw attention to dangers inherent in the Buddhist concept of the volitionless state.

There is room for much debate about whether this forms a sound basis for making a decision; but there is no doubt that what comes through, on the whole, is a respect for the sanctity of life and the repugnance that is experienced at any suggestion that there should be active intervention to terminate it.

An interesting contribution deals with the attitude of the economist in trying to calculate monetary value for something that, in my view, is incalculable. An admission was finally made, of course, that there are qualities which could not be quantitated, e.g. the sort of case that we meet in our professional capacities. Take the case of the quadruplegic who has survived a serious traffic accident. He is paralyzed from the neck down and even if, for a victim like this (and the cases I think of are tragically young people), the award of damages is in the 6-figure bracket, R100 000 or more, how can that *really mean* anything in the way of the compensation that this is supposed to represent?

One other quite unusual and startling point to emerge is that our concern about *how* people die is a product of Western medical technology which has been, or is being, imported into the oriental sphere. This is clear from the contributions, for example, made by those representing the Hindu and the Islamic views. So this problem is really one created by the Western world and its technology.

This brought us to the contributions from our legal friends, who were in the easier position of trying to define what we can call 'the definable'. There seems to be absolutely no doubt that active euthanasia is equated with the act of murder, however extenuating the circumstances might be. There seems to be a complete uniformity of view on this. There was no exception to that particular proposition and, of course, this is borne out by the decision in the recent Hartmann case which was heard in the Cape Provincial Division of the Supreme Court.

The other interesting point is the little debate that developed between Prof. J. van der Vyver and Prof. P. C. Smit on the nature of the contract into which the doctor enters when the patient approaches him, and creates a doctor-patient relationship. Prof. Van der Vyver thought that the doctor was obliged to carry on with the treatment which he had, as it were, contracted to do, or undertaken to do, and Adv. Smit took the slightly different view that there would come a time when a doctor could, without any impropriety either morally or legally, abandon the treatment that he was committed to because it was now useless treatment. From the purely medical point of view, and the layman's point of view, we would find this an acceptable proposition.

The other point to emerge from the legal contributions is that if the legal framework were to be modified in any way, this framework should be left as widely open as possible so that we could have an area in which the matter could be left to the conscience of the doctor. It should be made possible for him to regard it as his duty to respect the wishes of the patient who wants to die, without becoming involved in the prolongation of the patient's agony.

In the sociological section our attention was drawn once again to the Frankenstein of medical technology which has led to a shifting of our emphasis to the quality of dying. To me it was heartening to hear that the terminally ill patient and the doctor were not the only actors in this drama which was being enacted at the end of the patient's life. The policy for active euthanasia, if one is to be adopted, was described quite frankly as legalized murder and it would obviously need very careful scrutiny before any such development could be contemplated.

A useful suggestion was also made in this section. Prof. A. Weiss stressed the point that we are stuck with an inappropriate terminology which, for historical reasons, has got connotations which are not really justified when we use the term euthanasia, or when we use it as we have readily been using it in the context of this symposium. We use it in the sense of passive euthanasia, and that quite simply means allowing the patient to die.

I am afraid we are stuck with this, as we are stuck in medicine with so many words that we find unacceptable. They have come into such firm usage that it will be very difficult to replace them.

From the contributions to the medical section, it is clear that in some way or another we have reached the point at which there seems to be a perversion of the role of the machinery of maintaining life, or prolonging the moment of dying. After all, if we go back to first principles (this was not explicitly stated but I think it was implicit in everything that the doctors said), the role of the machine is to tide the patient over until he has reached the point where he can go on on his own, and if we cannot reach this point in a reasonable period of treatment, then there is nothing medically wrong with abandoning that treatment.

Doctors have been switching off artificial respirator machines ever since they were invented — and that goes back quite some years. The criteria which they follow are based on medical indications and I am sure that, however much we amplify the detail, this is the essence. The machine was never intended, and should not be intended, to keep a patient perpetually in this sort of limbo. This was not the reason why it was introduced, and this is not the function that it should fulfil.

The problem that this presented in the medical area was, indeed, raised by Prof. Jenkins, who exposed the dilemma by a ruthless pursuit of logic. He has certainly posed a problem for us. As I understand the Abortion and Sterilization Act, and I think he understands it in the same way, it is lawful up to the time of delivery to interfere with the hydrocephalic infant, i.e. while it is still in the womb of the mother, because it suffers from a physical and/or mental condition which will seriously handicap, physically or mentally, the child about to be born. So there is no legal problem although there may be a moral problem. But the profound issue which he raised, viz. that this same infant, once it has been born, cannot be disposed of in this way lawfully, is something that worries one, because his logic is unassailable: if you can do it just before birth, why can you not do it just after birth or a little later?

I can only express my reaction to the proposition, one likely, I think, to be shared by most, that there is a greater repugnance to taking the life of a child after it has been born than there is before it has been born, even though this may be rooted merely in irrational values or attitudes. However, it still represents a very real problem; perhaps this is one of the more acceptable uses of hypocrisy, because there is some hypocrisy in the attitude that we adopt. We are indebted to Prof. Jenkins for raising this point because it is something that we have got to think through; it is an issue that we are side-stepping at the moment. It obviously requires a profound change in the law. It means that we must accept the principle of 'selective infanticide' as Prof. Jenkins has called

it; and, after all, this opens the door to what happened in Nazi Germany. This is what makes us hesitate to allow it, or to permit this thin end of the wedge to be introduced into what is, in any case, a profoundly distressing situation.

The contributions of the sociologist and the criminologist can perhaps be taken together. They re-emphasize that positive euthanasia is common murder and agree that there is nothing wrong in withdrawing useless treatment. In fact, the criminological paper goes so far as to suggest that to withdraw useless treatment does not even come into the description of euthanasia. There is much force in that view.

Each particular case has to be decided on the particular facts and it is necessary to introduce safeguards to protect the doctor as well as the patient. The note of warning sounded is the danger that may arise — of diminishing the quality of our terminal care and encouraging what amounts to no more than assisted suicide.

I come now to the more general papers at the end of the symposium. Miss Brenda Robertson expressed the standpoint of the 'the woman in the home', but that of the Catholic woman in the home, and therefore perhaps a different attitude. As she eloquently puts it, the patient may well get into a position in which, when confronted with the officious intervention of both doctors and nurses, he may cry out, 'A plague on both your professions'.

The need for moral or spiritual standards is emphasized and attention is drawn to the departure from the moral standards on which the older members of this audience were raised. These standards have been replaced by new standards of conduct which have sorely tried most of us, as our youngsters have been growing up. But perhaps this is not quite fair to the younger generation, which has developed its own social code and its own morality, which imposes quite a strong restraint on these young people.

There appears to be no moral objection to passive euthanasia, and the following interesting question was posed: what happens to the patient who is the victim of cardiac arrest, for example, during a surgical procedure? This is not strictly part of what we are discussing and I do not, therefore, propose to pursue it, but it was brought out in many ways by many of the speakers, that whatever we may adopt as a guide (over and above what we do at present), we must not lose sight of the importance of the trust and the confidence which the patient has in the doctor and that nothing must be done which could erode that trust in this relationship.

One speaker made a very interesting suggestion, which ties up with the point which was afterwards raised by Professor Grant-Whyte, viz. the need to provide scholarships for both doctors and nurses to make a study of the ways of dying. Now this clearly has been a neglected area in undergraduate medical and nursing education. We have had to find our own way on a do-it-yourself basis, which is not always the best way to do things.

Professor Lamond stresses the need to communicate simply, not only with the patient, but (and this is equally important) also, with the relatives in their bereavement. The nurse is a person privileged to be able to assist the patient in all the ways that are necessary when he can no longer help himself; she sees this in its correct perspective as the duty of a partner in the health team. This view is also held by the sociologist. There is a role which the social worker can play as well, in sharing in this enormous responsibility, and in the very responsible acts which must be done at a time like this. Here, again, what emerges is support for the view that there is nothing improper about passive euthanasia. But a division of opinion emerged about the desirability of sharing the responsibility of decisions that have to be made with the relatives who are involved. This view, as you know, is controversial and is not shared by all the contributors. One should probably take a look at the facts of the particular situation, because clearly there are times when it would be necessary, as well as desirable, to consult with the relatives or the intimate friends, and there are times when this may not be at all desirable.

Apart from her view that the patient should be allowed to die, Dr Paterson also gives the very striking example of the patient on the kidney machine and the inadequacy of our medical training regarding how to handle the dying and the situation in which this occurs. This emerges very strikingly and emphasizes what has been stated (perhaps not as vigorously as it should have been) about the need to take care of that hiatus in medical and nursing training. Of course, she endorses the view that the patient's plea to be allowed to die is the one that should be honoured and respected.

Mr Balkisson's contribution from the psychologist's point of view raised the interesting statistics which indicate that it is the younger ones in the professions who choose euthanasia. This makes me think that the conscience is an organ in man which develops very late in life. Our revolutionaries, our terrorists, our political activists, are young people who would not hesitate to put their best friends up against the wall and shoot them if this was necessary in the interests of 'the revolution'. This zealous disregard for life and its sanctity seems to decrease as we grow older. Mr Balkisson did, in the end, also support the acceptability of passive euthanasia.

So from this discussion emerges the question of whether there is really any support for a programme of active euthanasia; whether there is, in fact, any need to ask for legislation to protect the doctor in what he is doing at present. It seems that there is a need for propaganda. There is need for education of the medical profession about what the proper approach of its members should be to the patient who has prepared a living will. But there may be dangers in trying to create some sort of statutory framework within which these things must be done. The art of government is to refrain from legislation sometimes, and this may well be the situation here.

Lastly, may I sum up with a point which I think we should distinguish both morally, medically and legally: there is a difference between abandoning treatment which is meaningless and useless, and going beyond that to perform an act of omission with the intention of ensuring the death of the patient. There is, too, a profound distinction in respect of the intention with which one approaches this problem. I am sure that this distinction is legal, and I think it is also moral and medical. If this clarification emerges, this in itself would be a valuable crystallization of our thinking on the subject, because this is what has been achieved in this very important debate.

The contributors have not hesitated to confront frankly the profoundly difficult issues in all spheres of our society — moral, ethical, religious, legal and medical. A discussion like this will influence the climate in which we in this country will henceforth think and act about these matters.